BOMBER OFFENSIVE

PEN & SWORD MILITARY CLASSICS

We hope you enjoy your Pen and Sword Military Classic. The series is designed to give readers quality military history at affordable prices. Pen and Sword Classics are available from all good bookshops. If you would like to keep in touch with further developments in the series, telephone: 01226 734555, email: enquiries@pen-and-sword.co.uk, or visit our website at www.pen-and-sword.co.uk.

Published Classics Titles

Forthcoming Titles

BOMBER OFFENSIVE

by

MARSHAL OF THE R.A.F.
SIR ARTHUR HARRIS
G.C.B. O.B.E. A.F.C.

PEN & SWORD MILITARY CLASSICS

First published in Great Britain in 1947 by
Collins Clear-type Press, London and Glasgow
Published in 2005, in this format, by
PEN & SWORD MILITARY CLASSICS
an imprint of
Pen & Sword Books Limited
47 Church Street
Barnsley
S. Yorkshire
S70 2AS

ISBN 1 84415 210 3

A CIP record for this book
is available from the British Library.

Printed and bound in Great Britain by
CPI UK

Pen & Sword Books Ltd incorporates the imprints of
Pen & Sword Aviation, Pen & Sword Maritime, Pen & Sword Military,
Wharncliffe Local History, Pen & Sword Select,
Pen & Sword Military Classics and Leo Cooper

For a complete list of Pen & Sword titles please contact:
PEN & SWORD BOOKS LIMITED
47 Church Street, Barnsley, South Yorkshire, S70 2AS, England.
E-mail: enquiries@pen-and-sword.co.uk
Website: www.pen-and-sword.co.uk

CONTENTS

5

Chapter One

FACING THE WAR

Arriving in England from Palestine in 1939. Certainty of war.
Appointment as Air Officer Commanding No. 5 Bomber Group.
My service career. Previous experience of air war. The last war
and "police bombing" in the East. The years of disarmament.
The Army Staff College. A journey to America. Palestine and
Montgomery. Looking ahead to a bomber's war.

IN THE SUMMER of 1939 I was on my way home from
Palestine, where I had been Air Officer Commanding R.A.F.
Palestine and Transjordan during one of the worst of the periodical rebellions resulting from the Anglo-Jewish-Arab controversy.
I had had there a busy year teaching the British army the advantages, and the rebels the effectiveness of air power. My wife
and I returned by ship and arrived off Plymouth on a bright and
blustery day. As we rounded the breakwater, some naval multiple
pom-poms—"Chicago pianos"—resumed their firing at sleeve
targets towed by an aircraft. I was depressed to see how ineffective
the shooting was. But, by contrast, after being abroad for a year,
I was struck by the warlike preparations on every hand as we
sailed up the Channel to Tilbury. I remember my wife asking
what was the purpose of the circular patterns in the foredecking
of the ship; I told her that it covered the sites which had been
stiffened for deck armament; the ship was obviously destined
to be an armed cruiser in the event of war. She was in fact the
Rawalpindi, and lies now at the bottom of the Denmark Straits,
an unpardonable sacrifice, like so many of these poor armed
merchant cruisers, to the parsimony of governments.

I was convinced that we should be at war within a matter of
weeks. As a professional fighting man I knew that I had absolutely
nothing to gain and everything to lose by war. If the regular
first-line fighting man is young enough when war breaks out
he is inevitably killed or crippled during the period when the
nation is getting its national forces ready to come to the support
of the regular forces. If he is too old for active service or a

9

specialist he will be employed on the staff or in high command. Whatever may be the result of the war it is a foregone conclusion that he will lose by it. For if the war is won, there will be a wholesale retrenchment of regular forces. This always happens after every major war, when it is assumed that everybody will be too tired for another major war within at least the next ten years. He will then in all probability be no more than half or two-thirds of the way through a normal service career, but he will nevertheless be thrown on the beach, a beach to which he is an absolute stranger and where he will find the utmost difficulty in picking up a living for himself and his family; moreover he will be at the wrong age to make another start. If the war is lost, he will be led to the nearest lamp-post and hanged, or given a debased pension. Those are the alternatives which major wars offer to the regular serving man, and to call him a militarist in the sense that he desires and encourages war in order to serve his own interests is nonsense. Yet it is a view widely held and disseminated by the loose thinking of interested parties and political demagogues, who blame the fighting man to conceal their own folly.

Before I undertook any new task at all I was determined to get a week or two's rest; all the more so because I knew how close we were to war and how difficult it would be in any war to get even such rest as is physically necessary. We went to our friends in Norfolk, Jean and Adeline Tresfon. Jean had been an officer in the Dutch army, and became a naturalised Englishman shortly after the 1914-1918 war. He is quite one of the ablest men I have ever met. He farms 1200 acres in Norfolk; it is better farming than I have seen anywhere in this country—and I am a bit of a farmer myself—but he does it as a spare-time job, a hobby, betweeen running half a dozen big firms and factories. It was nice to be back in the green countryside in the late summer.

On September 3rd, 1939, we were still with the Tresfons. We sat round the log-fire and listened to Chamberlain's uninspired and uninspiring broadcast; when he announced that we were now at war with Germany he was about as stirring as a schoolmaster confirming the fact that mumps had broken out in his prep. school. A lifeless call to the blood and tears, the toil and sweat of war. There was silence at the end of his speech, until Jean Tresfon turned to me and said: "How long will this one be?" I drew a bow at a venture and answered: "Five years." I do not know why I said five years, except that I knew we could not hope to reach our full effort before five years and that it would take at least our full effort to stop the Boche and consider-ably more to beat him.

I then went to the telephone and rang up Portal and told him that I wanted a job. I had finished with my holiday, no matter what might be said to the contrary. There was complete chaos on the telephone lines and I only got through to the Air Ministry by demanding "immediate priority"—a meaningless term and quite unauthorised, but one which had the desired effect. I had the mortification of kicking my heels for some days, which seemed like years, before I received a message telling me to report to the Air Ministry. There Portal, after ringing up Ludlow-Hewitt, Commander-in-Chief, Bomber Command, told me to go and take over command of No. 5 Group of Bomber Command at Grantham the next day, which I did. My task was made none the easier by the fact that neither the Command nor the Air Ministry had thought of informing the Air Officer then com-manding the Group that I was on my way to take over from him. As he was an old personal friend of mine and an officer for whom I have always had the greatest admiration and regard, it was for the moment an unpleasant situation, only relieved by the way he took it. He was fulminating against the idiotic procedure of bowling the useless 250 lb. bomb on to German battleships from a height of a few feet, which was what Bomber Command was doing at that time.

As I drove myself and my traps in a small borrowed Austin from Norwich to Grantham, which is without exception the worst cross-country route in England, I pondered on the really frightful and frightening military prospects of the nation. I knew that we had nothing to fight with, and that France had less; we at any rate had the heart to fight, but the French had not, rotted to the core as they were with the worst type of politician and politically-minded serving officer. I knew—how could I fail to know after two years of the Army Staff College and five years on the Committee of Imperial Defence and Joint Planning Committee?—that the navy had no idea beyond the long-defunct battleship; year after year they had reasserted in Parliament and outside it, with an entirely unjustifiable confi-dence, that the submarine threat was a busted flush and had been finally and effectively mastered; every year they reasserted that aircraft could be no threat whatsoever to any form of naval operation. I had seen the army preening itself, even as early as 1927, on having reduced the machine-gun content of its formations to near the 1914 level, and its artillery to such a point that at one time, by 1918 standards, I think they had about enough left to cover a limited advance on a front of a mile. By 1927 they had also succeeded, though not without opposition, in abolishing the Royal Tank Corps. They could thereafter settle down to what, I believe, was known as "real soldiering." I knew well enough the army's plan of campaign; it was a replica of the opening phases of the war in August, 1914, or as exact a one as could be produced, with the help, it almost seemed, of the original blue-prints, even to the point of "paying rent for the same trenches." But I also knew that the best of the army itself had no faith in that plan, and none whatever in the French army; they had agreed to adopt the same old plan again only because the French had intimated that they wouldn't fight at all if we didn't agree with their ideas. The French had also got us virtually to promise that in the event of an invasion of France we would use the whole of our bomber force to protect the frontier; they had no idea that a bomber force could be used for any purpose whatever except as long range artillery in support of their army. Their air force was hopelessly deficient in every way, a dire state for which their politicians were responsible. Their air force, too, was in complete subservience to their army.

I had every reason to know what the Germans possessed in the way of aircraft, tanks, artillery and anti-tank weapons, and I was also familiar with their ideas of warfare; on the other side an old and valued soldier friend had told me that we had only one type of tank that was any good, and only one serviceable tank of this type. No one would have thought that a quarter of a century before we had actually invented and been the first to exploit the tank. I was convinced that in these circumstances we were going to be thrown out of the Continent neck and crop just as soon as it suited the Boche to do it, but like everybody else I had not foreseen the possibility of the long "phoney-war" period. To say that I was depressed by the prospect was to put it mildly.

Apart from everything else, a rule had been first tacitly and then explicitly in force for some twenty years which could not have been more effectively designed to secure our unreadiness for war. This was the iniquitous "Ten Year Rule," as it was called. After the 1914-1918 war the Chiefs of Staff sought political guidance on which to base the establishments and plans of the three services. They were told to base their plans on the assumption that there would be "no major war for ten years." That was a simple and, at the time when it was made, justifiable ruling. But that rule remained in force year after year, and no one had observed the logical conclusion that the progressive plans should thereafter have been based on an amended ruling that there would be no major war within nine years, within eight years, and so on each year, to zero. Until Hitler was already in power the passage of the years was ignored, and as year succeeded year each was still assumed to be the first of the ten years of immunity from any major war. Then, with all the services still, through *force majeure* on the part of the Treasury, basing their plans on this ruling, it was in force one day and completely abrogated the next. It was this absurd procedure, as much as anything else, which had brought the Royal Air Force and the other services to the position they were in in 1939, when everything we had—and that was little—was in the shopwindow, with nothing behind it.

In 1923 there was a panic about the size of the French Air Force and the French occupation of the Ruhr. The French could safely ignore our protests, and they did, because we had no force with which to back them. In particular, the French had, in the previous year, 128 air squadrons, while our whole front line strength amounted to 371 aircraft. The Salisbury Committee, a sub-committee of the Committee of Imperial Defence over which Lord Salisbury presided, looked into the matter and recommended that the Air Defence of Great Britain should always be strong enough to protect us against air attack by the strongest air force within striking distance. The home defence squadrons were to be increased to 52—the whole front line strength of the R.A.F. at home and abroad was then 34 squadrons. At the same time the Salisbury Committee stopped a naïve scheme of the War Office which would have left the Air Ministry powerless to control anything except civil aviation, research and experiment, and the supply of aircraft, presumably for the use of the War Office. The perennial row between the Admiralty and the Air Ministry over the Fleet Air Arm was also smoothed over for a time, and, in fact, the Royal Air Force was given permission to exist. So far so good, but a year later the "Ten Year Rule" was officially laid down, and the result was that even in 1934 the home defence squadrons only numbered 42, of which only 29 were regular squadrons, and this in spite of the fact that, eleven years before, the Salisbury Committee had recommended the formation of

34 new squadrons "with as little delay as possible" to bring the Home Defence squadrons up to 52.

For some time we could not get across to the people who mattered the urgency of making preparations for war, but eventually Eden and Simon, in 1935, went to Germany and came back sufficiently staggered by what they had seen to cause them to ring all the bells. This started urgent discussions about increasing our forces at home. I was then head of the Air Ministry Planning Department, and as far as I recall the first I heard of the results of Eden's and Simon's visit was on a Saturday; I remember noticing with some amusement that by the following Monday, as I think it was, the tone of the Foreign Office had become distinctly more truculent, even slightly bellicose, presumably on the strength of the new air forces we had been authorised to get on with on the preceding Saturday.

By then it was already far too late to avoid the desperate condition in which we found ourselves in 1939. Four years was certainly not long enough, with modern industrial processes what they are, to get the factories built and tooled up, to get aircraft into production, and to get an adequate scheme of training organised. About a dozen new schemes for rearmament, each scheme more ambitious than its predecessor, succeeded each other up till 1938, but in 1939 almost everything was still on paper.

As I saw it, the position on the outbreak of war was that our fighters—what there were of them—were up to the standard of any that the Germans had produced, and that some of our bombers—especially the Wellingtons and the "Heavies" which were just getting into production—were going to be good. But what we actually had was not much good, being totally insufficient in number and with no reserves either of crews or aircraft adequate for any sort of sustained operations. Nor, indeed, was there any adequate organisation for training crews up to the standard or in the numbers required for modern war. As I felt convinced that neither France nor our own forces on the Continent would survive for long, I could see no possibility, after the inevitable *débâcle*, except a direct grapple between the Boche and ourselves alone. From a good deal that I had read about the previous war, and from what I had seen during the last peace, I felt confident that the United States would not come in unless she was pushed, and I could not for the life of me conceive that our enemies would again be fools enough to push her. Neither could I see Russia coming in.

But I never had any fear that the enemy would succeed in getting across the Channel, with the equipment then available. I knew we could and would stop him. All past experience of combined operations pointed to the impossibility, at that time, of a cross-Channel invasion on the scale that would be necessary in the face of anything approaching serious opposition. I could therefore see only one possible way of bringing serious pressure to bear on the Boche, and certainly only one way of defeating him; that was by air bombardment. It consequently looked as it was going to be a straight fight between our own and the enemy's production of heavy bombers. We might be helped by whatever we could beg, borrow, or buy from America, but getting aircraft from America was, as I well knew (I had been there to buy them some little more than a year before) at that time a matter of hard cash, and damned hard cash at that. Lease-Lend—"the most unselfish act in history"—was yet to come.

My belief in the heavy bomber as the predominant weapon for the war, and my views on the probable course that the war would take, were based on past experience, and to explain them I shall have to go back to the past. I may as well begin at the beginning.

My father was an Indian Civil servant, and my parents were on leave in England when I was born in 1892. I was not regarded as the most promising member of the family; at any rate, although one of my brothers was sent to Eton and the other to Sherborne, I went to a less well-known school. My father had always wanted to be a soldier, but deafness prevented him, and he fathered his ambition on us. He dearly wanted me to go into the army. I was dead set against it. And as it was either the army or the colonies, I plumped for darkest Africa. After some domestic discord over the matter I accepted a ticket and a fiver and went to Rhodesia. I was then sixteen. My first job there was gold mining. Then I took to driving coaches. They were horse coaches at first, but the horses were always dying of fever and we used mules and finally cars instead: I drove some of the very first cars that came to Rhodesia. I also took to general farming, tobacco, maize, and cattle. It was hard work, but the best of all lives. I was, and I still am, a Rhodesian. I never wanted to leave Africa. I have always intended to return, and now at last I am back there.

In August, 1914, I was away in the bush, and I did not hear about the war until the end of the month. When I got back to town and heard the news I tried at once to join the 1st Rhodesian Regiment. There was no room left. I pestered the regimental office again and again, to receive the same answer. At last I heard that there were two remaining vacancies for "specialists" in the regiment, one for a machine-gunner and the other for a bugler. I applied for the job of machine-gunner and was interviewed by Hope-Carson, the adjutant, a great man and still going strong. I was unable to convince him that I knew anything whatever about machine-guns—I had never seen one—so I demanded the job of bugler. During my days in the O.T.C. at All Hallows, I had become a good enough bugler to collect second prize in the annual Public School O.T.C. Camp. I landed the job, and the unkind have accused me of blowing my own trumpet ever since.

The 1st Rhodesian Regiment's first campaign was in German West Africa. In it we had to carry out a march over many weeks of such length—and on starvation rations—that it became famous even in the annals of the British Army. It was in fact the greatest marching performance of an infantry brigade in British military history. It made such an impression on me that to this day I never walk a step if I can get any sort of vehicle to carry me. When the 1st Rhodesian Regiment was disbanded, after we had carried the campaign through, defeated and collected the Boche, and occupied German West Africa, I sailed for England determined to find some way of going to war in a sitting posture. I thought of the cavalry, but I had no faith in horse warfare. The Gunners were full up. I thought I would learn to fly; even before the war I had toyed with the idea of joining the R.N.A.S. and might have done so if it had not meant becoming a professional sailor.

I therefore joined the R.F.C. To me it was just an incident pending the suppression of the Boche and the chance to get back home to Africa. I certainly had no idea that air warfare would be my life's work. I had an uncle on Kitchener's staff so I slid round the 6000 "waiting list"—it was sheer nepotism. I was appointed a second-lieutenant on probation, and learned to fly. During the war I had two main jobs. I formed and commanded a detached flight—and later a squadron—in the first Home Defence squadron of night fighters—in which Leefe Robinson shot down the first Zeppelin—and in France I commanded a flight in a fighter squadron protecting our artillery spotters. I was therefore engaged in defence rather than attack, but in point of fact it was the defensive aspect of the air war of 1914-1918 that first brought about the conception of an air force independent of the other two services, and of independent air operations. Daylight attacks on London by German aircraft in June and July of 1917 caused so much disturbance that General Smuts, then a member of the War Cabinet, was asked to get out a report on the whole subject. In this report he said that the air arm "can be used as an independent means of war operations. Nobody who witnessed the attack on London on 11th July could have any doubt on this point. . . . As far as at present can be foreseen there is absolutely no limit to the scale of its future independent war use. And the day may not be far off when aerial operations with their devastation of enemy lands and destruction of industrial and populous centres on a vast scale may become the principal operations of war, to which the older forms of military and naval operations may become secondary and subordinate."

I shall describe later how I showed General Smuts, when he visited us at Bomber Command, the proofs of the extraordinary accuracy of his prophecy. But the bomber was in no way an important weapon of the 1914-1918 war; the predominant weapon of that war was, of course, the submarine, and if the German admirals and generals had grasped this simple fact they would certainly have defeated us. As it was, they missed victory through submarine power by weeks. Aircraft were then tied to the long and bloody siege war in France, and though we had just got aircraft ready for an "independent" attack on Berlin when the war ended, it can hardly be said that there was any real use of air power during this period. Although the accuracy of gunfire was much improved by artillery spotting from the air it was still quite possible to fight effectively against an enemy even if he had command of the air over the battlefield and the contribution of the air to sea power was insignificant, compared with the outstanding possibilities of the submarine in those days.

While I was on anti-Zeppelin defence at Northolt I had a good deal of trouble, as I have had from time to time throughout my life, with inventors of lunatic weapons who too often obtain the ear of the authorities. One particular maniac had got the ear of the War Office—we were, of course, under the War Office then and the R.A.F. had not yet been formed—and I was instructed to give him *carte-blanche*. However, I demurred when he proposed sawing out a large part of the essential structure from my aeroplane as a preliminary to fitting in his anti-Zeppelin gadget. He eventually fixed this in with a reasonable degree of security

B.O. B

and he then explained its use to me. "You see," he said, "that you have on this drum 500 feet of steel cable and on the end of it this large harpoon. You get above the Zeppelin and pull the handle; the harpoon goes down through the envelope of the Zeppelin, opens its barbs and catches in the structure, and there you are." To which I made the obvious retort: "Well, where am I? The Zeppelin has 3000 horse power and I have 75, and what I should like to know before attempting this is—who goes home with whom?" Whereupon he said, "But then, of course, you see I have not quite completed this. My subsequent intention is to provide an explosive grenade on a ring. When you have harpooned the Zeppelin, you slide the grenade down the wire and it bursts on reaching the harpoon."

Seeing the chance to get rid of him for a time, I suggested that he should go home and complete his invention on those lines—which he did. That disposed of him for some three weeks or so. He then returned with his explosive grenade on the ring and explained it all again to me. I suggested innocently enough that when I had achieved the markmanship necessary to hit the Zeppelin with the harpoon in the first instance it might be a good idea to have an explosive harpoon rather than to go to the additional trouble of sliding a grenade down the wire to a captive harpoon. This kept him away for a few more weeks, but he eventually produced an explosive harpoon and then went through the whole process with me again. I then said: "Well, now we hit the Zeppelin with an explosive harpoon, what is the need of having 500 feet of wire cable, which is, after all, a fatal additional load and a great inconvenience in my aeroplane?" That suggestion he again accepted enthusiastically, whereupon I pointed out to him that the harpoon was not ballistically very sound. Why not give it ballistic properties to enable it to be more accurately dropped? To this he agreed, but not being knowledgeable on the subject of ballistics he asked me for my help. Whereupon I sketched for him on paper, instead of the harpoon, an article shaped exactly like a bomb. This, he agreed, should certainly do the trick, if it hit the Zeppelin. I replied: "That is precisely why I have four bombs hanging under my aeroplane at the present moment." He was furious, and went off in the local taxi. He was but one of a legion.

I more or less drifted into the R.A.F. as a regular after the war; I had been in the job so long that I thought I might as well continue. I had become a major by the end of the war, and was quite unexpectedly granted a permanent commission as squadron leader in the R.A.F. It was to me a heartbreaking decision not to return to Africa, but by then I had a family. I still felt the urge to return to the sunshine, and after many applications I managed to get transferred to India, where I commanded a squadron on the North West Frontier. In 1919 the Amir of Afghanistan launched a holy war against India, expecting that a general uprising of the Moslem population would follow. This did not happen and he was quickly driven back into his own country. One 20 lb. bomb in his palace grounds decided him. But his attempt exacerbated the normal troubles among the warlike tribes on the North West Frontier, and especially in Waziristan; these tribes have always been difficult to control; they intermittently sympathise and intrigue with the Afghans, inhabit the wildest of country where it is difficult to reach them, and are always glad of an opportunity to fight. The army had the job of controlling them but the Air Force contributed some squadrons of Bristol fighters and D.H.9s.

My service on the North West Frontier was always to remain in my mind as a bitter reminder of what happens when air forces, or any other forces equipped with new weapons, are put under the control of another and older service and subordinated to the uses of previously existing weapons. We lacked everything in the way of necessary accommodation and spares and materials for keeping our aircraft serviceable—the only thing there was never any shortage of was demands for our services when the trouble blew up on the frontier.

In the end I got so tired of having to fly myself and to send out my crews in aircraft which were utterly unairworthy that I resigned. My resignation was not forwarded from headquarters to the Air Ministry, because just at that moment Lord Montagu of Beaulieu, who was visiting India, came round the R.A.F. stations and saw for himself the appalling state of affairs that existed. For instance, it was not unknown for aircraft to take off on operations on wheels with naked rims, because there were no tyres, and with axles lashed on with doubtful country-made rope, because there was no rubber shock-absorber rope. We flew on single-ignition engines which the Air Force at home had long discarded as unairworthy. There were vast numbers of new dual-ignition engines available at home, where the Disposal Board were selling the latest engines as junk for a few pounds, but the army in India, on whose financial vote we were dependent, refused

to supply us with them. Any of the new equipment in the hands
of the Disposal Board could have been bought by the Indian
Government at scrap-metal prices to make good our terrible
deficiencies. It was no joke to fly over the mountains on the
frontier with worn-out and out-of-date equipment, where a
forced landing meant probably being killed outright in the crash
or, if you survived this, a still less pleasant death on the ground.
In this, as in all the R.A.F.'s many operations over savage
countries, including Germany, capture by the natives was one of
the worst things we had to fear.

Lord Montagu wrote a letter to *The Times* and this raised such
a stink at home that Sir John Salmond was sent out from England
to inquire into the charges. The moment it was known that
Salmond was being sent out, the attitude of the Army High
Command to us completely changed. They obviously panicked.
Mobilisation stores were opened up and all the spares which we
had been unable to obtain for a year and more in the past were
rushed up to us before he could reach India.

I well remember that during one of our expeditions on the
frontier, one of the less pleasant types of general came up to see
us from army headquarters. I was operating with my last four
aeroplanes, the last four in flying condition, if you could call it
that, in the whole of India. The general told us that we were
to stop operating until we got further operational orders from
headquarters, on which I said I would take my machines back to
Peshawar, get them under cover, and nurse them there until we
were wanted again at Miranshah. Whereupon the General went
off the deep end and made some unpleasant and entirely uncalled
for remarks to the effect that airmen could never do anything
unless they were coddled to the point of living in the lap of
luxury. Unfortunately for him, he added: "I suppose you must
get back to your spare parts before you can do any more." I
replied: "Yes, it was high time we got back to our ball of string"
—and that was about all the Army and the Indian Government
had ever supplied for our use. The General departed and reported
me to Air Force headquarters, who must have agreed with me,
for nothing more came of it.

I am sure that it was because of my personal knowledge of
the disgraceful technical conditions of the R.A.F. in India under
the Army that I was hurriedly posted to Irak. The posting coincided with Sir John Salmond's arrival in India to inquire into
our shortage of spares and equipment, a state of affairs not lightly

to be forgotten or forgiven, but I stayed on long enough to help put him wise.

Even if we had been able to make our aircraft airworthy, we should not have been able, while we were under the control of the Army, to use air power in an intelligent fashion. Bombing, our main task, was usually made part of combined operations, and the army's idea was much the same as in the 1914-1918 war, to control the frontier with troops, supported by long and vulnerable lines of communication. The convoys were frequently given air escorts; we were seldom given any chance to operate independently, though on occasion we were allowed to reduce a tribe to submission by independent action to the point where the Army could walk in at the last moment and take the credit and the K.C.B. Although this was up to a point a necessarily primitive essay in the "air control" we were later to use in Irak—the inhabitants were always given fair warning before their villages were destroyed, and casualties were extremely few—the special characteristics of the new weapon, its flexibility and its capacity to strike anywhere within a very wide area at any moment, were certainly and deliberately given no chance to show to advantage. A good example of what happens when old Services can suppress new weapons.

When I got to Irak, or Mespot as we called it in those days, Sir John Salmond had just taken over the "air control" of the country and most of the very large army forces which the British taxpayer refused any longer to support there had departed. A rebellion had broken out in 1920, because the Arabs had been led to expect complete independence and had got instead British Army occupation and a horde of Jack-in-Office officials; the British Army forces occupying the country were then being heavily reduced for economy's sake, but they were still numerous enough to get the rebellion under after some months of hard fighting with heavy casualties on both sides. The military control of Irak was transferred from the army to the R.A.F. entirely in order to save money. At that time the newspapers at home were running a campaign to cut down overwhelming and world-wide expenditures and were suggesting that we should abandon such useless and expensive responsibilities as Irak. If we had done so we should have been hard put to it for oil during Hitler's war. The decision to hand the control of the country to the R.A.F.—which was of course Winston Churchill's—was made in 1921 and took effect on the 1st of October, 1922. Four infantry battalions remained, and Air Vice-Marshal Sir John Salmond was in command of these as well as of the R.A.F. units in the country, which consisted of eight squadrons and four armoured car companies. We had to form our own armoured car companies because the army refused to put theirs under the R.A.F. Salmond gave me command of one of the first two troop carrying squadrons, No. 45 Squadron. We were equipped with Vickers Vernon and subsequently Victoria aircraft. My Flight Commanders were R. H. M. S. Saundby and R. A. Cochrane, whom I then met for the first time. They were both outstanding men and later both of them held high posts under me in Bomber Command. By sawing a sighting hole in the nose of our troop carriers and making our own bomb racks we converted them into what were really the first of the post-war long-range heavy bombers.

During our first year in Mespot the Turks made a determined attempt to regain the Mosul Vilayet. They began this before the R.A.F. took over and had already roughly handled a column of Imperial troops. Wars were very unpopular in those days and as a result hardly anything appeared in the home newspapers about this particular war, though the Turks eventually sent large forces over the frontier to make a determined and deliberate invasion of the Mosul area. Sir John Salmond, by concentrating all the squadrons up at Mosul and sending us straight on to the Turkish columns as they crossed the border, very quickly impressed upon the Turks that they were not getting the place without a fight, or without heavy casualties, as they had hoped, or indeed at all. They withdrew and gave it up.

The truculent and warlike tribes which occupied and still controlled, after the rebellion, large parts of Irak, also had to be quelled, and in this our heavy bombers played a major part. We were hundreds of miles up river near Baghdad and in the very centre of thoroughly turbulent and wholly unpacified tribes on whom we were endeavouring to impose government of local Baghdad i Effendis whom the tribesmen have naturally held in utter contempt from time immemorial. When a tribe started open revolt we gave warning to all its most important villages, by loud speaker from low-flying aircraft and by dropping messages, that air action would be taken after 48 hours. Then, if the rebellion continued, we destroyed the villages and by air patrols kept the insurgents away from their homes for as long as necessary until they decided to give up, which they invariably did. It was, of course, a far less costly method of controlling rebellion than by military action and the casualties on both sides were infinitely less than they would have been in the pitched battles on the ground which would otherwise have been the only alternative. At last we were able to plan our action so that the air weapon worked in complete independence of the ground, except when it was necessary to come to the rescue of the Iraqi army, which was gradually being recruited with a view to the eventual handing over of control of the country.

Never shall I forget the appalling climate, the filthy food, and the ghastly lack of every sort of amenity that our unfortunate men were compelled to put up with in "peace time," for two years at a stretch, away from their families. A main result of the economy campaign in the home newspapers was to deprive us of the most meagre and essential comforts; for example, we lacked even adequate bathrooms, though these had been in the original estimates. The swimming pool in Hinaidi Cantonment, an essential to relaxation in such a place, was economised on until it became too unappetising to use, and meanwhile it had infected numbers of men with the dread Bilharzia.

After two and a half years in Irak, 1922-1924, I came home and went through the Army Senior Officers' School. I was then given command of No. 58 Squadron at Worthy Down. This was the first heavy bomber squadron to be reconstituted as such after the war and the first to get back to night training for night operations. There again I had Saundby as Flight Commander. I believe the squadron did more night flying at that time than all the rest of the world's then existing air forces put together. It was already becoming obvious that the need to get on with the job was urgent.

In 1927 I went to the Army Staff College, where I learned a great deal about horses and thoroughly enjoyed two years' hunting with the Camberley Drag and the Garth. I contemplated with some surprise the fact that, while we were cut to the bone for every essential requirement in the Air Force, and indeed in all three services, the army at Camberley was allowed to run a stable of some 200 picked hunters, labelled as chargers. I had a magnificent first-class hunter entirely to myself the whole time, and when one horse was killed in the hunting field it was immediarely replaced by another, equally good.

It was while I was at Camberley that I first realised, with some depression but no astonishment, that since the last war the army had reduced its artillery and machine-gun content to almost pre-1914 level in addition to abolishing the Tank Corps. I used to get into trouble there occasionally. I remember a one-time C.I.G.S. giving us a lecture in the course of which, looking pointedly at me as the sole surviving airman on the course, he, to all intents and purposes, dared me to challenge his assertion that Gibraltar was so small that a bomber could not even hit the place; he then asked me what percentage of hits on Gibraltar I would consider reasonable. I replied 99 per cent, allowing for a 1 per cent hang-up on the bomb racks. He was much upset at this answer, which created considerable amusement among the students on the course. But he asked for it. In the same way I remember getting into hot water when I was asked in my turn, after a week's intensive study of tank warfare (and this at a time when the army had just got rid of the Tank Corps) to give my opinion of the week's work. I included in my answer a remark to the effect that, after I had watched the army mind at work disposing of the tank as a useless thing because it could not do exactly what the cavalryman and his horse had always done and in precisely the same way, I was sure the army would never succeed in choosing a tank that would meet all their requirements until somebody invented tanks that ate hay and thereafter made noises like a horse.

I was at least once asked to leave, during my first year, but after the second I was asked to stay on another two years as an instructor. That prospect appalled me. Nevertheless, I made many very good friends there who have since stood me in good stead, not excluding Monty, who in those days was an instructor. I had the greatest admiration for his precision of statement and lucidity as a lecturer and also for what I, as an airman, considered his ability and breadth of view as a soldier. But he appeared to me to be regarded with grave suspicion for holding what I understood were heretical, though they seemed to me very reasonable, views about the conduct of future war. As a stranger in a strange land I kept my own counsel, but I left the course with a very definite impression that in Monty we certainly had a soldier who knew his onions, no matter what the "high-ups" in the army might officially think of the smell.

I was also full of admiration for the hard-working and highly intelligent type of army officer who as a general rule went there as student, but it was borne in upon me in no uncertain manner that the motto of the place was "be orthodox or perish"; and being orthodox appeared to mean holding on to every tenet of warfare that had turned out to be a busted flush between 1914 and 1918 and ignoring all subsequent technical development.

After the staff college course I again felt a nostalgic urge to clear out and return to Africa, but I accepted instead an appointment in Egypt as senior air staff officer. When I returned, three years later, Sir John Salmond sent me, as he had long promised that he would do, to command a flying boat base and squadron. I had three aims, to do something to break what we called at that time "the flying boat trade union," to clear the black magic out of the trade, and to help solve the difficulties they were having with night flying. The flying boat branch of the service had succeeded in surrounding itself with an esoteric atmosphere, based on largely spurious nautical lore, and wished it to be understood that there were so many difficulties in the way of taking up a flying boat by night that for ordinary human beings to attempt this feat was suicidal. It did not take me long to discover that the only difference between night flying in a flying boat and in an ordinary aeroplane was that it was in every way much simpler and safer in a flying boat. The sea landing areas provided aerodromes of comparatively unlimited extent, and a flying boat could be flown down on to the water blind in conditions in which no land-based aircraft could, at that time, be landed. Don Bennett, afterwards A.O.C. of Bomber Command's Pathfinder Force, was one of my Flight Commanders in the flying boat squadron and from there I got him his subsequent job, when his short service commission expired, with Imperial Airways. He was, and still is, the most efficient airman I have ever met.

I have always looked upon that as the most enjoyable year I had in the service. There was the delight of plenty of boat sailing, and the flying boats themselves I regarded with great affection as almost entirely useless but splendid yachts for the upkeep of which somebody other than myself had to pay. Nothing could have been pleasanter, but I knew that I was wasting time and that time was short. I was not in the job for long. I was sent to the Air Ministry to serve as Deputy Director of Operations and Intelligence, and after a year I became head of the Air Ministry Planning Department, which meant that I was a member of the Joint Planning Committee, with Ronald Adams and Ted Morris at various times the army representatives, and Tom Phillips and Daniels at various times the naval representatives. I stayed at the

Air Ministry until 1938, and was therefore in a position to know exactly what was being done to prepare for the coming war. We had a very good idea about what was going to happen. One cannot divulge state papers, but when I look back on the Joint Planning Committee's 1938 paper forecasting the war and the way it was likely to develop, I think that the three of us who, fed with the facts from our respective ministries, were finally responsible for the paper—the other two were Tom Phillips, Vice-Admiral who went down with the *Prince of Wales*, and Ted Morris, Major-General, who commanded a division in Italy—can almost claim to be among the major prophets, except, of course, that neither I nor anyone else predicted, or could have predicted, all the incredibly stupid mistakes that Germany was going to make. In point of fact, I do not know why such papers should not be published by the Stationery Office, if only for the purpose of showing that the Ministry staffs of the fighting services are not quite so incompetent as they are widely believed to be.

It was while I was at the Air Ministry, in 1935, that the specifications for the heavy bomber which later developed into the Manchester, Stirling, and Halifax were laid down. Three years later it was decided that all the main bomber force should be of this type. In 1936 the shadow factory system came into being, a method of using the automobile and related industry in Britain as a second line behind the aircraft industry, and in the same year the R.A.F. was divided up into the various commands, Bomber, Fighter, Coastal and Training Commands.

In 1938 I took command for a short time of No. 4 Bomber Group, in Yorkshire, which was just forming and sadly lacked every sort of equipment. We did cross-country flights and night bombing training in Whitley aircraft, but we were up against every conceivable sort of trouble when we tried to get training areas for bombing. We wanted Abbotsbury, but the use of this as a bombing range was postponed by prolonged and bitter opposition, with a vast correspondence in the Press; the objection was that the swans at Abbotsbury would not lay eggs if we used this as a range. In actual fact, once the site was given to us and we started bombing, the swans laid more eggs than they had ever done before. The reason was that they soon learned to regard the aircraft and the practice bombs as harmless things which served, at the same time, to keep unwanted human beings away from their nests. Until one of them was killed by a direct hit, and I doubt if this ever happened, they had no reason to be anything but grateful for the change. We experienced more difficulties and opposition when we urgently needed Holy Island as another training site, apparently on the grounds that we might disturb the shades of some of our less reputable ancestors. It was hard indeed to keep patience with that sort of spirit when we knew what an appalling and imminent catastrophe threatened. I see that this sort of thing has already started again; there has lately been trouble about the use of an island to which some gannets appear to have established a prior claim.

I was then posted as Air Officer Commanding Palestine and Transjordan, and I was literally on the point of embarking when I was stopped by Sir Cyril Newall, then Chief of the Air Staff, as I left the Air Ministry; I was sent on a mission to America to buy aeroplanes. I took a technician and a test pilot with me, and we were afterwards joined by Sir Henry Self, a civil servant, to see that everything was done in proper form and order. Mr. "Jimmy" Weir came with us as an industrial expert to judge whether the factories to which we might propose to give our orders actually had the right equipment to enable them to carry them out. The result of this visit was the purchase of the first batches of Hudsons and Harvards. The Hudsons beyond doubt pulled us out of the soup when we used them for anti-submarine patrols in the first years of the war, and the Harvards broke the back of our problem in finding training aircraft.

I was much impressed with the American business efficiency, not least in one respect. We had a private conference amongst ourselves for a whole afternoon in our own hotel sitting-room, and drafted out a cable giving our final decisions to the Air Ministry. I kept the only manuscript note of the cable we proposed to send in my pocket pending dispatch, and there was no other copy of it. After the conference we retired to the bar and one of our party went to a telephone booth to send a message for us to New York; there he overheard, on a crossed line, an American voice on the transcontinental wire giving a complete account of the whole of our discussions and decisions to an interested industrial party on the other side of America. An examination of our hotel sitting-room revealed the source of the leakage; this I will not divulge. In later days, when I had a highly confidential conversation with Lord Beaverbrook, we talked in his bathroom, which seemed reasonably safe even though the seating was unconventional.

My reason for giving the order for Lockheed Hudsons was not

only that I was much impressed with the aircraft itself and thought it highly suitable for reconnaissance work; it was also that I was immensely struck by the ability and energy of the comparative youngsters who were running this then very small factory, and I could see they obviously knew their business from A to Z.

For instance, I remember saying at the end of our discussions that it was all very well expecting me to give them such a large order, but I had only been shown a purely civil version, which was all they had, of the aircraft, and I would have to take their word for it that they could alter that version to suit our military requirements. They asked me to come back in a few days to see a mock-up which they would produce. This I could not do because I had no time: I had to go elsewhere to see flying boats and Fortress bombers. To my astonishment, only twenty-four hours later a car arrived to fetch me out to the Lockheed works, and there I saw a mock-up of all our requirements in plywood, fitted complete in every detail, with two alternative noses hinged on to a real aircraft all ready for our inspection. The first alternative was our idea of our own requirements, and the second was Lockheed's idea of the same thing, but showing how it could be better done by themselves—and it was this second alternative that we chose. As I was well aware that at home we were never able to get a mock-up of any description produced in less than months, I was entirely convinced that anyone who could produce a mock-up in twenty-four hours would indeed make good all his promises—and this Lockheed's most certainly did.

I met one very efficient aircraft manufacturer who was afflicted with verbal diarrhœa to an extent I have never known before or since. He talked me into a coma and, when I was just about to pass out, invited us to lunch with him at his home. The prospect appalled me, but there was no polite way of getting out of it. When we got to his very pleasant house outside the city and were introduced to his very charming wife, I could not help thinking, while I was still in a daze and the continuous babble went on, that it was astonishing that any woman could possibly live with a man like that. Some time later I learned the explanation. She was very deaf but an expert lip reader; she did not have to listen unless she looked, so she didn't look. Afterwards I expressed to General Arnold my astonishment at this gentleman's capacity for talking. "Talk," he replied, "you have never heard him talk. You ought to see him on his knees in my office, with the tears running down his face at the prospect of gaining or losing aircraft orders, and still talking."

When the rest of the mission left America I stayed on for another week to try and see a few things in the American Air Force and to investigate the possibility of getting certain navigational instruments and other equipment that we needed. I was allowed by Colonel Olds, then commanding a bomber squadron, to look over his "Forts." I had a long and very interesting afternoon with him. I was not impressed with the armament then carried by the Fortress; in particular, the gun-mountings were wholly impractical. When I later headed the R.A.F. delegation to Washington the fruits of the discussion with Olds were already visible in the newer types of Fortress.

When I got home in 1938 I was told to my great disappointment that my posting as A.O.C. Palestine and Transjordan had been cancelled and that I was to go as Senior Air Staff Officer to Fighter Command, under Dowding. I had a prolonged argument with the then Chief of the Air Staff. Eventually, by telling him that I had just got married and that my wife's trousseau was entirely tropical I persuaded him to let my oversea posting stand. Needless to say I had other reasons besides that.

I spent the next year in Palestine. While there we made considerable progress with new methods of army co-operation, at first against suspicion and opposition, but later with the most enthusiastic co-operation of the junior army commanders. The Air Ministry had assumed a special responsibility for Palestine and Transjordan in 1919, but only because this was considered administratively more convenient. It had never been proposed to exercise the same kind of air control over Palestine as over Irak. The result was that in the troubles which came about, just before the 1939 war, as a consequence of Arab-Jewish controversies, it was mainly the army's job to police the country, though with air co-operation. At first the army used to carry out laborious encircling movements over the extremely difficult mountain country, and generally found, when the circle was complete, that they had drawn a blank. We then did the encircling with aircraft, and we did it at a few minutes' notice anywhere in the country; we dropped messages to the encircled village or area telling the inhabitants that no one would be hurt if they did not try to get out of the ring. After that the army, instead of struggling over the hills for forty-eight hours, could have a proper breakfast before they started and arrive in buses; by such means we were assured of far larger hauls of rebels and arms, and we obtained them. We called this system the "Air-Pin."

While I was in Palestine, Monty arrived to take command of a division at Haifa; I remembered him well from my two years on the Army Staff course. I met him at Headquarters, where he had come to discuss the military aspect of the rebellion with the G.O.C. He greeted me with his usual precise intonation: "aircraft, aircraft, this is no job for aircraft. It's a job for policemen." I answered that while I recognised that it was a job for policemen and not for aircraft, or for soldiers for that matter, the strength and determination of the rebels and the weakness of the police in arms and numbers were in themselves sufficient reason for using all the few military and air resources available. But I said that if he himself did not require air assistance I should be only too pleased to allot the share we should otherwise have held for him to the other army commanders; their calls for assistance from us were incessant and their appreciation of its value unqualified, if only because of the saving in effort and casualties to their troops. I felt a certain mild amusement not long afterwards when Monty became as urgent in his requests for air support as the rest of them, indeed he was more insistent than most of them, since he appreciated realities more quickly.

I always pride myself that Monty, who is only too willing to learn anything new and learns at speed, got his first real understanding of air co-operation from me, during his very short term of office in Palestine in 1939. It was short, because he was taken desperately ill not long after his arrival in the country and left for home on a stretcher. Knowing that more serious war was close upon us, I thought with dismay that we were to lose a man whom I considered to be one of our best generals. But whatever bug it was that bit Monty on that occasion—and it bit him so hard that we never expected him to reach home—he got the better of it.

The rules for rebellion in Palestine appeared to me to get simpler every day. For the British forces they amounted to this; you must not get rough, no matter how rough the "enemy" is. If the "enemy" gets particularly rough and you get rougher and kill any noticeable number of his men, even if only with the aim of saving your own men, then it is just too bad for you. My advice to all young commanders in all services is, whenever you see any prospect of being called out "in aid of the civil power" in any part of the world, to get to hell out of there as quickly

and as far as you can. If you fail by being too soft you will be
sacked; if you succeed by being tough enough, you will certainly
be told you were too tough, and you may be for it. Therefore I
say that the best thing to do is to take long leave, or to get transferred, or to retire and buy yourself a farm; do anything, in fact,
sooner than get involved "in aid of the civil power." There are
two things you can get from aiding the civil power, and two
things only—brickbats and blame. If you do not mind either of
these things it can at times be quite amusing, especially if you
are in a position to watch the machinations and the wrigglings
of "the civil power" itself.

Such, in brief, was my service experience before the 1939 war,
and to sum up my view of the country's prospects on the outbreak
of war, I could see only one vista through the wood which seemed
to end in the faintest gleam of daylight. That was the bomber
offensive. But in any case I knew that this would only be undertaken *faute de mieux*, after older methods had failed. Considering
the state of France and the fact that she had nothing that could
even be called an air force I saw no hope of successful military
operations on the Continent. It never entered my head that the
Germans, even after we had been thrown out of the Continent,
would succeed in crossing the Channel; what I feared was
complete stalemate, with the politicians eventually deciding to
call it a day and Germany left free to refresh herself for the next
step. Who was to imagine that Germany would be so idiotic as
to attack Russia? Or Japan so idiotic as to push America into the
war when she had every opportunity to do as she liked with our
Eastern possessions while we were entirely preoccupied with
Germany? In the circumstances that I foresaw—by ourselves, as
I thought we should inevitably be and for a long time were—
the bomber offensive would be our only hope of getting at
Germany, and I determined to see to it, as far as I could, that the
offensive got there, and got where it hurt.

I certainly had faith in the bomber offensive—if it could be
got going, and if the Germans did not find effective counter-
measures before we had built up the force. The surest way to win
a war is to destroy the enemy's war potential. And all that I had
seen and studied of warfare in the past had led me to believe
that the bomber was the predominant weapon for this task in this
war, as the air was already the predominant factor in other
operations either on sea or land.

In the 1914-1918 war, England being an island and there being no air force capable of really heavy attack, the Germans had the opportunity to defeat us by sinking our ships in the U-boat campaign. This would have had the same effect as destroying the country's industries, just as air attack on German communications eventually had an effect similar to the actual destruction of enemy industries. The submarine was therefore the predominant weapon of the war of 1914-1918 and if the Germans had had any strategic insight they would have used it as such. Before that, and for a very long period, the battleship had been the predominant weapon and British sea power had destroyed the war potential even of continental countries by blockade. But in 1914-1918 the submarine had ousted the battleship from its long authority. By the same token, in 1939 the bomber was the new weapon and the submarine was already getting out-of-date. How long the authority of the bomber would last I could not tell, but for the time being it seemed secure, and it was all we had, in the light of probable developments, that was suited to our purpose and to circumstances. Even before the war we heard of German attempts to develop yet newer weapons, but it is just as essential not to use the unready weapons of the next war as it is not to use the outclassed weapons of the last.

Meanwhile, in the first few days, the immediate and the worst anxiety was that if the war broke out at the tempo that we expected we should certainly run out of aircraft and crews in a matter of weeks, if not days. I expressed my feelings at that time to one of my oldest service friends. "Every time you pass a lamp post," I said, "take your hat off, because if the war starts seriously the blame is going to be put on us and that is where we shall finish."

This was my mood as I turned the borrowed Austin into the gloomy gateway of St. Vincent's, Grantham, the headquarters of my new command. Like everything else in England it was a skeleton formation with not enough meat on the bones to prevent a rattle which would be audible to the enemy. I had come to make bricks, and there was no need for my predecessor in the Command to advise me of the lack of straw.

Chapter Two

THE FIRST BOMBING

The Hampdens of 5 Group. The bomber groups. Operationa. Training. Ludlow-Hewitt. A change of command. The leaflet raids. The magnetic mine. 5 Group's minelaying. Our defence-less aircraft. The Battle of France. The Battle of Britain and the invasion barges. The beginnings of strategic bombing.

I HAVE in the course of my lifetime rarely been so depressed as when I arrived at Grantham to take over command of No. 5 Group. For one thing, the Group itself was equipped with an aeroplane which failed to meet many requirements of the normal specifications, especially with regard to comfort for the crew. It appeared to have little to recommend it except a very reliable brand of engine and the fact that this particular aeroplane, the Hampden, had at least materialised in a hurry, and was available in some numbers; most of the other types were still largely on paper. The crews made the best of it and, being strong and reliable, the aircraft did a sterling job.

At this time there were five operational Groups in Bomber Command, mainly equipped with Battles (one-engined bombers which were sent to France with the Advanced Air Striking Force to be available for direct support of the French Army in the event of an invasion of France), Blenheims, Wellingtons, Whitleys, and Hampdens. The system of Groups, each commanded by an Air Officer subordinate to the Commander-in-Chief, was an excellent one, and proved to be so throughout the war. Owing to the weather and other factors there was seldom more than a day's notice for laying on any ordinary operation and it would have been impossible for the Command to give all the necessarily detailed orders directly to its stations. The Command issued the orders to the Group Headquarters giving the target and the general plan for co-ordinating the whole attack, and the Groups themselves issued detailed orders to the units. So much was this decentralisation necessary that towards the end of the war it was found that even the Groups themselves had too much to handle;

we had to go still further and split the Group organisation up into Base organisations, each base dealing with an average of three airfields. The Group Commanders sent to the Bases more detailed explanations of the orders they themselves had received from Command, and the Bases in turn expanded the orders they had been given by Group Headquarters. The Group Commanders were given absolute freedom within the limits set by the necessity of co-ordinating an attack. At the beginning of the war, before concentration of attack made it necessary for Command itself to plan routes and timing very exactly, the Groups had even greater freedom in planning an operation.

During peace-time the enormous organisation and the large number of airfields and aircraft needed to train an adequate number of crews up to operational standards could not be provided within the limits of the endurance of the British taxpayer. Flying Training Command and the Empire Training Scheme provided us with recruits trained up to a certain standard, but very far from being fit for operations; for one thing, none of these men had yet been trained to work together as a bomber crew. This was all right when we had bombers, such as the Battles, Hinds, and Vickers Wellesleys, which usually had only a crew of two, but with the newer types, carrying crews of four, five and six, such training of the men as individuals was wholly inadequate. All the rest had to be done by Bomber Command itself, and there had been no provision for such training in peace-time outside the squadrons themselves—which in war could not undertake both training and operations.

On the outbreak of war we had, in consequence, a force almost without reserves and without any adequate training organisation behind it; any sustained campaign in the autumn of 1939 would very quickly have brought us to the end of our small supply of trained crews. And even what we had in the shop window, though there was nothing behind it, had to be bled white if we were going to provide the instructors, aircraft, and unit organisations for the training that was essential to maintain the force for the bombing offensive of the future. Only the most experienced pilots and other aircrew were fitted to serve as instructors, and these experienced men were all, of course, in the front line. Minute as was the bomber force with which we started the war, we had at once to convert a number of front line squadrons into operational training units, each unit consisting of the squadrons, usually two, of one bomber station. We began with eight such operational training units, and this was, of course, a very serious drain on our front line strength, even though this training organisation was nothing like adequate for building up a large enough force to do the enemy any real harm; at the peak of our training effort, in December, 1943, we had 22½ operational training units to meet the wastage of a front line strength of some 1000 aircraft.

During the first year of the war we were therefore tied down to an absolute minimum of operational work and operational risk, and it would have been the same whether or no we had taken squadrons from the front line for training; the only difference would have been that if we had had no O.T.U.s there could have been no bomber offensive in the future.

Air Chief Marshal Sir Edgar Ludlow-Hewitt was the chief of Bomber Command at that time, and we could not have wished for a better leader to serve under. He was a man with a minute and detailed knowledge of every aspect of his job. He was far and away the most brilliant officer I have ever met in any of the three services. If he had a fault, it was that he had such immense knowledge of every technical and operational detail of his subject, of every aspect of air warfare, that he sometimes appeared to think too much about details. Never have I come across an officer in any of the services who so completely commanded and earned the faith and respect of his subordinates.

I vividly remember the wave of black despair which overwhelmed me when, as I left one of my stations with him in his car, he told me " before it was announced" that he was leaving. My comment was: "My God, a disaster, a catastrophe!" I understood then, and I have since heard nothing to make me alter my mind, that the main reason for this change in the command was his positive insistence on the formation of the operational training units which would necessarily deprive the front line strength of the aircraft and skilled crews needed to form and man the training units. This was an essential process of "ploughing-in," which nevertheless irritated less knowledgeable authorities. Without these units, the dog would of course have eaten its own tail to hurting point within a few weeks and would have been a dead dog beyond all hope of recovery within a few months. Ludlow-Hewitt saved the situation—and the war —at his own expense, and did it, as he does all things, with good grace, and without thinking of himself or what effect it might

have on his career. In all wars commanders are faced with decisions which are unpalatable to politicians, though often enough
such decisions have to be made as a direct result of the previous
sins of omission of the same politicians. In the early stages of
every war commanders are therefore more often than not
removed; they are sacrificed either to provide some sort of
smoke screen to hide the shortcomings of those who are really
responsible for the country's unpreparedness, or merely to satisfy
some public demand made in necessary ignorance of the true
facts.

In losing Ludlow-Hewitt, we lost the finest of commanders.
But our loss in the end was to the gain of the Service as a whole,
because as an Inspector-General, with his immense technical
ability and practical knowledge, Ludlow-Hewitt had an influence
during the rest of the war on design, production, development,
and organisation which was of incalculable value throughout the
service. Without him I am sure we should never have prevailed.
Inspector-General in the R.A.F. is too often merely a job given
just before retirement, but with Ludlow-Hewitt it was very far
from being this. We reaped where he had sown and no man
deserved better of his country than he did.

As I said before, we all expected violent fighting to start at
any minute and to bring us quickly to the end of all our resources.
Instead, there was the "phoney" war, and this saved us. We could
never have produced the aircraft or the organisation to train the
crews but for the breathing space this gave us.

In the earliest stages of the war we were not allowed to bomb
anything on land, and our only possible targets were therefore
warships, which we could attack only by day. Our losses from
enemy fighters and flak were prohibitive and we therefore desisted
before we had done ourselves or the enemy much harm. Meanwhile the Whitleys and Wellingtons were put to the questionable
employ of dropping pamphlets all over Europe, a game in which
we never had the slightest faith. My personal view is that the
only thing achieved was largely to supply the Continent's requirements of toilet paper for the five long years of war. You have
only to think what any man of sense would do with an obviously
enemy pamphlet when he picked it up, how he would regard it,
and how he would react to the statements in it. Our reaction to
enemy pamphleteering had always been to jeer and at the most
to keep some of their leaflets as souvenirs. News to occupied
territory was another matter.

Years before, the idiotic expansion of secret files at the Air Ministery once drove me to send a minute round pointing out that at the rate we were going we should be making newspapers secret next. But never did I think to see the day when not only were newspapers made secret, but moreover newspapers expressly produced for the sole purpose of being delivered as rapidly as possible and by any and every means to the enemy. Yet they still had to be handled under all the complicated secret document procedure on our bomber stations and, in spite of repeated applications, we could never get these instructions withdrawn. Many of these pamphlets were patently so idiotic and childish that it was perhaps just as well to keep them from the knowledge of the British public, even if we did risk and waste crews and aircraft in dropping them on the enemy.

I suppose that propaganda of this kind, properly timed and efficiently turned out, might have the effect, in certain circumstances, of shortening a victorious and overwhelming offensive by a day or two. Leaflets are said to have had some effect right at the end of the previous war, though such claims generally originated with those who got the leaflets out. But if so, why go to the trouble of inoculating your enemy at the very beginning of a long war against a weapon you might conceivably use with some profit at the end of it?

The first magnetic mines began to take effect round our coasts and ports in October, 1939, and I remember the alarm and despondency which this caused. We then had the extraordinary task of bombing the flare path on the sea from which the German minelaying aircraft were supposed to take off. Actually we did some good, but it is an amusing sign of the country's political attitude to the air war that we were not allowed to go and bomb the aerodromes on land from which other minelayers took off in case we hurt somebody. This ban was temporarily lifted when German aircraft dropped some bombs on Scapa Flow and three nights later we attacked, by way of reprisal, the seaplane base on the island of Sylt. It had been originally intended to make the seaplane base on the island of Borkum the target, but some politicians discovered that there were half a dozen civilians in the neighbourhood. The then Secretary of State for Air, Sir Kingsley Wood, interrupted his speech in the House of Commons that night with dramatic effect to announce that at that very moment our aircraft were dropping bombs on Sylt. There was a good deal of surprise when it was discovered that no worthwhile damage had been done to the seaplane base; it was, of course, a most unsuitable target for attack by night for a force of 50 aircraft dropping a negligible load of bombs, and however heavily and successfully it had been attacked it could have been repaired in a few days, during which the enemy could have used a number of alternative bases.

I was much interested in this German minelaying campaign. Years before, when I had been head of the Operations and Intelligence Branch of the Air Ministry, I had put out a specification for the magnetic mine, virtually in the form in which it afterwards appeared. I concluded my original minute on the subject, which is still in existence, by pointing out that the introduction of this weapon would be very much to our detriment as a seafaring nation and that logically we should therefore do our utmost to develop this weapon, because it is only by developing and experimenting with weapons that it is really possible to arm yourself in time with the antidote. This proposal of mine led to a furious fight between the Air Ministry and the Admiralty about which of the two was to make the magnetic mine. The Air Ministry asserted that the mine was airborne and therefore their responsibility, while the Admiralty said that as it fell in the water it was theirs. I was not personally involved in this dispute, which was no doubt as futile and silly as most other inter-service disputes and rivalries and caused long delay in getting on with the job. But now that the weapon had started showering down around our coasts and blowing the bottom out of our own ships I rang up Ludlow-Hewitt and told him that I had started people thinking about the magnetic mine years ago with the idea of finding an antidote to it—as they did not appear to have found the antidote, had we yet got as far as producing the mine itself? Because, if so, I should like to give the Germans some of their own medicine. Inquiry elicited the fact that the Air Ministry and the Admiralty had eventually agreed to allow the mine to be produced by a naval shore establishment which I have always found an extremely efficient and capable organisation and where the torpedo and mine experts of the Navy work. Not only had this establishment agreed to produce it, but prototypes had in fact been produced, with the usual speed and high skill that I have always found in the technical departments of the Navy. They very soon got the mine into production and then— poetic justice—it was discovered that my particular aircraft, the Hampden, was the only aircraft that would carry the mine; this was exactly what might have been expected of it, since in general it would do little and carry little that our specifications had demanded of it, but it would do a great deal else, including this minelaying.

The one really bright spot in No. 5 Group's operations was the minelaying that followed. This was the beginning of a highly successful campaign which forced the enemy to divert more and more of his war effort to anti-minelaying devices, and shipbuilding for replacements and repairs, and, before the end of the war, drove him to engage 40 per cent of his naval personnel in minesweeping; it also put an immense strain on the enemy's alternative communications.

When the Germans invaded Norway we attempted some daylight operations against the enemy, though only the southernmost part of Norway was within range. The Hampden was cold meat for any determined enemy fighter in daylight, as I knew it would be, and we got one or two pretty serious knocks. The Hampden was then a most feebly armed aircraft with a single gun on top and a single one underneath, manned by a gunner in a hopelessly cramped position, together with a gun firing forward which, as it was fixed, was of no value at all. The mounts of the two moveable guns were rickety and had a limited traverse with many blind spots.

I saw that something would have to be done, and done quickly, to get some sort of reasonable armament for my aircraft. I had not served for 25 years without knowing that it is quite impossible to get anything drastic done through the proper channels within reasonable time, and I had not dealt directly or indirectly with the Treasury for almost as long without realising that if you order things otherwise than through the proper channel you find yourself made to pay for them. That is, you find yourself made to pay provided the bill is small enough to make repayment conceivable out of the meagre salary of a regular officer. I have therefore learned long ago that if you want to do anything drastic on your own in the Service, you must do it on a large enough scale to put it beyond the bounds of practical possibility for you to be forced to pay for it. With these facts in mind I collected a technically-minded Station commander in my Group, E. A. B. Rice, and we forayed forth into the countryside to visit the nearest manufacturing town, Gainsborough, where we discovered a typically English "family" firm, Alfred Rose and Sons. This is the sort of firm which can do anything without any fuss and with a comparatively minute staff in the design and drawing office. It is the sort of firm where the workers greet you with a smile wherever you walk and where they address the owner and the managing-director by their Christian names with Mr. or Master in front of them, as appropriate. It took Rose's no more than a fortnight to produce designs for gun mountings which got rid of all the fearful disabilities of the official type, doubled the effective fire power of the Hampden, and eliminated the blind spots. It was but a few weeks before the gun mountings were in full production and going into action. Through the normal channels it is most unlikely that they would ever have materialised. When asked why I had ordered two thousand of these mountings with no authority to do so I replied that if I had ordered twenty or two hundred I should have had to pay for them myself, and that anyhow they were necessary—as indeed they were.

Later in the war Rose's—that is, Alfred Rose himself, Curtis the designer, and Fred the foreman—together with Rice, who was by then a Group Commander—were again to pull us out of the soup with beautifully designed and made .5 turrets, when official channels had let us down completely and spent much of their energies protesting that nothing could be done while we and Rose's got on and did it.

When Germany opened the offensive in the West most of our information about the Battle of France came from what we read in the newspapers. The Command's effort was directed, or misdirected, to the task of blocking the enemy's communications, and for my Hampdens this mostly took the form of attempting to push down houses in French towns in such a manner as to block the important crossroads. With the bomb load that my aircraft could carry and the lack of navigational aids this was, of course, a quite impracticable employment; and except in the brightest moonlight we had no conceivable means of identifying a pinpoint target like a crossroads, or even, for that matter, an averaged-sized town. At that time it was almost impossible to hit any inland target by night except when there was a bright moon; on the coast one could find a target on dark nights because the shore line and the surf showed up. Even in moonlight it was difficult to find an inland target unless this had some identifiable landmark beside it, such as a thick wood, a river bend, or a lake, or unless there was a very big open space or park in the middle of a densely built-up area which had some definite shape. The principle of blocking crossroads by bombing was sound, and this eventually proved an important contribution of the bomber force during the Allied invasion of Europe, but during the Battle of France we were attempting the impossible with the equipment then at our disposal.

Before the war the French were promised that the whole of the R.A.F.'s bomber force would be used to resist an invasion of France, and that all our bomber squadrons should operate, in the event of invasion, under the general direction of the French High Command. This included, not only the Advanced Air Striking Force of short-range bombers which was actually based in France, but also the longer-range bombers in England. The French had been much afraid, before the war, that the English would proceed at once to the strategic bombing of German industries and leave the air support of the French army to the French; this was naturally an alarming prospect, the French air force being what it was, but they were reassured, and promised everything we could give them. At the same time we had to warn them not to hope for too much from the bombers. We knew that the enemy would have vastly superior numbers of aircraft, that most of our bases would have to be far from the battle-front because we should not have the facilities for handling even a force of medium bombers in France, and that the Germans would have at their disposal an immense and therefore at that time an indestructible network of communications. Nevertheless the French continued to expect much from the bombing of railways behind the German lines and were inclined to think, when our bombing proved as ineffectual as we had said it would be, that this was because the R.A.F., in spite of all its promises, had concentrated on targets east of the Rhine.

Oddly enough, in spite of the French insistence on the support of the whole bomber force for their army, when the invasion started, it proved impossible to persuade General Gamelin to permit the use of bombers at all. Gamelin was quite rightly afraid of the effect of bombing on his own army and he suffered from the extraordinary delusion that if he did not use the bombers, the enemy, by a sort of gentleman's agreement, would also omit to use them. Eventually Barrett, the Commander-in-Chief of the British Air Force in France, had to order his squadrons into action on his own initiative. It was soon discovered that the French High Command was really quite incapable of directing any bomber force at all, and the British Air Staff had to do most of the planning for them. There were occasions when the Air Staff had to refuse to attack targets chosen by the French Command because we knew that the attack would have caused us heavy casualties without having any influence whatever on the course of the battle.

From the point of view of Bomber Command the Battle of France was a complete muddle, and, even if we had had a large enough force to intervene with success, we should seldom have had enough information to plan our attacks. The influence, actual or potential, of our bombers on this battle was much exaggerated, but later on, during the Battle of Britain, the influence of the bomber force has been much underrated; all the credit for preventing the invasion of Britain has been given to Fighter Command, and the significance of Bomber Command's share in the battle, which was, of course, the bombing of invasion ports and the barges in them, has been largely overlooked. I am very far from wishing to belittle the achievement of Fighter Command, though it must be pointed out that once we had confirmed what we were already sure of, that the eight-gun fighter could in fact catch the almost unarmed German bomber, then the destruction of the German bomber squadrons outside their own fighter cover was very similar to shooting cows in a field, and our own casualties showed that this was so. Almost the only danger was from the German escort of fighters, and the escort was by no means always there. In point of fact, Fighter Command's losses were very low as compared with the normal casualty rate for our bomber operations.

The Germans never make a small mistake, because they are cautioned against all small mistakes in their manuals, without reference to which they seldom do anything whatever. But they can always be relied upon to make all the imaginable large and catastrophic mistakes, together with a good many that only a German could think out. No one but a German would have thought of attacking Russia quite needlessly before the rest of the world had been finished off. Nobody but the Germans would have thought themselves so clever at designing aeroplanes that they could afford to use almost unarmed bombers against us; they never grasped the simple fact that even a bad fighter is bound to catch the average bomber. At the beginning of the Battle of Britain the German bombing was certainly very good, but they were then using their regular and highly trained crews;

as they were flying in almost defenceless aircraft the supply of really good crews soon began to run out.

The facts about the projected invasion of England came out at the Nuremberg trials and here may be briefly summarised. Hitler issued to Keitel and Jodl a directive for the invasion of England, a landing operation, on July 16th, 1940. The first essential condition for the landing was that the English Air Force should be so effectively overcome that it could no longer "show any considerable aggressive force against the German attack." By the beginning of September Hitler was beginning to think about attacking Russia instead of invading England; Raeder said that this was because Hitler feared that control of the air over the Channel in the autumn of 1940 could no longer be attained. What Hitler wanted was protection from air attack for a seaborne invasion and at that time our fighters could not have been a serious threat to shipping. In those days there were no rockets or bombs on fighters, and the protection he wanted was therefore against bombers.

It was definitely Bomber Command's wholesale destruction of the invasion barges in the Channel ports that convinced the Germans of the futility of attempting to cross the Channel, especially as Fighter Command's victory meant that our bombers could have fighter cover over the Channel if necessary and so could attack by day in addition to their normal operations by night. Our attacks on the barges began in July of 1940, well before the main air battle of Britain developed, and were highly successful. They were carried out by night and here it was of decisive importance that we could identify and hit coastal targets, even on a moonless night, unless the weather was very unfavourable. The Channel ports proved such easy targets that it eventually became the custom to allot the routine bombing of these ports to crews in the final stages of their operational training, freshmen, as they were called. Wing Commander Guy Gibson, V.C., has described in his book *Enemy Coast Ahead* how the ports were allotted to bomber stations and the individual basins in the ports to squadrons. The crews studied photographs of the ports taken day by day and were easily able to count the barges they had smashed. Stations and even squadrons had their own "private" docks—and great was the competition to bust all the barges in them.

In the past I had done a good bit of ditch-crawling in the French canals and rivers and sailing round the French coasts.

While doing so I had been continually impressed by the magnificent power-driven barges, of which there seemed to be an unlimited supply on the Continent, and I had realised how valuable they would be in any invasion across the Channel. Before I drew the attention of General "Bob" Haining to the threat which these barges constituted, the War Office seems to have lacked appreciation of how they could be used to put troops across the Channel or of the enormous number of them available.

During the summer and autumn of 1940 we began the strategic bombing of German industries, though on an infinitely small scale. Before the war there had been a great deal of theoretical study of the problem of attacking industrial targets, all of it based on the assumption that the precise identification of targets would be far easier than in fact it proved to be. This was partly because it was more or less assumed that much of the strategic offensive would be carried out by day, and partly because the difficulties of navigation by night were not fully appreciated. Manuals of bombing tactics, which might have done us more harm than they did if we had been as manual-minded as the Germans, went to great pains to pick out the more vulnerable parts of specific factories and to recommend various elaborate sequences of attack with different kinds of bombs. The more vulnerable parts of gasworks, for example, were considered to be the power plant, exhausters, pumping station and benzol plant; it was understood that these parts of the plant were usually to be found standing together in line and were easily distinguishable by the scrubbers. Since it was assumed that bombs could be readily directed at the more vulnerable parts of a plant, the use of ridiculously small bombs was recommended, the 250 lb. general purpose bomb, for example, was considered best for the preliminary stages of an attack on certain sections of fuel production plants—this would include synthetic oil plants—to be followed by incendiaries when the high explosives had spilled the inflammable oil out of the tanks and pipes. Even smaller bombs would do for smaller targets, as, for example, the 40 lb. general purpose high-explosive bomb for the smaller electric transformer stations.

It was very much a gentleman's war that our manuals contemplated; houses, for example, were conceivable targets but they were described as of two kinds, multi-storeyed, such as barracks, and single storeyed, such as the smaller types of dwelling houses used as billets by troops. The right method of attack against billets was by 40 lb. general purpose bombs, to be followed if necessary by incendiaries. Incendiaries, it was held, should always be dropped at the end of an attack when inflammable debris has been scattered and could most easily be set alight; this particular doctrine persisted during the first two years of the war, though anything less easy to set alight than a heap of rubble it would be hard to imagine.

In 1940 the Ministry of Economic Warfare was in its glory, planning a campaign against Germany's synthetic oil plants, together with factories making aluminium, and aircraft works. There were several factors which tended to conceal the futility of planning such a campaign during the early stages of the bombing offensive. The forces we were able to send against such targets were extremely small and their bomb load negligible, but it was known that this could be remedied in time and meanwhile our weakness could be considered sufficient reason for the failure of any campaign. At the same time we were using a number of regular and highly-trained crews who were much better able to find their targets by night than the average crew, and the defences of Germany were then in a rudimentary stage, so that it was possible to come down low and visually identify targets even in the Ruhr; this suggested that there was nothing radically wrong with the idea of bombing individual German factories one by one. But, like the greater part of our economic warfare at the beginning of the war, the whole plan of attack overlooked the fact that Germany was not effectively encircled as she had been in the last war.

To begin with, there was the blockade; as the German people had chosen guns instead of butter they obviously had no butter, and as blockade had starved them in the last war, it was obvious that it must be effective in this. It may be remembered that very early in the war somebody thought he had discovered that the Nazi war leaders were having butter and other luxuries sent in from abroad, and that this revelation was given the widest publicity; it was supposed to show that everyone except the Nazi leaders was enduring frightful privations. This argument overlooked the fact that Germany could get pretty well anything she wanted from Russia under the terms of the non-aggression pact and had only to give a rather meagre allowance of war material in exchange. In June, July, and August of 1940 aircraft were sent to attack quite a number of aluminium plants, because it was thought that Germany had started the war with insufficient stocks of aluminium for the aircraft industry, but the rather obvious fact that Germany had just conquered France, where there were huge stocks of bauxite, in addition to aluminium plants, was forgotten. The bombing of synthetic oil plants had a much longer history, which I shall discuss later, but it is worth remarking here that Germany had captured Poland, where there were some oil supplies, and could get oil from Rumania and Russia.

Anyone of the three classes of industrial target—synthetic oil plants, aircraft factories, and aluminium plants—attacked by Bomber Command in 1940 would, in the later stages of the war, have had to be given first priority for attack by both Bomber Command and the U.S.A.A.F. for a considerable period if a campaign against them was to have any chance of success. But in 1940, besides these industrial targets, we were also required to bomb German communications, both railways and canals, in the area of the Ruhr and Rhineland. This was really a continuation of the campaign against communications which Bomber Command had been required to carry out during the Battle of France, when any damage we did to railways, bridges, and the like was quickly repaired or easily by-passed. But it was probably not until we ourselves had experience of bomb damage to railways during the Blitz that it was fully understood how very quickly all but the heaviest and most widespread and continuous damage can be repaired.

Throughout 1940 and the first half of 1941 attacks continued to be made on the marshalling yard at Hamm, which never was and never could be a bottleneck in the German railway system; there are far too many marshalling yards in the Ruhr area for any practicable attack on them to have any decisive or lasting effect on the running of the railways, and this fact was to be fully appreciated in the successful attack on communications which eventually brought the German war machine to a stop. As it was, it is very doubtful if our attacks in 1940 had any appreciable effect, even for a few hours, on the efficiency even of the one marshalling yard at Hamm.

It was appreciated, even at this early stage, that no attack on German communications could be effective unless it included coastal traffic, which was being attacked by minelaying, and inland waterways as well as the railways. The autobahnen which Hitler had built could be neglected because road traffic can never supply the place of railways and shipping, especially when there is anything approaching a shortage of oil and rubber, and because in any case roads are wholly unproductive targets for bombing. It so happens that there is a genuine bottleneck in the German system of inland waterways; this is the Dortmund-Ems Canal, and it is vulnerable to air attack at points where there are aqueducts or where the canal passes between embankments over low lying ground. This canal is the only link by water between the Ruhr and Eastern Germany or the North Sea and the Baltic; iron ore from Sweden inevitably goes through the canal to the Ruhr, and its barges carry millions of tons of freight to and from the Ruhr. The canal was accordingly attacked several times in 1940, and Hampdens from my Group succeeded in damaging both of its aqueducts in low level attacks against very heavy flak. Five Hampdens were dispatched on one attack and all of them were damaged by gunfire, two of them being shot down at once. The pilot of the last of the five, Squadron Leader Learoyd, was rightly awarded the Victoria Cross for his determination; it was his bombs that hit the aqueduct. But any operation which deserves the V.C. is in the nature of things unfit to be repeated at frequent intervals, and it was obvious that the Dortmund-Ems canal could never be blocked for long unless accurate attacks could be repeated at frequent intervals to keep pace with repairs.

It might be argued that since it must have been clear that we could do the enemy no harm by bombing his industries and communications in 1940 we should not have wasted men and aircraft on these attacks, but should have conserved our strength for use in a possible invasion of England and for offensive action in the future. But after the Battle of France strategic bombing at once became the central point in Allied strategy, so that it was necessary to begin attacking at once, on however minute a scale, if only for the purpose of testing and probing the enemy's defence. A policy of conserving our front line strength until such a time as it could be used on an effective scale would have meant that we should have had no chance of keeping pace with the enemy's counter-measures. As it was, we were able to appreciate without any sudden and catastrophic rise in casualties, the effect of the enemy's growing defences; we were able, for example, gradually to increase the height at which our bombers operated and eventually to find means of identifying the target even from such great heights as became necessary. And in one sense we were conserving our strength for the future by setting aside so many squadrons for training; for a long time to come our operational training units would have been able to put up as many crews and aircraft as the front line squadrons. To resist invasion, that force would have been available, and it did in fact contribute to the bombing of the invasion barges in the Channel ports.

Chapter Three

IN THE AIR MINISTRY AND U.S.A.

Appointed Deputy Chief of the Air Staff. Cutting down our staff. The Blitz in London. We plan for 4000 bombers. Strategic bombing a British idea. The Air Force and the Army. Lunatic weapons. A visit to America. "Imperial Troops." Bomber Command's operations.

WHEN Ludlow-Hewitt left Bomber Command in 1940 he was succeeded by Portal. Portal then sent for me at Bomber Command Headquarters to tell me that he had just been appointed Chief of the Air Staff and was to take up his new duties at the Air Ministry within twenty-four hours. He had been considering what sort of team he wanted to work with him and he asked if I would go with him as Deputy Chief of the Air Staff. After an active command in the field the prospect of returning to the Air Ministry horrified me.

The working hours were appalling. As D.C.A.S. I used to leave my flat at 8.30 and start with a meeting at nine o'clock every morning. I never got back to bed until one a.m. at the earliest, often not until three or four, sometimes not at all. This went on continuously for three to four weeks without a stop, and then I had just 48 hours in which to go home and get my breath back.

My first impression on arriving at the Air Ministry was that the staffs of every department were fantastically bloated. Junior officers were to my mind quite needlessly named directors of this and that, and they all imagined themselves as commanders in the field of the commands they were supposed to direct—a very nice job too, because they thought—mistakenly—that they were running the show without having to take the responsibility for the results. As far as my own staff was concerned, I quickly disabused them of that attitude. I stopped subordinates from writing to Commanders-in-Chief saying that they were "directed" to say this, that, and the other. I looked upon Commanders-in-Chief in the field as responsible people who were not to be bothered by the trumpery opinions of young Jacks-in-office who felt that they could blow themselves up with the full authority of the Air Council. But the same thing began again when I left the Air Ministry and was myself a Commander-in-Chief.

It has always been my principle to prevent negative-mindedness amongst my staff and wherever I have held a Command, until the time when I went to Bomber Command, I always issued a definite order that, while the head of any branch of the staff could say "yes" to anything which the units asked for from headquarters, I was the only person entitled to say "no." At Bomber Command itself I had slightly to modify that rule; the force and the staff were too large and the pace too hot for it to be workable. But I always instructed the heads of departments to reserve negative replies for themselves and to disabuse their juniors of the idea that they were running the show, or were there for any purpose but to help the Units.

I was greeted on arrival at the Air Ministry with stacks upon stacks of files from every department of the Air Staff, each file arguing from the general to the particular against the reduction of any member of the staff in a particular department. Much of the Air Ministry, in fact, seemed to be spending the greater part of its time in justifying its own existence. This was a legacy from my predecessor, who had suggested reducing the staff. It was quite obvious that to discuss every individual appointment mentioned in the files would offer no solution and would take up all my time. A much simpler and more effective way of reducing staff was suggested to me. This was merely to issue a fiat that the whole of the Air Staff should be reduced by so much per cent, and no back answers; 40 per cent was put forward. We issued the fiat and as the missive crept round the corridors I almost thought I could hear the wail of despair with which the *embusqués* in the bowels of the building were greeting it. The next morning my office was filled, not with a deputation, but with a crowd of deputies, each sent to argue the case of his particular branch or department. I was adamant, and so were others. Some of the heads of branches thought they had found an unanswerable objection when they were able to point out that some vital job was being done by one man; they got the unsympathetic reply that any job done by one man could be given as additional work to two men who were doing some other job.

The consequence was that there was an enormous and very suitable clear out and that all the essential work was not only still being done, but done with much more efficiency and speed; the grimly long hours were reduced and a number of people who were doing nothing to justify their existence were shoved off somewhere where they could do some useful work. It was fun while it lasted, but I fear it was not long before they crept in here and there again. One thing I never succeeded in doing was to produce any impression whatever on the number of civil servants in the place; for instance, I always had far more clerks and typists than could possibly find full employment and I entirely failed to get rid of any of them. A sure way to promotion in the civil service, and often in the services, is to get the establishment of one's department increased, and some civil servants are masters of the art of empire-building.

I well remember the worst nights of the Blitz. I watched the old city in flames from the roof of the Air Ministry, with St. Paul's standing out in the midst of an ocean of fire—an incredible sight. One could hear the German bombers arriving in a stream and the swish of the incendiaries falling into the fire below. This was a well-concentrated attack, though the number of aircraft which actually got to the city and the weight of bombs they dropped was a mere nothing as compared with our subsequent attacks on German cities. Even on the worst night the majority of the German aircraft failed to reach the actual target area.

As I watched I turned to the sentry on the roof and said: "The last time London was burnt, if my history is right, was in 1666," and I told him he was looking at history. This seemed not to make the slightest impression on him; he did not even answer beyond sucking his teeth. I asked him how long he had been there, and he said for the whole of the war, as he was over-age for active service. I asked him whether he wasn't very bored on ordinary nights, and he said that he wasn't, because he was a student of natural history. That seemed to me a somewhat extraordinary pursuit to engage in on the roofs of Whitehall, and I asked him to explain what he meant. He said that there were some 40 to 50 cats from Government offices on the roofs at night, and that what with the fights and one thing and another there was plenty to see, especially as there was an "unexploded tom" amongst them.

All the same, though the sentry was uninterested, the Blitz seemed to me a fantastic sight and I went downstairs and fetched Portal up from his office to have a look at it. Although I have often been accused of being vengeful during our subsequent destruction of German cities, this was the one occasion and the only one when I did feel vengeful, and then it was only for the moment. Having in mind what was being done at that time to produce heavy bombers in Britain I said out loud as we turned away from the scene: "Well, they are sowing the wind." Portal also made some comment to the same effect as mine, that the enemy would get the same and more of it.

If the Germans had gone on using the same force for several nights against London and if the majority of aircraft had got to the target they would have got the whole of London in flames. The fire tornado they would have raised would have been worse than anything that happened later in Hamburg and the whole of London would have gone as Hamburg went.

We were then well in the war and entirely on our own. There was no reason why anybody should be fool enough to join us. Nobody then anticipated that the Germans would be idiotic enough to kick Russia into the war, though in fact Hitler had already made his plans to do so, or the Japs idiotic enough to kick America into it; it looked then like a complete show-down between Germany and ourselves alone. That being so, it was obviously outside the bounds of possibility to invade the Continent, though the British army wished to make plans for doing so, and there therefore remained three alternatives. The first was to give in, which was unthinkable. The second was just to sit down, accept a stalemate, and defend ourselves, which in the long run would be impracticable and absurd and mean eventually a victory to Nazidom. The third was to get at Germany by the only means left to us, which was by the bombing offensive.

I most certainly regarded this, not only as the only alternative then available to us, but also as an entirely practicable method of beating the enemy, provided only that we got on quickly enough to keep ahead of the enemy's counter-measures. But in the light of our experience I was not at all happy about our ability to beat the enemy's growing defences; we ourselves seemed to have been quick enough in finding methods of confusing or beating off the German attacks on Britain, by interfering with the enemy's radio beams for navigation at night, by starting dummy fires, and later on by equipping our night fighters with the first of the radar devices which enabled them to find the bombers in the dark. I did not then have that high regard for the ability of our scientists that I subsequently acquired as the war progressed and as I saw their inventions pull us time and again out of a mess.

If we could keep ahead of the Germans, I was convinced,

having watched the burning of London, that a bomber offensive of adequate weight and the right kind of bombs would, if continued for long enough, be something that no country in the world could endure. I knew also that others besides myself, including Portal and Winston Churchill, were convinced that to carry out a bomber offensive was about the only thing we could hope to do in the foreseeable future. It was, of course, anybody's guess what effort would be required and over what period the offensive would have to be continued, but working it out as best we could on the data then available we asked for a front-line strength of some 4000 heavy bombers, about three times the strength we were ultimately to achieve. It was not, of course, in any way my decision to build up a force of this size; to put so large a part of the nation's war effort into the production of one weapon was a decision that could only be made by the War Cabinet advised by the Chiefs of Staff.

It is worth remarking that no other country in the world had at that time conceived the possibility of using an air force in this way, to fight a war by itself and, within certain limits, win a war outright. The French believed that bombers could only be used to serve as long-range artillery for the army and had very vague ideas even about how this artillery should be used; in any case, they had no bombers and left it to the British to give this support to their army. The Germans completely subordinated their whole air force to the land operations of a Continental army. The Russians never seriously attempted strategic bombing after they had entered the war against Germany or in their war against Finland. They had neither the knowledge nor the productive capacity to equip a heavy bomber force, so that it may be supposed that they either had never entertained, or had rejected, the idea of using an air force on independent operations; in any case the Germans have stated that the Russian air force was comparatively ineffective even when reinforced by large numbers of British and American aircraft flown by Russians. The Japanese entirely subordinated their air force to the operations of their army and navy. And it is certainly true, as Major Alexander de Seversky has said in his published report on Pacific Air Power, that the United States, as well as the Japanese, had not originally visualised the use of aircraft in any but a close strategical-tactical role; undoubtedly they took the main idea of the strategic use of air power from the R.A.F. and only because of the incredible efficiency of their industrial organisation were they able to produce strategic bombers in time for them to take part in the war against Germany and Japan. Seversky says that the tactical use of aircraft was "the only role at first visualised by military leaders of all warring nations including our own," but this was certainly not true of the British. General Smuts had reported to the War Cabinet in the last war that air power could and would be used strategically before long and the R.A.F. was using air power strategically in Irak in 1922. The idea was a natural one for a country which has never maintained an army of Continental proportions, has a large empire which must be defended as cheaply as possible, and has in the past largely won its wars by the strategic use of sea power working as an independent weapon; the same principle of strategy that made England a sea power in the past had only to be applied to the new weapon which had rendered obsolete the old one, the battleship.

Winning a war by bombing, as at that time we were proposing to do, can mean several things. It may mean bringing the enemy's war effort so completely to a standstill that you are invited into the country to clear up the mess; in which case the only army you will need will be a well-trained police force. Or it may mean little more than softening up the enemy's defences, communications, and war industries so effectively in advance of a well prepared invasion that that invasion goes according to plan; in which case you will need a large and very well-equipped army. And, of course, it may mean, and probably does mean, something between these two alternatives. As things were after Dunkirk, it seemed inconceivable that any army we could raise and equip in Great Britain would ever be able to get back on the Continent unless there was some internal rot in Germany or effective revolt in the German-occupied territories. Certainly those responsible for the war did not seem to need convincing that this was so; if we had had any allies, or had expected any, the situation would have been different. After Dunkirk it became obvious that the army would need for the re-invasion of the Continent, something like 15 armoured divisions and 70 other divisions over and above what might be needed to defend Great Britain or any other part of the Empire. To raise such a force by ourselves was wholly impracticable; we should never have had the man power to recruit such an army or the shipping to mount so vast an invasion.

It was, of course, the army's business to think in terms of the moment when they could get back on to the Continent after the enemy had been sufficiently weakened, either by bombing or by some other means, for this to be possible. When the moment for invasion came air power would probably not have finished its work, but would still be needed; in fact the soldiers had been convinced by the swift succession of German successes that it would be absolutely indispensable at this stage, and they asked for a huge force to serve as a specialised air component of the army; such an air component, they believed, had been largely responsible for the German victories. We in the R.A.F. had to point out that the highly specialised types required by the army would not be able to hold their own against a powerful air force, and perhaps not even against powerful ground defences. The Germans had won their victories in circumstances entirely different from any that we could contemplate for our own forces; they had used their air force against armies which had scarcely any air protection or air support and were very ill-provided with anti-aircraft guns, but this would not be the case if we encountered the German army in the future. Admittedly the specialised army co-operation types of aircraft might be rather more suitable on special occasions than the general-purpose bombers and fighters we were proposing to build, but they could not by themselves gain or maintain air superiority. The German dive-bombers were a case in point. They were no doubt accurate and alarming when used against undefended troops, but they were so easily shot down by efficient anti-aircraft fire, or, of course, by any normal fighter, that they were rapidly becoming obsolete at the very moment when a " why no dive bombers?" campaign was being run in the Press and in Parliament; even in Russia, it was not long before the Germans found they could only use them by night. It would, of course, be a good thing if we could afford to build all the specialised types as well as the main air force, but here again we altogether lacked the man-power and industrial resources to do anything of the kind. What we therefore proposed to do was to build a force which, acting independently against the enemy's air force and other defences, would, it was hoped, gain air pre-dominance, and then, when that was achieved, could work in close co-operation with the army; for this co-operation there would eventually be special training and exercises.

There were some doubts at the beginning of the war, whether any such air force could, in fact, be sufficiently flexible to do all the work that might be required of it. In particular it was gravely doubted whether any one type of bomber, or crew trained in one way, could serve for strategic bombing, close support of the army, attacks on capital ships, and sea mining. In the event, the heavy bombers proved so extremely useful in all these roles that I had the greatest difficulty in preventing them from being continually switched, to meet the demands of one or other service or of one or other of the Government departments, from one duty to another. It was much like my experience in Palestine over again; at first nobody thought our aircraft would be of any value, and then there were incessant demands for the use of them.

Rather naturally the soldiers wanted the specialised air component to be as much a part of each army corps or army as its tanks or artillery. It had to be pointed out that this was not in point of fact how the Germans had used their air force in their successful campaigns, and that it overlooked the main advantage of an air force, that it can be concentrated at very short notice at the point where it is needed. This concentration of the force at the decisive time and place cannot be brought about if the force is split up into penny packets; unified control of all the available air power is necessary because, with the rapid changes of situation that are always characteristic of air warfare, a number of small and separate air components will always provide too few or too many aircraft at any given time and place.

At this time, when those who were responsible for the conduct of the war had to all intents and purposes placed the whole management of all offensive action in the hands of the Royal Air Force, Portal, as the Chief of the Air Staff, had immense responsibilities. It was not only that he had to see that the offensive was correctly planned, and with the odds as much against us as they were then the least blunder seemed likely to prove fatal. He had also to decide exactly how much air power should be allotted to defensive operations at the expense of the coming offensive. Of course the Chiefs of Staff have almost as much responsibility in putting the facts before the War Cabinet as the War Cabinet has in deciding what to do in the light of those facts. Portal could not, for example, delegate the real responsibility for the overall running of the bomber offensive to me or anyone else; that it was carried out as it was was finally the decisions of the War Cabinet, acting on the advice of the Chiefs of Staffs, and when America entered the war the decision of the British and United States Governments advised by the Combined Chiefs of Staff Committee on which Portal acted for the R.A.F. and General Arnold for the United States Air Force.

At the conferences of the Chiefs of Staff, the Chief of the

Air Staff, as in the matter of deciding what provision should be made for the air support and defence of the army, has to hold his own against the very natural demands of the other services, whose heads were just as anxious to prove that sailors or soldiers could win the war as airmen were anxious to prove that their own weapons would be decisive. Portal had great strength, though he seldom showed it. His intellectual powers were outstanding; nobody could be more lucid; nobody could write a better minute. And he was a fighting man through and through, in spite of his quiet and modest manner. At Bomber Command his calm confidence during the Battle of France, when the bomber force was enduring heavy casualties and it was clear that its efforts could do no good, was exactly what was needed to sustain the courage of those under him.

I noticed at the Air Ministry that there was a marked tendency —not on the part of Portal—to go cap in hand to the other services. In the early stages of the war, the R.A.F. very definitely had an inferiority complex; it seemed unduly conscious of lacking tradition—though no tradition is worth having in a fighting service except a tradition of success—and over anxious to prove that there were no real grounds for doubts. They were up against the fact that the average soldier or sailor undoubtedly had in his mind a sort of composite picture of a typical air marshal, to which I may perhaps have contributed one or two features, which was by no means flattering. The attitude of the Air Ministry led the R.A.F. to give up far more than it should have done on several occasions. Very soon after the war started it should have been obvious that the weapon the R.A.F. had—air power—made the air force by its possession, if for this war only, the senior service.

I do not know exactly how we could have got this obvious fact recognised, but to put forward one's point of view as though one was asking for a favour is not the way to do it. Of course I am not here talking about any question of prestige, which is rubbish in war time or at any other time except in so far as it gets you what you want, but about getting those in authority to recognise what we could do and therefore to give us the job and the weapons with which to do it.

In this respect we have not been very lucky in our Secretaries of State; we have occasionally had some good men, but the other services seem to have got men who could put their case much more effectively. I know that Sir Archibald Sinclair, for example, always had the welfare of the service at heart but he did not have the power of convincing people in the mood that they were in during the last war; whenever he spoke, he made a speech, which is a very different thing from the kind of convincing assertion that Churchill made. In the House of Commons he should have been far more forthright than he was. It was, for instance, a long time before he described the kind of bombing we were doing. I personally thought that this was asking for trouble; there was nothing to be ashamed of, except in the sense that everybody might be ashamed of the sort of thing that has to be done in every war, as of war itself.

As D.C.A.S. I had, of course, a good deal to do with the air defence of Great Britain, which at the beginning of the Blitz was practically non-existent except against daylight bombing. The navy had far more on their own plate than they could effectively deal with, but they could not forbear interfering with ours. They produced *inter alia* a scheme for laying mine-carrying balloons to destroy the German bombers. The Air Ministry protested, but this had no effect, and in the event a vast amount of time, material, and manpower was wasted on this fatuous scheme. The sailors, being complete amateurs in air matters, had overlooked the fact that the weather systems are circular— hence the terms cyclone and anti-cyclone. When, after a very long time, a large scale test was at last carried out, it merely proved what we already knew that a large number of balloon-borne explosives would, if launched at any given place, eventually come home to roost. This did no sort of good to the area from which they were launched, and, in point of fact, greatly disturbed the telephone and electric grid systems and created widespread alarm and despondency—but not to the enemy who were put to no inconvenience whatever. But the test had no effect on the enthusiasts for this weapon. Eventually we were goaded into retaliation and worked out for the War Cabinet the astronomical number of men, wires, balloons, lorries, cylinders and gas needed for the use of this weapon; it was a quantity vastly in excess of the sum total available in the country. And then, and only then, did the enthusiasts succumb, not indeed to argument, but to *force majeure*.

But it was not only the sailors who produced such amazing contraptions. So great was the urge to find some cheap and quick defence against the Blitz that even scientists of repute were guilty at times of equally impracticable ideas. Such was the scheme of towing mines behind an aeroplane in the path of the raiders. For many months unfortunate Harrows—obsolete bombers—attempted to drag miles of piano wire with mines attached about the sky—this particular weapon had the code-word "Mutton." Though the scheme was invariably unsuccessful, those who pushed it could not be persuaded to abandon it until on one occasion all the mines in one of the "Mutton" aircraft prematurely exploded inside it when it was in the air. Even then the intention was to continue with the experiment until at a conference I interposed with the remark that if all the mines had exploded at one and the same time inside an unfortunate old Harrow without even discommoding it, I did not see how in the very unlikely event of one of them catching a German aircraft it could be expected to have a lethal effect.

However, these things did serve to give us some relief from our desperate cares, and they were indeed no worse than the idea of the gentleman in the last war who perpetually hawked round a scheme for freezing clouds and mounting anti-aircraft guns on them. Nor were they any worse than the idea of the man who wanted me to harpoon Zeppelins in the last war, a story already told.

I was still D.C.A.S. when it was decided, late in May of 1941, to send an R.A.F. delegation to the United States, and the C.A.S. suggested that I should lead this delegation, at least for a time. The object was to expedite the delivery of the warlike stores which the R.A.F. was hoping to acquire there and therefore to send serving officers who could deal with the American serving officers on equal terms. If there was one thing that depressed me more than the idea of going to America, as opposed to getting a command on the field, it was the thought of staying in the Air Ministry, and, as this was the only alternative, I agreed to head the delegation.

I had the selection of my own personnel, including the civilians, among whom I certainly chose two winners. One was Harry Weldon. He had been dean of Magdalen College, Oxford, and was one of the many dons who had been put for the duration into the higher ranks of the service departments of the Civil Service. To judge by his decorations, he had been a gunner of no mean order in the last war, but he was considered too old to be anything but a civilian in this. The other was a professional civil servant, of exceptional quality even in a service where quality runs high, George Cribbet, a man of immense application and ability. He was so completely devoted to his duty that, although he was a healthy specimen by nature, he worked himself to a shadow.

As America was not then at war I knew well, from my previous experience there when I spent six weeks buying aircraft in 1938, that we should have to do a considerable amount of return entertaining. But there was the usual frightful struggle with the Treasury to obtain the wherewithal even to exist in the country, let alone to do any entertaining. In all such battles the Treasury plays the same game. They find out the date when you are due to leave and then fight to the last ditch to prevent any decision before you go, with the idea that when you are out of reach you cannot argue effectively by post while they can always delay any decision.

I anticipated this usual tactic of theirs by getting the V.C.A.S. to inform them, before I was due to leave, that it was impossible for the mission to go on the terms the Treasury proposed; it was suggested that they should find some member of the idle rich who could be turned into an ersatz airman and head the delegation, since nobody else would be able to afford to go on the Treasury's terms. This at last brought them to their senses, though in such matters it is perhaps an exaggeration to speak of the Treasury as having senses; they are purely opportunist and have no qualms whatever about grinding the faces of the poor, that is, of the serving officer.

I was delighted when I heard that I could take my wife and small daughter with me, and still more so when we were offered passage in a battleship, H.M.S. *Rodney*. At one time we thought we had missed the *Rodney*. because we found she had already left for a much needed overhaul in the U.S. naval yards on the other side of the Atlantic. But she was then involved in the *Bismarck* fracas and had to return to England for more fuel before going on to America for her overhaul, so we caught her after all.

The navy looked after us with their usual hospitality and efficiency in such matters; my daughter, then aged eighteen months, had a six-foot-four marine as nanny. The only trouble with battleships as passenger vessels is that they roll like blazes, and although I am a very good sailor—this is nothing to boast about but is due to malformation of the inner ear—my wife is not. Dalrymple-Hamilton, who commanded the *Rodney* when the *Bismarck* was sunk, gave us an interesting account of the action. It will be remembered that a single torpedo from an aircraft had hit the *Bismarck's* screws and rudders and reduced them to such a state that she could only steam in a circle. While she was thus running round in circles the *Rodney* plugged most of her ammunition through the hulk. The *Rodney* closed to such short range that she had in the end depressed her guns so low as to tear up her own deck planking and slightly depress the steel decking underneath. The *Rodney's* great guns were all still blistered and peeling and you could see where her deck planking had been patched up, but apart from this she had no other damage from this encounter except a hit by one shell fragment which went through the screening of a searchlight station on the after structure of the ship. Nevertheless it must have been a fairly hair-raising task for this ancient old battle wagon to wade into the *Bismarck*, especially as this was within a few hours of the *Bismarck's* having disposed of the *Hood* at extreme range and apparently with only one salvo.

Somewhere and some time in the past the *Rodney* had been hit by a German bomb, apparently of about 2000 pounds weight, which had failed to explode. I saw the dent in one of the workshop flats where the bomb had finished up. I must say I was rather depressed by the attitude of the enthusiastic sailors who showed me round; it was obvious that they had not yet learned to take aircraft as seriously as their later experience forced them to do.

I think it was on the second night out that when we were at dinner in the Admiral's flat we heard a tremendous racket and roar overhead. There was also a shower of white paint and cork fragments off the deckhead above; the "Chicago piano" or multiple pom-pom anti-aircraft gun on the quarter deck had opened fire. The Navy run these things so well that I felt quite sure they would not open fire while we were having dinner down below merely in order to practise. Admiral Sir Charles Little, the head of the Naval Mission to the United States, who was also present, suggested that I should go up and see the fun. But the figure of a duffle-coated snotty appeared in the doorway and reported without a blink at my presence; "The Captain's compliments, sir, but we were only firing at a friendly aircraft." This seemed so normal to me that I required no further reassurance, but as a matter of curiosity we went up to have a look. A poor innocent old Whitley was then circling round that part of the Atlantic; it appeared that she had come out of the low clouds and had been received in the usual manner by the Navy, and no questions asked. I must say it annoyed me a little; the airman is shot at by everybody, and usually without the slightest justification. Certainly there can be no mistaking the Whitley; its design was so cock-eyed that it always flew in the most astonishing and unusual attitude with its tail right up behind its ears.

We had a couple of destroyers with us, one of them of the old American type. The journey took us seven days on a zigzag course, calling at Halifax and arriving at Boston in the dark. I recall the staggering effect, after the months of black-out at home, of the lights and neon signs shining miles out to sea.

At Washington I found the only accommodation that could be got for me not much to my liking. I discovered something better, but it seemed difficult to get rid of the rooms that had long been reserved for us. However the problem was solved in an amusing way. After a stay in the country my wife arrived at the hotel and asked for the keys of my room. The reception clerk denied that there was any such person as myself staying in the hotel. As my wife had been there with me before she went to the country, she, of course, insisted, and even gave the number of my room. The reception clerk replied that that room was occupied by "a young lady who just come up to Washington for one of the conventions." Just at that moment I turned up myself; we had a bit of a laugh about the situation and thought no more of it.

The weather was then extremely hot; as few people who have not been to stay there realise, in the summer Washington has just about the worst possible of tropical climates. I normally sleep without much on, but in such climates I sleep naked under an electric fan. During the middle of the night there was a rattle at the lock of the door and in came the young lady from the convention. We were amused, but the young lady was somewhat startled. It was quite obvious that she had been given the key of my room by the management in spite of the fact that I had been staying there for nearly a month.

Next morning we moved into our new rooms; I pointed out that my wife was first informed that a young lady up for a convention was staying in my rooms, and secondly that the young lady had been given a key to my rooms while my wife was away. How did they expect me to explain this to my wife? My lawyer would call for the answer to that problem. I found no difficulty in moving out.

We had rather a similar experience with a young lady whom we christened Olga Petrovska, the beautiful spy. She continually tried to get in touch with me for some purpose best known to herself, and gave my wife and me some amusement. She never realised that my wife was with me. Her final effort was to ring up about one o'clock in the morning and urgently demand admission to my room for the purpose of telling me something of the greatest importance. I must say I was too tired to find out what this was. We never learned what her purpose was; it was not the usual one, and we had little doubt that it was either blackmail or something on behalf of some foreign power.

While I was in America I found that our Government's habit of issuing communiques in which the phrase "Imperial troops" was invariably used had the effect of convincing all Americans that in North Africa, where our troops were then putting up a good show, all the fighting was being done not by the British but by "colonial troops," and probably black ones. I raised the matter at one of the periodical Embassy meetings over which Lord Halifax presided. I do not know what the word "Imperial" means in official circles in England, except that the words "Empire" and "Imperial" are never uttered at all by Dominion Office officials, if they can possibly avoid doing so, in case some one should feel insulted. But I do know that all the rest of the world, including America, believes "Imperial troops" to mean troops who come from outside the British Isles. We made representations which, I believe, put things right to some extent, but the damage had been done—and it sticks.

I am to all intents and purposes a colonial myself, so I feel myself at liberty to say something about this. I am always astounded by the idiotic behaviour of the British islanders in crying down their own efforts and giving all the credit to others. I do not myself ascribe this habit, which is a widespread one, to any highfalutin ideas about decency or "old school tie" behaviour or anything of that sort. I regard the habitual reluctance of the British to claim their own rights and seek credit for their own good points as a manifestation not so much of diffidence but as of of stupidity.

Our newspapers were always full of the wonderful fighting qualities of Australians, New Zealanders, Canadians, South Africans, Rhodesians, Gurkhas, and what have you—anybody except the British. It has, in fact, become a parrot cry to praise our admittedly magnificent fighting men from the colonies and dominions at the expense of the British Isles. And this has been done, not only recently in the latest war but ever since the dominions and colonies made any serious contribution towards the wars of the British Empire. I have been amused to read, as one does in almost every history or novel about Empire wars of the past, what magnificent horsemen and "natural good shots" the colonial troops were, as compared, by implication, with the British cavalryman or the British infantryman. Now I have ridden with colonial troops and shot with colonial troops and been shot at by colonial troops, and I have no hesitation whatever in saying that the dominion and colonial troops are on the average, with remarkably few individual exceptions, damned bad horsemen and damned bad shots unless and until they have been put through the standard riding school procedure, in the days when horsemen meant something, and the standard musketry drill of the armed forces. After which they are no better and no worse than the British themselves. I have myself watched with great amusement a complete regiment of these colonial "crack shots," over 500 of them, open fire at half a dozen 5-foot-square targets out in the desert at 500 yards range with 5 rounds apiece. Later I examined the targets for myself and found that out of 2500 rounds fired precisely three hits had been scored. Yet I have no doubt that if they had been put through a British musketry course these 500 "hard riding hard shooting" colonials would have been just about as good as the ordinary British infantryman —and no better.

There is, in fact, nothing to choose between trained British and colonial or dominion troops except that the British, being in general better educated and more amenable to discipline, are apt to be quicker in the uptake during the complicated training which has to be given before troops can handle modern machines of war.

I have had under my command tens of thousands of fighting men from every part of the Empire and from every part of the British Isles, and I say without hesitation that the finest fighting aircrews of the whole lot were beyond doubt the British crews; when I say this, it is in no way to belittle the magnificent performance of crews from other parts of the Empire. The fact is that an ordinary mixed British crew from all parts of the British Isles is as brave as any crew from any part of the world, and is much better disciplined, and certainly better educated than the average colonial and dominion crew.

In America it always used to make me laugh inwardly when the Yanks told me—and even President Roosevelt once seriously impressed this on me—how quickly the average American could pick up flying and crew duties, "because you see our boys are all used to mechanical things—they can all drive a car long before they are legally allowed to"—and so on and so forth. Well, the answer to that sort of statement is that any moron can drive a motor car and it is generally the moron who takes most delight in doing so.

This diffidence, or as I call it stupidity, of the British, still continues and is really a serious menace to them. When so many people are told that the British are inferior as fighting men to everyone, from a New Zealander to a Gurkha, they are apt to believe it, coming as it does, over and over again, more or less straight from the horse's mouth. History shows that the British are as good fighters as any and better than most.

I saw nothing while I was in America to shake my belief that the Americans were not going to get into the war. Of course, they were doing a great deal to help us to get weapons, but we had to do a great deal as well to get them made in America; for instance, we had to build factories there, and Lease Lend—"the most unselfish act in history"—coincided with the expenditure of our last dollar. I heard the news of Pearl Harbour as I was going up in a lift in Washington (in 1945 I was in the same lift when I heard that the Japs had surrendered—I am not sure whether it was the same lift-man who gave me the two items of news).

The Americans were very raid-conscious after Pearl Harbour. My wife and I were having lunch in our apartment when we tuned in the radio to get the local news and heard a running commentary on a most terrible air raid on New York which was apparently then going on. We got quite worked up about it, but it turned out that it was only a training aircraft that had gone slightly adrift over the Bay. We had understood that casualties were not negligible. Early war fever twice in one war (we had enough at home) was an odd experience.

I was also rung up by an old and much valued friend of mine who owned a factory at Trenton, New Jersey. He told me that he was making up the factory's A.R.P. layout and wanted my advice about how to deal with incendiary bombs—would I tell him what they did in England? So I explained that one got a long-handled shovel and, holding the lid of a dustbin as shield, one picked up the bomb and put it in a heavy iron bucket or slung it out of the window. I concluded by saying that if he would then wrap it up and send it to me I would eat it and every incendiary bomb that fell on America in the war.

Here is a story the Americans tell against themselves. After Pearl Harbour a lot of anti-aircraft guns and dummy guns were mounted on roofs of buildings. It appears that the anti-aircraft guns at Los Angeles one night let off thousands of rounds of ammunition at an imaginary aircraft. The explosions took off a number of roofs in Hollywood, and Hollywood replied in kind, also firing at imaginary aircraft. Then they got a message from McArthur, who was *in extremis* on Bataan: "If you can hold out for 36 hours, I will reach you with reinforcements."

The first effect of the entry of America into the war was rather to nullify the efforts which the R.A.F delegation had been making in Washington. The United States at once put a total embargo on the export of munitions to the allies, being driven to do so by the very serious position in which their own forces found themselves. For the time being the effect on the R.A.F. was serious and especially on the bomber forces, which it had been hoped to expand very soon by sending aircraft from America. We were sending large quantities of aircraft to Russia, the situation in the Middle East required every possible aircraft that could be sent to give support to the army whose plans were based on American deliveries, and we had an entirely new and vast sphere of operations in the Far East. An economy campaign was at once begun in England, every effort being made to conserve aircraft by cutting down the accident rate. The position was rather complicated by the fact that the American embargo had at all costs to be kept secret from the enemy, and so it was impossible to let flying personnel know exactly why they were required to be more careful than ever before not to waste a single aircraft.

I returned to England in February, 1942, and was appointed Commander-in-Chief, Bomber Command. Though I myself had not been connected with the bomber offensive since I left 5 Group at the end of 1940, it would be as well for the sake of continuity to give a brief account of the Command's operations in the meanwhile, up to the point when I took over in February, 1942.

In December of 1940 the Command gradually began to drop its policy of attacking with entirely inadequate forces keypoint factories which were supposed to constitute a bottleneck in the German war industry. That month an attack was made on an industrial area—a genuine industrial area where there were scarcely any houses but a lot of factories, railway yards, and so forth—in Mannheim. All the Command's available aircraft were put into a single attack, whereas previously it had been the policy to send small batches of aircraft to a number of different targets on the same night. This attack on Mannheim may be considered the Command's first attempt at a concentrated attack; the principle that all the available force should be concentrated on one target seems an obvious policy for a very small bomber force, but it was not given effect until then. It seems to have been thought that 100 aircraft were too large a force for an attack on an individual factory, and, in fact, the reason given at the time for attacking a group of industrial targets instead of single ones was that the Command had expanded. Afterwards we discovered that a force of two or three hundred heavy bombers—the Command had none of these in December, 1940—was not too large for an attack on a single important factory.

The attack on Mannheim caused an appreciable amount of damage and in consequence attacks were carried out by the whole available force on similar areas in Bremen, the naval bases of Wilhelmshaven and Kiel, and elsewhere.

During the Blitz there was a most natural demand for retaliation against Berlin, and the Command had to make great efforts to attack this very difficult and well defended target. The railway stations were usually aimed at. An acute and intelligent report by an American observer on the spot reached the Command after the attack on Berlin had been resumed in the late summer of 1941; during the summer it was not, of course, possible to attack so distant a target in the short hours of darkness. This report was undoubtedly disturbing. It pointed out that the damage in Berlin was very slight and had been greatly exaggerated in newspaper and broadcast reports in this country, that the enemy's morale was not seriously affected by our raids, that our bombing was inaccurate but did not appear to be wholly indiscriminate, and that the attacks seemed to be carried out in such a way as to give the enemy's defences the maximum advantage.

In the first two years of the war a good deal of information was brought out of Germany by business men and others from neutral countries, and their reports often led to the belief that our attacks were causing considerable damage. No doubt they were often based on rumours which the visitors had overheard and were therefore thoroughly unreliable. It is also the case that isolated examples of bomb damage, when seen from close at hand, always look impressive; the observer does not consider how much there is undamaged, though this is immediately apparent in photographs taken from the air. At any rate, the clear and unbiased report from Berlin was salutary.

Though our strategic bomber force would in any case have been very small throughout 1941, it was to all intents and purposes greatly reduced when the battle cruisers *Scharnhorst* and *Gneisenau* arrived in Brest in March of 1941. The two battle cruisers went to Brest after a successful foray into the Atlantic where they sank 22 ships. The presence of these warships in a base from which they could easily make forays into the Atlantic gave a new meaning to the phrase "a fleet in being"; instead of containing a hostile fleet, they contained a large proportion of the bomber force which might have been used to attack Germany.

In Brest the ships were usually in dry dock and always in shallow water and therefore could not be sunk; they could be and were damaged, but damage to warships, even when this is serious enough to make them unfit for operations, is extremely difficult to detect in air photographs, and the Admiralty took a lot of convincing. In June of 1941 the heavy cruiser *Prinz Eugen* also arrived in Brest. Towards the end of July the *Scharnhorst* made a brief excursion to La Pallice, some way to the south of Brest, and there was a chance of sinking her. Daylight attacks, in which a few four-engined bombers took part, were made both on the *Scharnhorst* at La Pallice and on the other two warships at Brest. The *Scharnhorst* was hit and the damage was severe enough to send her back to the dry dock at Brest.

The hits on the warships that were obtained from time to time while they were in dry dock, under heavy camouflage, were enough to keep the ships from operating for eleven months. Then, in February, 1942, the enemy decided that it was useless to keep the ships any longer at Brest, since they were obviously going to be damaged at frequent enough intervals to keep them out of the Atlantic. They were patched up sufficiently to enable them to go to sea, but not to fight, and in weather too bad for any successful bombing attack they were rushed through the Channel and taken back to Kiel. Naturally enough the Germans waited for just such weather. But mines laid by Bomber Command ahead of them damaged both the *Scharnhorst* and the *Gneisenau* on their way back. I was therefore lucky enough to take over the Command when it had just been relieved of an incubus which had exasperated everyone for a long period. One of my first attacks was on the *Gneisenau* at Kiel. We hit her hard and she was subsequently towed to Gdynia and dismantled.

In March, 1941, Blenheims of No. 2 Group began a campaign of low-level bombing against enemy coastal shipping, which could not be attacked by the Navy without risking prohibitive losses from attack by shore-based enemy aircraft. These attacks were hazardous in the extreme; the enemy's anti-aircraft fire was deadly and our losses were very heavy. The gallantry of the Blenheim crews was beyond praise and their determination never wavered though I know that many of the men felt that they were being sent to certain death. It proved extremely difficult to estimate the exact degree of success in many of these attacks, because of the very low height from which they were carried out; oblique photographs of the target were taken at the moment of attack and as the aircraft left for home but these could seldom be interpreted with any degree of certainty. It was believed that about 70 ships were sunk in a period of about six months.

Minelaying was continued by Hampdens of No. 5 Group and continued to be a most effective weapon against the enemy's shipping.

Chapter Four

BOMBER COMMAND

Appointed C.-in-C. Bomber Command. The bomber force in
1942. What we were up against. The need for speed. Attacking
German morale. Area and Precision bombing. Previous failures.
Target finding by night. Using the wrong bombs. Early
bombing tactics. The principle of concentration. The lesson of
the Blitz. Bombing policy.

I BECAME Commander-in-Chief of Bomber Command on
February 23rd, 1942. The headquarters of the Command was
about five miles from High Wycombe, in Buckinghamshire.
It was the only Command headquarters in this country to be
built as such; work was begun on it before the war, though it
was not ready until the spring of 1940—before that the Command
was at Richings Park at Langley, near Iver. The site near High
Wycombe was chosen because the country thereabouts was thickly
wooded, and the headquarters themselves were right among
beech trees and almost impossible to spot from the air. About a
quarter of a mile from the headquarters buildings the officers'
mess, married quarters and other buildings had been laid out to
look like a housing estate. Although the Germans knew perfectly
well where the site was, we were never molested by the enemy.
One incendiary bomb was dropped, of course entirely by accident,
on the W.A.A.F. quarters; we also had some flying bombs in
the country not far away, but these were overshoots from London.
We also had some parachutist scares and some definite information of a plan to make away with me when our attacks were at
their height. The Commander-in-Chief's house, Springfield, was
about five miles from the Command headquarters; I drove to my
office at nine in the morning, but there was, of course, a direct
line from my house to the Operations room and I was in constant
touch during the night. I lived at Springfield, a pleasant old-
fashioned house, with my wife and daughter, and before long
Saundby had his quarters there, as well as my P.A.—personal
assistant, the equivalent of an A.D.C. in the army—and Harry
Weldon when he became my personal staff officer. We had
over five thousand visitors at Springfield for a meal or more
during those years, so that it was always a busy house.

Air Vice-Marshal R. H. M. S. Saundby, now Air Marshal Sir Robert Saundby, was then Command S.A.S.O.—senior air staff officer—and had had that job since November, 1940. My first contact with him had been in 1922, in Irak, when he was one of my Flight Commanders in No. 45 Squadron, though we had both been in the same job during the 1914-1918 war, flying night fighters for the defence of London. I knew him to be an out-standing man in Irak, and since then he had done first-class work. He had been a lecturer at the Staff College, and had a great deal to do with planning the eight-gun fighter and so with the win-ning the Battle of Britain. His ideas about bombing were absolutely sound, and naturally I relied enormously on his experience when I first became Commander-in-Chief, as I did throughout the war; he was with me at Bomber Command the whole time, and left at the same time as I did. He was a keen fisherman, which was why all the main German towns that were our targets had the names of fish for code names, Whitebait for Berlin, Trout for Cologne, and so on. He had lately taken up collecting butterflies and moths and had debated whether to give their names to our German targets, but there were not enough short names of butterflies and moths to go round and it would obviously be inconvenient to use words like "Broad-bordered bee hawk." He was one of the hardest workers I know, and this moth-collecting in the evenings was a necessary relaxation for an hour or so. His habit of prowling round the country near Springfield once got him into trouble with the village policeman; he was investigating a hedge when he felt a hand on his shoulder. When Saundby had explained what he was doing the policeman said that he thought Saundby was after birds' eggs; there was quite a trade in these—they were sent up to London and used by the restaurant in salads. Saundby naturally wanted to know why, even if he had been after birds' eggs, this should have been considered a crime; the policeman said that those who go after birds' eggs for the restaurants are not the sort of people who stop at that. He did not in the least mind being seen in his Air Marshal's uniform chasing a butterfly with a net, and when he went to London used to stop his car near Lord's cricket ground to search there for an addition to his collection.

Saundby had less side than almost anybody I have known; out of office hours anyone could talk to him and he would talk to anybody; a pilot officer could have played with him. He was liked by everybody in the Command, and his sociability in the mess, where he lunched and also had a drink in the evening before driving to Springfield, was a great help to me, as it was quite impossible for me to see as much of my officers as I should have liked. More important still, I should have liked to have been able to see far more than I did of my air-crews, but it was quite out of the question for a Commander-in-Chief during the war to get round to most of the stations. At Springfield we had a continuous succession of visitors whom I had to convince of the vital importance of the bomber offensive; if I had not been able to persuade those in the charge of the conduct of the war as a whole that we were really hurting Germany we should not have got even that small fraction of what we needed that was eventually granted us. And this, of course, had to be done in what time I could spare from my real work, the strain of which I do not think had ever been fully understood.

For that matter I wonder if the frightful mental strain of commanding a large air force in war can ever be realised except by the very few who have experienced it. While a naval commander may at the most be required to conduct a major action once or twice in the whole course of the war, and an army commander is engaged in one battle say once in six months or, in exceptional circumstances, as often as once a month, the commander of a bomber force has to commit the whole of it every twenty-four hours; even on those occasions when the weather forces him to cancel a projected operation, he has to lay on the whole plan for committing the force. Every one of these operations is a major battle, and as much depends on the outcome, success is as vital and disaster as grave, as on any other occasion when the whole of a force engages the enemy. In addition, there is the continuous and fearful apprehension about what the weather may do, especially in the climate of North-West Europe. Meteorology is an inexact science; in fact it is still in the condition of being rather an art than a science. This being so, and our climate being what it is, I should have been able to justify myself completely if I had left the whole force on the ground, if I had done nothing whatever, on nine occasions out of ten. But this would have led to the defeat of Britain in the air. The whole of the responsibility, the final responsibility, for deciding whether or not to operate falls fair and square on the shoulders of the Commander-in-Chief, and falls on them every twenty-four hours. For all he knows he may lose the whole of a very large proportion of the force by weather alone, to say nothing of enemy action. It is best to leave to the imagination what such a daily strain amounts to when continued over a period of years.

When I took up my Command the bomber force had played its very great part in stopping the projected invasion of England, but had done nothing else worth mentioning to injure the enemy. The force had been too small for that, and was still, in February, 1942, much too small to achieve anything lasting, it was also poorly equipped. On the day that I took over there were 378 aircraft serviceable with crews, and only 69 of these were heavy bombers. About 50 aircraft in the force were not even medium bombers but the light bombers of No. 2 Group. These, apart from making intruder attacks on airfields, could take no part in the main offensive and were mostly used as bait by Fighter Command; they took part in fighter sweeps over France in an attempt to make the German fighters accept battle. In effect, this meant that we had an average force of 250 medium and fifty heavy bombers until such time as the Command really began to expand. Equipment was no more impressive than these numbers. The German defences were so strong that it was impossible to operate regularly or with any sizable force by day, so that all our main operations were confined to the hours of darkness. But at night the bomber crews were hardly ever able to find their targets even though, before I took command, it had already been decided (it was a decision with which I had nothing to do) that all our main attacks should be against large industrial areas, which meant, of course, large industrial cities as a whole. Up till then the Command had had no radar navigational aids, though the first of these was just being issued, to enable the bomber crews to navigate or find the target without seeing the ground, and it had become glaringly obvious that the average crew in average weather could not find their way to the target by visual means alone. It had also become obvious to all who had studied Bomber Command's previous operations that it would be necessary to concentrate the force in time and space, both for its own protection against enemy defences, and to ensure the destruction of the target. But the tactical and technical problems involved in achieving such a concentration had scarcely been tackled, nor was it realised what degree of concentration was necessary; it was hoped eventually to reach a total of a hundred aircraft over the target per hour. There was also a serious deficiency of trained crews.

This then was the force with which I had to begin an immediate offensive against Germany ; it was also the only force in the west which then could take any offensive action at all against Germany, our only means of getting at the enemy in a way that would hurt at all. I knew well from what I had seen in America and from what I knew of our own difficulties at the beginning of the war that it would take the Americans at least a year and probably two before their might could really begin to make itself felt in the air or on the ground, and at that time America had been in the war less than three months.

The importance of beginning the offensive as soon as possible could hardly be overestimated. The bomber offensive, or rather what could be made of it, was the only means we had of actively helping the Russians, who, though the German offensive in Russia had been halted, had every appearance of being *in extremis*. Even if this could not be done directly, by destroying the enemy's war industries and communications, at least it could be done indirectly, and to a very material extent, by forcing the enemy to keep his fighters in Germany. In the same way, if not directly, then indirectly by containing the enemy's air force and compelling it to be used for the defence of Germany, the bomber offensive was at that time the only means we had of doing anything to give any measurable help to our armies engaged in a desperate struggle in the Middle East; a bomber offensive would also have the effect of making the enemy keep his anti-aircraft guns at home, and every German anti-aircraft gun was a dual-purpose weapon, convertible at will into an anti-tank gun.

By the bomber offensive, and only by this means, could we force the Germans to keep any large proportion of their manpower for defence; a serious bomber offensive would compel the enemy to keep many hundreds of thousands of men on active and passive defence, in the night-fighter force, in the anti-aircraft batteries, in the fire-fighting services, demolition squads, and so on. In the same way Bomber Command, by getting on with its minelaying campaign, could put a large part of the German navy on to the work of minesweeping, and many workers on to the repair of ships.

A bomber offensive was the only means that I could see, and the results eventually bore out this conclusion, of preventing the allied armies from suffering enormous casualties when they eventually invaded the Continent. And it was then under consideration to invade Europe, not in two but in one year's time, in 1943.

I knew very well that the Germans were preparing all sorts of secret weapons against England, and that these would give us a very bad time indeed unless we could get the enemy down first and destroy his industries. There is no doubt whatever that but for the bombing we should have had such a dose of V-weapons as would have made London completely uninhabitable, would have inflicted frightful damage on the whole of the southern part of England, and would have greatly prolonged the war. I knew well that this was also Winston Churchill's opinion. Above all I had in mind two things, uranium and heavy water. Some of us knew by then that the race for the atom bomb was on, and we knew that the Germans had just as much chance of getting it, and just as good facilities for making it, as anyone else. In no circumstances whatsoever did there seem to be any means of preventing Germany from making progress with the atom bomb except by bombing industry generally in the hope that this would hit where it was most likely to hurt the production of the atom bomb. Parachutist attacks on the production of heavy water in Norway might certainly cause delays, but if the Germans chose to give priority to atom-bomb research, and to the manufacture of the materials needed for it, they could always get ahead of such attacks on individual plants or facilities; only in the event of industry in general being badly dislocated by bombing would attacks on such individual targets count for more than brief damage. Here we came up against the same problem and the same objections that I had to make when panacea targets, as I called them, were so frequently put before me, targets like synthetic oil plants, ball-bearing factories, molybdenum mines and the like; I shall go into this later.

I knew at the same time that the ever-increasing demands from the Middle East, as well as from elsewhere, and of course, the inordinate demands of the Admiralty for every conceivable thing to be turned to their use, would bring any bomber force offensive to a standstill. In 1941 the Air Force had already had a tough struggle with the army who were asking for an army air component for the invasion of Europe rather larger than our whole front line strength at that time. They were good enough to say that they wished this to be arranged in such a way as to cause the least possible hindrance to the expansion of the R.A.F. for strategic action; it would, of course, have stopped this expansion altogether.

I was also fully aware that such large demands would be made

by other services and for the purpose of conducting other campaigns as would wholly prevent the projected expansion of the
bomber force. And even if the force did expand, I was well aware
that there would immediately be demands for every conceivable
dispersal of effort, in almost any direction except the right one.
If these demands should be answered, we should never catch up
with the German repair squads; as was obviously happening at
the beginning of 1942, the German war potential would increase
far more rapidly than our capacity to damage it. I had to prove,
and prove quickly, to the satisfaction of those who mattered, that
the bomber force could do its work if it was large enough and
if its efforts were not frittered away on objectives other than
German industry as a whole.

The general idea at this time on what civil servants always
call "a high level," was that the main and almost the only purpose
of bombing was to attack the morale of the industrial workers.
This was to be achieved by destroying, mainly by incendiary
bombs, the whole of the four largest cities in the Ruhr, and thereafter fourteen industrial cities elsewhere in Germany. The idea
of attacking morale might be described as a counsel of despair,
based on the previous failure of night bombing, and the break-
down of the theory of precision attacks on key factories, a theory
which got much publicity when our attacks on Germany first
began in 1940. But it also implied an unbounded optimism, not,
indeed, about the strategic effects of a bombing offensive, but
about what could be achieved at this moment. Portal and I, when
we discussed the bombing of Germany during the London blitz,
had thought in terms of a front line strength of 4000 heavies.
We were now expected to use a force of 50 heavies and 250 medium
bombers to knock out whole German cities; three months, it was
suggested, was a reasonable time in which to destroy the four
cities in the Ruhr. As we had done nothing more than scratch
at the Ruhr in the previous two years and as attacks on targets
in this area had almost without exception failed in the past, such
a degree of confidence in the future requires some explanation;
the explanation is that the non-visual aid to navigation which
had the code name of Gee was just being introduced into the
Command, though as yet, and for some considerable time to
come, only a small fraction of the force could be equipped with
it. Far more was expected of this extremely useful device, one
of the many really brilliant things the scientists gave us, than it
could in fact achieve. And, of course, far more was expected of

a very small bomber force than was at all reasonable, even if the new Gee equipment should come up to the most optimistic forecasts; so I had to prove, not only what an adequate and adequately equipped force could not achieve, but also what a small and inadequately equipped force could achieve. I had to dispose of all wishful thinking, while at the same time making perfectly clear the grounds of my complete confidence in a bomber offensive if this was given a real chance.

The switch over from precision to area bombing, from attacking key factories, or even individual sections of key factories, to attacking large industrial towns as a whole, had been made some time before I took over the Command. The decision to concentrate on the complete destruction of four Ruhr cities, with a view to breaking German morale, was conveyed to the Command just before I took over, but attacks on whole cities and an offensive primarily against morale were under discussion in the summer of 1941, when I was in America. At least by the early summer of 1941 everyone who had anything to do with staff policy knew that the great majority of our attacks on Germany were, in fact, though not in intention, area attacks; the area concerned was, more often than not, a very large one in open country. Very little material damage could be seen in the photographs, taken by the photographic reconnaissance unit, but as against this the Germans were showing definite signs of agitation. The large bombs we were dropping, the 4000 pounder and a very few 8000 pounders, were obviously having some effect on morale. The principle of attacking morale was at any rate half-admitted, though proposals to concentrate exclusively on this were turned down; the idea was to keep on at small targets for their strategic importance but, to put it crudely, not to mind when we missed them, or at any rate to regard a miss as useful provided that it disturbed morale. Just before Germany invaded Russia a scheme was worked out for attacking German railways; it had become obvious that no good could be done by attacking synthetic oil plants, partly because we always missed them and partly because Germany could then get the oil she wanted from elsewhere, so the plan was to prevent the enemy from getting oil and other supplies to the places where they were wanted. The targets chosen were in congested industrial areas and were carefully picked so that bombs which overshot or undershot the actual railway centres under attack should fall on these areas, thereby affecting morale. This programme amounted to a halfway stage between area and precision bombing. This being the position, there was inevitably a good deal of evasiveness and contradiction when the object of an attack was described, some of this being due to the belief that if air-crew got the idea that it was permissible to bomb anywhere in a given built-up area they would soon feel it was permissible to bomb anywhere in Germany. The aiming points in a large number of towns were then chosen at the Air Ministry, and the theory was that they should be in themselves well worth destruction as well as being in such a position that damage all round them would have the maximum effect on the economic life of an industrial city. Unfortunately for this argument, though some of the aiming points might be railway stations, garrisons, or post offices, others were large open squares. In point of fact a good many of them were chosen because it was hoped that they would be easy to see, and the fact that they were often particularly difficult to see does not affect the argument. It was also decided in 1941 that aircraft should not bring their bombs back from Germany; it had previously been the rule that this should be done if the target, or a specified alternative, could not be identified.

The idea that the main object of bombing German industrial cities was to break the enemy's morale proved to be wholly unsound; when we had destroyed almost all the larger industrial cities in Germany the civil population remained apathetic, while the Gestapo saw to it that they were docile, and, in so far as there was work left for them to do, industrious. But it seemed quite a natural opinion in 1941. The argument was that the German nation had been enduring a frightful strain since 1933, when it first began to work for rearmament. The quick and easy victories they had been promised did not always come and certainly did not bring the end of the war; meanwhile, their menfolk were dying by the hundred thousand in Russia. England, with America's help, was getting stronger every day; the U-boats were not stopping this inevitable process. They had been told that England was defeated, and, before that, they had been promised they would never be bombed; what, then, must be the effect of English bombers dropping four thousand pounders night after night? It was also believed that in the last war the rot started from within; this belief, that Germany had been defeated in 1918 because of a crack in morale on the home front had, of course, been vigorously put about by the Nazis themselves. There was also the fact that after the policy of attacking key factories had broken down, no obvious alternative except an attack on morale presented itself at once; it was only after careful study of the blitz in England that it was observed how immediate and serious was the effect on war production itself of the destruction of large town areas. Added to this was the fact that the Air Force, through no fault of its own, had unfortunately got itself a good deal mixed up with political warfare, and so with questions of morale, in the beginning of the war. First there were the leaflet raids, then the attack on Sylt, then the fact that an exaggerated importance had been attributed to our early attacks on Germany in order to cheer up London and other cities under the blitz, while now, towards the end of 1941, the bombing of Germany assumed great political importance as a means of persuading the Russians that we were doing all we could to come to their help.

I do not, of course, suggest that bombing is not a useful weapon against morale. On the contrary, the Germans themselves used it as such with great effect in 1939 and 1940, though their attempts to break the morale of Britain by bombing altogether failed. And there is no doubt that the panic caused by Bomber Command's attacks on industrial cities in North Italy, though the weight of the attack was insignificant compared with that of the offensive against Germany, did as much as any other single factor to bring about the downfall of Fascism in that country. But "morale" bombing was comparatively ineffective against so well organised a police state as Germany. The German leaders themselves admitted after the war that morale was bad after our attacks on their towns, but they distinguished between the morale and the conduct of the workers; conduct, they say, was not affected. In other words, there was nothing that unarmed Germans could do about it, with the Gestapo standing by, with obedience part of their very nature, and with the concentration camp round the corner.

A scheme for the precision bombing of key factories had been worked out before the war. As an abstract theory, in the void, it had its points; Germany had built up what seemed to be a highly artificial economy, using factories to produce raw materials synthetically at vast cost in labour in order to be self-sufficient. But the theory did not, of course, take into account the possibility of Germany overrunning Europe. Nor did it take into account the practical impossibility of hitting their factories, by day because of the German air defence, and by night because we could not find them in the dark. Our attacks on German naval units during the "phoney" war had shown that we could not operate by day over Germany without completely prohibitive casualties for day fighters, and we at once began to prepare and train for bombing at night. The immense difficulty of this task, unless some effective non-visual navigational aid is provided, is seldom appreciated. The only aids then available to the navigator, who was then also the bomb aimer, were his compass, map, sextant, and direction-finder loop, together with what he could see of the ground by starlight, moonlight, or by the light of an occasional flare, which was not then shaded as flares afterwards were and so more often than not proved so dazzling that he could see better without it. It was hard enough by such means to get to the target area, but if and when the aircraft got there, the navigator had the still more difficult task of getting a visual fix, either of the target itself or of some landmark which he could positively identify and from which he could make a run of a few miles by dead reckoning to the target. This search for a visual fix almost always took half an hour or so, and sometimes lasted for more than an hour; to spend so much time in the target area was just possible when the German defences against night attack were in their first and rudimentary stage, but it would have been fatal from 1942 onwards.

These difficulties were fully understood, though it was hoped by a period of intensive training, during and after the period of the "phoney war," to overcome them. What was not understood was how often a crew genuinely thought they had found the target when they had bombed miles away from it. When one looks back at this period in the light of later knowledge one can only be surprised by such successes as were gained; that the results achieved were even as good as they were is proof of the courage and determination of the pioneer crews of 1940 and 1941. But that was not realised for a considerable time, mainly because night photography was little used. And there was, I think, a general reluctance to disbelieve air-crew who genuinely thought they had hit the target; there was no great enthusiasm for checking the reports of captains of aircraft by independent evidence. As the Command was slowly—very slowly—equipped with night cameras there was a natural tendency to give these to the best crews, which meant that the photographs were not a fair sample. When there had accumulated a sufficient body of evidence from night photographs taken in the act of bombing, and accordingly showing the area within which the bombs had fallen, it was possible at last to appreciate the enormous possibilities of error in navigation by night.

Complete and accurate assessment of the success of an operation, the first necessity if a campaign is to be adequately planned was not possible until all aircraft in the Command had been equipped with cameras, and this was not until the autumn of 1942; like everything else cameras were in terribly short supply. But a year and more before then, there was enough evidence to show that the odds were enormous against hitting individual factories in Germany with the equipment the Command then had, or with any equipment it was likely to get in the near future. With the equipment then available it would be extremely lucky to hit a large town by night. This did happen occasionally; for example, some 30 aircraft bombed Stettin in September, 1941, and got 80 per cent of their bombs within two miles of the aiming point, or rather, 80 per cent of the photographs taken were plotted within two miles of the aiming point. But this was wholly exceptional, and had to be regarded as such. Night photographs taken during June and July of 1941 showed that of those aircraft reported to have attacked their target in Germany only one in four got within five miles of it, and, when the target was in the Ruhr, only one in ten. The proportion of total sorties, including those aircraft not reported as having attacked the target was, of course, much lower. The situation would have seemed hopeless if it had not been known that radar aids to navigation were in existence and would eventually be provided, if and when the necessary priorities were allotted to Bomber Command.

Night photography revised or reversed a good many views that were previously held. Lakes and rivers, previously considered valuable landmarks and very popular with crews, proved most unreliable. Coastal features, and especially docks, were much more easily identifiable. Investigations showed that to identify, or to believe that one had identified, a single landmark was very seldom enough; it was only when crews claimed to have identified more than two landmarks that their claims were borne out by the night photographs. As one might have expected, photographs proved that moonlight and clear weather were indispensable to a successful attack at that time; in poor weather very few aircraft indeed got within five miles of the target. Coastal targets were easier to attack than inland towns, and the

Ruhr was a quite impossible target, because of the industrial haze over the whole area and the lack of any good landmarks.

If the bombs used in the early stages of the war had found their target, they would have done it very little harm. High explosive bombs were invariably too small, and of the wrong kind; the standard 250 lb. general purpose bomb, as it was called, was a ridiculous missile. High capacity bombs, blast bombs, were hardly considered, although these have the advantage of bringing down a large number of buildings in proportion to their weight and at the same time of causing few casualties, provided the population is in shelters. When the Germans used them, and they were a long way ahead of us in this, it was supposed to show their unmilitary mania for indiscriminate terrorism; it was considered that the really sound thing to do was to drop bombs which consisted almost entirely of metal, fragments of which would do great destruction among factory machinery. By 1941 the R.A.F. had the 4000-lb. high capacity blast bomb. This was designed as a direct result of observing what the Germans did with their blast bombs in this country. For some reason the enemy's high capacity bombs were called land mines, perhaps because, like our airborne sea mines, they were fitted with parachutes instead of tails. The first of our high capacity bombs was, in fact, a modified sea mine, also equipped with a parachute. It was carried in a Hampden, the aircraft then mainly used for sea mining, and there would have been no room for the huge tail that would have had to be given to this 2000-lb. bomb. A most ingenious device enabled the 4000-lb. bomb to be aimed without the huge tail that it would have had to have if it had been designed on normal principles. A Wellington could just manage to carry one of these bombs, and half a dozen of them in one attack was considered a good effort. Eight thousand pound bombs, to be carried in Manchesters, were produced not long afterwards ; on the whole these were not worth as much as two four thousand pounders.

We also had the 4 lb. incendiary bomb, which proved throughout the war the best weapon for destroying large industrial areas. This had all the shortcomings that result from thoroughly bad ballistics; it was impossible to aim it accurately with the sights with which our aircraft were equipped, or for that matter with any known bombsight, but in spite of that it was extremely effective for its purpose.

In the early days of bombing our notion, like that of the

Germans, was to spread an attack out over the whole night, thereby wearing down the morale of the civilian population. The result was, of course, that an efficient fire brigade could tackle a single load of incendiaries, put them out, and wait in comfort till the next came along; they might also be able to take shelter when a few high explosive bombs were dropping. There was, indeed, little else that our bomber force could do at the beginning of the war; aircraft each took their individual route, and the timing was necessarily vague. But it was observed that when the Germans did get an effective concentration, probably more by luck than by cunning, then our fire brigades had a bad time; if a rain of incendiaries is mixed with high explosive bombs there is an irresistible temptation for the fireman to keep his head down. The Germans again and again missed their chance, as they did in the London blitz that I watched from the roof of the Air Ministry, of setting our cities ablaze by a concentrated attack. Coventry was adequately concentrated in point of space, but all the same there was little concentration in point of time, and nothing comparable to the fire tornadoes of Hamburg and Dresden ever occurred in this country. But they did do us enough damage to teach us the principle of concentration, the principle of starting so many fires at the same time that no fire fighting services, however efficiently and quickly they were reinforced by the fire brigades of other towns, could get them under control.

The principle of concentration in time and space would have been forced upon us in any case by the growing strength of the German defence. It may seem surprising, in view of the weakness of our bomber force in numbers and equipment, that the Germans should have reinforced their defences in 1941, but they were looking ahead. Moreover German strength and war production was still increasing and there was so much to spare that ample provision, as the enemy thought, could be made for the defence without robbing the armies who were taking the offensive. It was not till the following year that there was any need to take any of the German army's fighters and bombers for the defence of Germany.

With the occupation of France and the Low Countries the Germans were able to build up a formidable system of defence. They set up an early warning system along the coast, as well as on the coast of Denmark, together with a belt of stations for the control of fighters from the ground through Denmark and

Holland and down the Western frontier of Germany. Each ground station controlled one fighter within a rather small "box," and the belt consisted of a whole succession of these boxes touching each other. When the coastal radar stations gave warning, the fighter in each box was ready to intercept any single bomber coming into its box. If a bomber force was scattered, many single aircraft would naturally be entering a large number of boxes at any given time. But if it could be arranged that many bombers passed through one box at the same time, the fighter in that box would only have time to attempt the interception of one of them. A continuous searchlight belt covering the Ruhr made it easier for fighters to intercept the bombers passing through it, and here again it would be better for the bombers to get through this belt in a continuous stream, with the fighters only able to concentrate on one or two of them, rather than to go through it at long intervals and be picked off one by one. The same principle of saturating the defences applied to anti-aircraft guns and to the searchlights operating in conjunction with them.

A few ground control stations were probably working at the beginning of 1941, but by the end of the year they had become numerous and efficient, and bomber casualties were rising fast. The difficulty was to bring about any real concentration. "Gee" the first radar aid to navigation, was the real answer, but even before we had the Gee equipment in any quantity it was possible, on a bright, clear night, to plan the route and the attack so thoroughly that the bomber stream became compact. At first even the minute figure, as it seemed later, of 100 aircraft an hour, over the target and along the route, was only an idea, and very seldom achieved; for one thing, captains of aircraft were so used to being told to search for their exact target or aiming point until they found it, that it seemed contradictory to order them to bomb and leave the target area at a particular moment. Along with much else from the past it was necessary to abandon the idea of searching first for the primary target, then for a specified alternative target, and, if this could not be found, for a self-evident military objective; military objectives were not apt to be self-evident, but that was the term, usually contracted into "Semo," that was often and solemnly used. Quick as well as definite identification of the target became of increasing importance towards the end of 1941, and at that time most of the methods we afterwards used were under discussion, the training, for example, of special squadrons to find the target, the use of marker bombs with a distinctive colour to be dropped on the target, at the beginning of the attack, and so forth. Whether or no to begin an attack with fire-raising aircraft was much debated. It had been a widely accepted belief that the right time to drop incendiaries was at the end of an attack, and that at other times incendiaries did not do much harm; there was also, of course, the very real danger that crews trained to bomb fires might go straight for the enemy's dummy fires. At this stage, in fact, the whole theory of bombing tactics was being submitted to agitated revision. Even the principle of concentration had its opponents, on the grounds that, except on really dark nights, this helped the "cat's eye" night fighter, and because it led to congestion at home bases on landing. There were also serious fears that it might lead to collisions and to aircraft dropping their bombs on each other.

The question of the risk from collision was not finally settled until we put 1000 aircraft over Cologne in an hour and a half. Before this attack was planned the nature and extent of the risk from collision and falling bombs was investigated and found to be small, much smaller than many had expected. It was obviously much better to accept such a risk, which might mean that two or three aircraft were lost in a really heavy attack, if by doing so we could prevent the loss of 40 or 50 aircraft from night fighters and flak. Precautions had, of course, to be taken; the aircraft had all to orbit the target in the same direction, and aircraft with different operational heights had to attack at different times, so that the bombs of aircraft flying high should not hit other aircraft flying below them.

It would have taken Bomber Command longer to learn how to attack Germany if it had not been for the lessons of the German attack on Britain. We learned as much from their few successes as from their failures, from what they did as from what they did not do. The blitz was another instance of the German capacity for making every possible big mistake and no small ones. After the almost incredible folly they showed in the Battle of Britain they at last saw the hopelessness of facing up to our fighters in daylight and said, "Well, we will do what the British do and bomb by night." This was the final disastrous mistake they made in the air campaign against Britain, and they never recovered from it. Had they known anything about the exercise of air power—and they certainly knew very little—they would have known that night bombing requires not only a vast amount of specialised training, for which they had left themselves no time at all, but also very special aircraft and equipment, which they had made no attempt to produce. They had, in fact, no strategic bombers at all, since their whole force of well over a thousand bombers was designed for army co-operation work and was only used for attacks on cities when not required to support the German army. Even in day-time it was fitted only to carry out the work of a tactical air force, not strategic attack; the bombers were too small, and they were not equipped for weight-carrying. By night, the bomber force was well adapted to wreck itself, without any assistance from the British. We know now that in one month of the London blitz they lost 260 bombers from crashes on the return to their airfields. Kesselring then harangued the German air force leaders and said that not even the Luftwaffe and the entire resources of the Reich could stand that rate of loss. This, then, was why they abandoned the night blitz when it had just reached its most effective stage and when we knew that more of it would prove fatal to the continuance of normal life in London, with all that that meant.

Not only did they have no strategic bombers; they had no real plan of strategic attack on industries and communications. Between the Battle of Britain and the invasion of Russia the enemy left himself no time for the systematic campaign that alone could reduce a country from the air. The enemy remained, in fact, in the stage through which some people in this country were going in 1941, the stage of supposing that the primary object of bombing, when not directed exclusively towards small military objectives, was to break morale. But this did mean that the Germans, as soon as they were defeated in their aim of hitting military objectives by daylight, passed at once to area bombing. And in this they had such successes as must inevitably come, with however little forethought, when a large force attacks an almost undefended country.

The Germans invented the blitz without appreciating its strategic possibilities; in Britain, on the other hand, we were only too well placed for understanding them. In the attack on Coventry, which seemed to the enemy so successful that they proposed to make it a standard of all bombing and call any city "Coventrated" if it had endured similar damage, about one hundred acres in the centre of the town were devastated. Coventry was a large and important town, with the great majority of its inhabitants engaged in war industries; the light engineering industries of Coventry were almost indispensable to the production of a great range of weapons and war equipment. On the day after this attack production in all the war factories of the town was one-third of what it had been before. Some damage had been done to the factories themselves, but it was very slight compared with non-industrial damage. The loss of production was almost entirely due to the interruption of public utilities, the dislocation of transport, and absenteeism caused by the destruction of houses, and many other causes. There was very heavy damage, for example, to sewers, water supply pipes, electric cables, gas pipes and so forth, and this had an immediate effect on production. Output was back to normal again in about two months, but there were special circumstances which led us to believe that production would not recover so quickly in Germany as in England. War industries in Britain were not fully expanded at the time of the German attacks on us, and there was therefore much labour to spare for the work of repair. A large army was also standing idle in Britain, with nothing to do except to train for a second front which then seemed infinitely remote; many hundreds of sappers could therefore be spared and they were at once rushed to Coventry to carry out immediate repairs.

After the extent of devastation in a number of towns had been compared with the loss of output in these towns over a period of months, a definite correlation was found between acreage of concentrated devastation and loss of man hours; the one was a function of the other. Scattered damage, produced over a long period, had, as one might expect less effect on production than concentrated damage and the relation between the two was more difficult to estimate. It was also found that production took longer to recover after a second successful attack on a town than after a first. On the whole, output which had been cut down as a result of industrial damage was less quickly restored than output which had been cut down as a result of non-industrial damage, but on the other hand non-industrial damage always caused greater loss of output than industrial damage in the first weeks after an attack. What could not be fully appreciated from any survey of air raid damage in Britain was the cumulative effect on industry of its extensive destruction in a large number of towns; this was the point at which the comparison broke down between the small scale German bombing and the much heavier attacks that Bomber Command proposed eventually to deliver. There was every reason to expect not only that one thousand acres of devastation in a town would cause more than ten times the loss of output resulting from the destruction of one hundred acres, but also that when a large number of towns was similarly devastated the total loss of output could not be estimated merely by adding together the various acreages of devastation in all the towns. It was obvious if air attack was continued a time would come when factories in an undamaged town would stand idle for want of materials that should have been supplied by the factories of a damaged town.

As a matter of strict calculation it was therefore obvious that the policy of destroying industrial cities, and the factories in them, was not merely the only possible one for Bomber Command at that time; it was also the best way of destroying Germany's capacity to produce war material. The morale of the enemy under bombing could be taken as an imponderable factor. Just possibly a break in morale might lead to the collapse of the enemy, and more probably bad morale would add to the loss of production resulting directly from air raid damage, but it was not necessary to take these possibilities into account; bombing, there was every reason to suppose, would cripple the enemy's war industries if it was carried out for long enough and with sufficient weight. There was no reason, of course, to confine our bombing exclusively to the large industrial cities; if this should at any time be possible it would be of great advantage to attack key-point factories outside the cities as well. And in point of fact within a month or two of my taking over the Command the force was able to seize the opportunity to bomb two key factories, one in France and the other in Germany, with a large measure of success. Moreover, now that the Americans were in the war with us, their bombers, operating by day, would be able to attack just those factories in open country or on the outskirts of towns which we could not as yet hope to attack by night in normal circumstances. The American campaign and that of our bombers would be exactly complementary, but all the facts at our disposal showed that it would not be sufficient, even if by any chance it became possible, to attack only the key factories. When the Americans came to bomb Japan in force, although they had begun the war as one hundred per cent advocates of "precision" bombing, they also discovered that it was necessary to carry out area attacks.

There is a widespread impression, which has often got into print, that I not only invented the policy of area bombing but also insisted on carrying it out in the face of the natural reluctance to kill women and children that was felt by everyone else. The facts are otherwise. Such decisions of policy are not in any case made by Commanders-in-Chief in the field but by the Ministries, by the Chiefs of Staff Committee, and by the War Cabinet. The decision to build a great force of bombers for strategic attack on industries and communications was made long before the war; the prototype of four-engines bombers we used against Germany was designed in 1935, which gives some idea of how long it takes to organise a bomber force. The decision to attack large industrial areas instead of key factories was made before I became Commander-in-Chief. But whenever anyone wishes to blackguard me, as the *Economist* and the *Daily Worker* have done (a compliment from such sources), they accuse me of being not only the executor of the bombing policy but also its author. The idea is that when I went to Bomber Command I said, "Let there be thousands of bombers and let there be tens of thousands of crews and let there be all their ancillary equipment and the personnel enlisted and the aerodromes made." Whereupon, rather as in the first chapter of Genesis, I obtained all these things by sheer force of blarney in the space of a few months. What actually happened was that by the end of 1942, the first year of my Command, I had as few aircraft as when I took over.

Chapter Five

THE PRELIMINARY PHASE

A year of preparation. The first navigational aid. The history of *Gee*. Excessive optimism about its use. Experiments over the Isle of Man and Wales. Building up the force. Thirteen squadrons taken from Bomber Command for Coastal Command and overseas. The failure of the Manchester. The Lancaster produced by accident. Some critical operations. The thousand bomber attack on Cologne. A night of suspense. Churchill hears the result. A spurious broadcast.

I WAS unable to begin any real bomber offensive for a whole year after I took over the Command for lack of aircraft, proper equipment and trained crews, and also because I was compelled to use what force I had for many other purposes besides the strategic bombing of Germany. Besides destroying four Ruhr towns in the next three months, I was required to attack targets of immediate strategic importance—a euphemism for targets chosen by the Navy—to support combined operations when asked to do so, and to attack a list of factories in France, with the object of discouraging the French from working for the enemy.

But in the first few months the attack on the Ruhr was my chief concern. Everything depended on the new navigational aid, Gee ; it will be remembered that without it only one aircraft in ten had been able to get within five miles of any Ruhr target. This fact was perfectly well known by those who laid down the campaign I had to undertake, and the whole idea of beginning this attack at the present stage rested on a theoretical estimate which had already been made, not by Bomber Command, of the accuracy and usefulness of Gee.

The principle of Gee had already been worked out before the war, and we could have had this device much earlier if every priority had not been given to the air defence of Great Britian and to the defence of our Atlantic communications. It was not only that priority had hitherto been given to the manufacturers of radar-equipment for Fighter and Coastal Commands, and for the Navy, but also that the rather few scientists who were able to devise such equipment were entirely preoccupied with defensive measures; priority in the use of brains was at least as important a matter as priority in production. The principle of Gee is simple enough. Two stations, a master and a slave station, simultaneously transmit a radar pulse signal. The Gee apparatus in the aircraft measures the difference between the times at which the two signals are received, and so indicates the difference between the aircraft's distance from one station and its distance from the other. This shows the navigator that the aircraft is somewhere on a certain line, and this line is marked on a chart prepared for use with the Gee apparatus. But the same master station and a second slave station—there are three stations in all—also transmit another pair of synchronised signals, from which, by the Gee apparatus, the navigator can place aircraft on a second line on his chart. The actual position of the aircraft is therefore at the point of intersection of the two lines.

Theoretically this should have made the navigator independent of any sight of the ground, and navigation by night less dependent on the weather than it had been before. If the apparatus worked as well as it was expected to do, it looked as if it would be unnecessary to carry out that long search for landmarks in the neighbourhood of the target which was not only extremely dangerous, and not only almost impossible at any reasonable operational height, but also tended to prevent any effective concentration of attack. And unlike the various radio—not radar—devices and beams which had been in use before the Command had any radar aid to navigation, the Gee stations could give a force of any size any required number of fixes.

It had been decided in 1941 to equip every aircraft in the Command with the Gee apparatus as soon as it could be got into full production. In June, 1941, a few experimental sorties by aircraft equipped with Gee had been made over enemy territory, but it was then ruled that no more such sorties should be made until Gee could be used on a larger scale; this was because it was essential that the apparatus should not fall into enemy hands or the fact of its proposed use be otherwise disclosed. For it was a serious drawback to Gee that, as we knew, the enemy would be able to jam the transmissions of the ground stations when he discovered them. It was taken for granted that this would eventually happen and from the first the system was given, as a working hypothesis, an operational life of anything up to five months. As an extra precaution, in the hope that the enemy would attribute the increased accuracy of our attacks to the use of a radio beam, beams of this kind were transmitted from various points on the east and south coasts of Britian at the same time as Gee was introduced; they were, in any case, useful for homing aircraft. After the enemy had begun jamming Gee the Command would have to use one of the other radar aids to navigation which were in course of development some time before the operational use of Gee; in point of fact there was a long gap, which might have been very serious, between the jamming of Gee and the introduction of the later radar aids.

Another limitation of Gee was that it would only work efficiently within a range of 350-400 miles. This limitation was considered so serious that there was at first considerable reluctance on this account alone, to equip the force with Gee. But a range of 350 miles meant that Gee fixes could be got in the Ruhr area, and, by using Gee up to the limit of its range aircraft, could be flown to more distant targets with greater accuracy than before.

But the real question was, not whether Gee would or would not be very useful to a bomber force, but just how accurate it was. Was it, in fact an aid to navigation, enabling the navigator to get within a mile or two of the target but leaving him to find the rest of the way by using his eyes? Or could Gee be used for blind bombing, that is, would it give the bomb-aimer so accurate a fix that he could release the bombs on this alone, without sight of the target? Opinion at the Air Ministry was that Gee could definitely be used for the blind bombing of large industrial towns, though not of individual factories. It was believed that a large town could therefore be attacked through ten-tenths cloud; the estimate was that if Essen was attacked through cloud, nearly half of all the bombs dropped would fall on the city. With the independence of weather over the target that this would give, it would be possible for the force to operate on something like seven times as many nights as before. In effect, this would be equivalent to multiplying my force of 300 aircraft by seven, and quite a lot can be done with 2100 bombers, especially if half their whole bomb load can be trusted to hit even such a difficult target as Essen. Hence the expectation that I should be able to destroy completely Essen and three other towns in the Ruhr within a period of three months. On the other hand, only a small proportion of the force was so far equipped with Gee, but presumably it was thought that there would be some way of getting round this.

Up to the end of 1941 a front line strength of 4000 heavies, or more, remained the objective at which the Air Staff was ultimately aiming. Many thought it a fanciful figure, the main objection being that we should never get the training establishment, the maintenance personnel, or the aerodromes to run such a force. It was also objected that England was far too small an island on which to base such a force. It must, of course, be remembered that if we had had no allies and the bomber offensive had been our only method of attacking the enemy, we should have had to get the men for the force at all costs and the other services would have had to give them up. As to England being too small, the Americans based great numbers on far smaller islands in the Pacific, and, in point of fact, something like 4000 heavies, when the U.S.A.A.F. bombers were added to Bomber Command, did eventually operate from England in the later stages of the war. However, we now had Russia and America for allies, and the prospect of an all-out bomber offensive was receding and an eventual invasion of Europe becoming more and more feasible. The target figure of 4000 heavies was therefore allowed to drop.

Just before I took over command, two exercises in the use of Gee were held, one over the Isle of Man and the other over North Wales. These were not carried out in cloudy weather and were therefore no real test of the value of Gee for blind bombing. The idea was to discover how a small number of Gee-equipped aircraft —and it looked as if only a small number would be available for some time to come—could best lead the main force, unequipped with Gee, to the target. The Isle of Man was chosen for the first exercise because the accuracy of Gee in relation to the ground stations was about the same in that area as it was expected to be over the Ruhr. Twelve aircraft equipped with the Gee apparatus were to arrive at a given time and each of them was to drop a single flare over the aiming point. Then they had to orbit the aiming point, make a second run up to it, and after the crews had made every effort to identify the aiming point visually, drop a second flare. These flares had a double purpose; they were to attract the main force, the aircraft which were without Gee, to the target area, and, when this had been done, they were to make if possible to identify the target itself visually by their light. Each of the Gee-equipped aircraft was, in all, to drop six flares, orbiting the target six times, six times running up to it, and so giving the bomb-aimer six chances of identifying the target by sight. This would keep the aiming point lit up for twenty minutes.

This exercise, which was called Crackers, went wrong because of a fault in one of the ground stations, as a result of which the flares were laid in two groups some miles apart. It was held on the night of February 13-14th, 1942, and a few days later a second exercise, Crackers II, was held, on the night of February 19-20th, with the railway station at Brynkir, North Wales, serving as target. Even with the flares serving the double purpose of lighting up the target as well as attracting the main force to the area, and only the second of these two functions would have been performed by the flares in a blind-bombing attack through ten-tenths cloud, photographs taken at the time of the exercise suggested that if bombs had been dropped most of them would have fallen within a radius of two to three miles of the target. There was no cloud, but some haze, and in these conditions, which were rather better than could be expected in the Ruhr, the flares proved so dazzling that it was difficult to see the ground. Thus from the beginning there was some reason to suspect that bombing by Gee might prove nothing like as accurate as the theoretical calculations of the Air Ministry had predicted it would be, especially as much less accuracy could be expected over a heavily defended area in enemy country than during an exercise in Great Britain.

I laid on an attack on Essen at the earliest opportunity, which was on the night of March 8-9th. Essen was the first on my list of Ruhr towns, as it was the largest city in that area and industrially the most important. Two hundred and eleven aircraft were dispatched, 74 of them being equipped with Gee. The weather was good, though there was, of course, the usual industrial haze which never disappeared until Bomber Command had put out of action Krupps and a number of other factories in Essen; it was not until then that we were able to get any clear photographs of the place. Photographic reconnaissance not long after the first attack with Gee showed no damage whatever in the target area. The causes of the failure were investigated and it was established that, although most of the flares had been dropped in the right place, a large proportion of the main force, loaded with incendiary bombs, had arrived after the flares had gone out; these aircraft dropped their incendiaries over a wide area, mostly short of the target, and the incendiaries burning on the ground in turn attracted the bombs of more aircraft of the main force. Within the next three months there were eleven more major attacks on Essen, all made with the use of Gee, though with a considerable variation of tactics from time to time. On the night of the 10-11th March, the Gee-equipped aircraft dropped 250-lb. incendiaries instead of flares, these large incendiaries being intended to serve as a beacon to guide the main force. During this three months no serious damage was done either to Essen or Krupps, even though one of the eleven attacks was carried out by 956 aircraft; this was in the second of our three "one thousand bomber" attacks.

The bombing, it was discovered, was about a third as accurate as the results of the exercises carried out over Britain. For every hundred aircraft attacking Essen no more than between five and ten sticks of bombs could be expected, by the use of Gee alone, to fall on the built-up area of Essen and only two or three sticks on Krupps itself. But clearly the fault was not entirely that of the Gee apparatus, for in the interval successful attacks had been made on other towns by the use of Gee. None of the targets we attacked successfully was, however, in the Ruhr, and the obvious conclusion was that our attacks on this area failed because of its special characteristics, first, the invariable smoke and haze, and secondly the absence of any good landmarks. In the Ruhr it was extremely easy to mistake one town for another and this was often done; on the night of March 9-10th, 1942, Bomber Command attacked Hamborn by mistake for Essen. There was also the fact that the enemy used many decoy fires with good effect in this area. During March of 1942 a serious proportion of the whole bomb-load fell on decoy fires lighted at Rheinburg, about 20 miles from Essen. The large incendiary bombs dropped as a beacon on the night of March 10-11th did not provide the distinctive mark that had been hoped for, and though our flares were satisfactory when the weather was perfectly clear, their light was invariably scattered by haze; the crews said that the effect was so dazzling in the Ruhr that it was almost easier to see without them.

Clearly Gee was quite inadequate as an instrument for blind-bombing; our attacks succeeded when the target could be identified visually after Gee had brought the aircraft into its neighbourhood; they failed when visual identification was impossible or very difficult, as it was now clear that it always would be in the Ruhr. So for the time being the only thing to do was to get all the good we could out of Gee, but, until the new aids to navigation, Oboe and H2S, came along, to concentrate on improving the visual identification of targets. We had to accept the fact, not always fully recognised in 1941, that visual identification of targets was impossible except in moonlight and clear weather, and this meant that we had for the time being to accept a high casualty rate from fighter and flak. And we had to accept the fact that the Ruhr was for the time being impregnable, because in this area industrial haze made visual identification almost impossible.

The advantages to be got from Gee, at any rate as soon as the whole force was equipped with it, was very great. Concentration along the route, as a protection against night fighters, and over the target, as a protection against flak and fighters and as a method of increasing the damage, demanded accurate track and time-keeping, and Gee was indispensable for this. With such a concentration, large numbers of bombers had to be landed at the same time, and here again this could not have been done without Gee, which increased in accuracy as the aircraft got nearer home so that a large force could be marshalled with great precision over England. Hitherto the last lap had been one of the most dangerous parts of an operation, for many aircraft would be damaged, the crews would be tired, and landing by night was always perilous. With Gee most of these dangers were removed. Whereas in 1940 and 1941 it often happened that more aircraft and crews were lost by crashing in England on the return flight than over Germany, in 1942 Gee progressively reduced this wastage until it became almost insignificant. When it is remembered that the Germans had to give up the night bombing of England mainly because they lost so many· aircraft and crews in crashes on returning to base, the immense advantage we derived from the use of Gee will be understood.

My first step was to ask for two things, a marker bomb or target indicator, and the introduction of a new member of a bomber's aircrew, a bomb-aimer or air-bomber whose job would be to relieve the navigator of the task of identifying the target visually. The use of a target indicator bomb was obviously necessary; the leading aircraft had to be able to draw the rest of the force to the aiming point by marking it with some sort of firework or coloured light which could easily be distinguished. Fires were no good, because they could not be distinguished from the enemy's decoys; moreover aircraft which had got into difficulties could not be prevented from jettisoning their incendiaries at some point along the route, and it was always possible for these to be mistaken for the beacon fires of the leading aircraft. At the beginning of March, 1942, I wrote to the Air

Ministry and asked for target-indicators as an urgent requirement; I had, in point of fact, pressed for their development many years before. The Air Ministry and all the other departments and ministries concerned interpreted the word "urgent" in their own way, and we did not get our first target indicator until January, 1943. Meanwhile we had to content ourselves with various types of incendiary as a substitute, and these proved wholly unreliable.

There was an equally obvious need to introduce the air-bomber into the crew. The navigator had more than enough to do if he was to get the aircraft within a few miles of the target, especially when making the run-up to the target with Gee fixes. Apart from all the other difficulties involved in suddenly beginning a new and highly specialised task when near the target, the work he had done as a navigator left him no time to get his eyes conditioned to the darkness, which he would have to do before trying to spot the aiming point. We had to apply to the Air Ministry to get permission for the principle of introducing an air-bomber, but when once this was granted, in March, 1942, everything else could be done in the Operational Training Units under my Command. The problem was quickly solved. Up till March, 1942, the crews training in Wellingtons and Whitleys at the O.T.U.s consisted of two pilots, a navigator, and two wireless-operator air-gunners, one of them manning the rear turret. It was impossible to give the two pilots an equal amount of training unless the whole crew went through double the number of flights, circuits, and landings they needed, and the result was that neither pilot was trained to the standard that was rapidly becoming necessary, the standard required for the heavy bombers. So the second pilot was left out of the crew, and the air-bomber put in his place. At this time all night bombers carried front guns, so the air-bomber was trained to man the front guns, and he was also given a small amount of training as pilot, so that he could at a pinch take over the controls. Another change was also made at the same time; only one man was from then on trained both as wireless-operator and air-gunner; the fifth member of the crew was trained as a full-time gunner. The O.T.U.s then settled down to a five-months' course involving 80 flying hours, and maintained this standard until the end of the war; there were times when it looked as if we should have to reduce the length of the course, but in the end we got through without lowering the standard of training. It would, of course, have been easy at any time to improve the standard of training at the expense of the front line. The length of the course could have been increased, all the best air-crew could have been taken off operations at an early stage in their career and sent back to the O.T.U.s to serve as instructors, and new equipment could have been allocated to the O.T.U.s before the operational squadrons got it so that the new crews could all have been fully trained in the new devices. But this would have had a profound effect on our front-line strength and would therefore have lengthened the war. A balance had to be struck, and I am convinced that it was the right one. As it was, we had to reject some crews who learnt slowly because there was simply not time to persevere with training them, although if there had been time they might well have made good crews in the end. But it was in this, and not in any falling-off in the standard of training of the average crew, that the pressure of events showed itself.

I ought perhaps to explain that the training at O.T.U.s only comes right at the end of a long period of flying training for each individual; the training we gave in Bomber Command was for the crew as a whole; it was a specialist course in bomber operations. The education of a member of a bomber crew was the most expensive in the world; it cost some £10,000 for each man, enough to send ten men to Oxford or Cambridge for three years.

Training was of tremendous importance in 1942 because a formidable increase in the strength of the Command was expected to occur during the year. At the same time many medium bomber squadrons were to be re-equipped with heavy bombers, and this involved the re-training of all their air-crew. At first it was thought that the conversion of a crew to a different type of aircraft could be quickly and easily done, but it was soon seen that there was much more in it than this. It is not generally realised how astonishingly good was the work of the O.T.U.s. They produced an endless flow of crews whose ability to cope with every conceivable sort of weather was far in advance of what any pre-war crew, civil or service, could have achieved. All this was done by instructors during what were called their "rest periods" between operational tours, and it was not done without casualties. It was quickly realised that only air-crew with actual experience of operations could train the O.T.U. crews, and until the last year there was a continual shortage of men who could serve as instructors, and particularly of pilots with operational experience, so that they all had to work overtime. In the most dangerous flying conditions the instructors and instructional crews ran almost as much risk as the fighting crews, and they ran these risks over a much longer period than that of an operational tour. It was and is a matter of great distress to me that recognition of their work and of the risks they ran was refused.

In preparation for the expansion of the Command the O.T.U.s and the heavy conversion units—these were the units which trained crews to operate heavy bombers—did magnificent work during 1942. During the whole of that year the Command and the O.T.U.s and conversion units struggled to raise new squadrons, complete with crews. But as far as the offensive against Germany was concerned, the greater part of all this work might as well not have been done. As fast as each squadron was raised, it was transferred, not to the front-line strength of Bomber Command, but to the Middle East or to other Commands not concerned with the offensive against Germany. In all, 19 new squadrons were formed in the Command during 1942, and 13 of these were taken from us. And of the new squadrons that were left to us, three were on more or less permanent loan to Coastal Command and engaged in anti-submarine patrols. From May, 1942, to the end of February, 1943, additional aircraft lent to Coastal Command made 1000 sorties while engaged in this work.

At the same time the crews in the squadrons we succeeded in keeping were never, until May, 1943, at more than 80 per cent of the proper strength. This was due to the inordinate demands for crews overseas, and especially for the Middle East, where large numbers were misemployed in a very extravagant way. Few people realise that amongst all its other duties Bomber Command had until well towards the end of the war to raise and train every bomber crew for the whole of the Royal Air Force all over the world. In these circumstances, when one Command is supplying the cloth for another Command to cut its coat out of, the coat cut is naturally of generous, and even luxurious proportions. This supply of crews to overseas was an additional strain on top of the supply of 13 complete squadrons in 1942, and it could only be done by keeping the crew-strength of our own squadrons at twenty per cent below what it should have been. There were times when we sent as many as 50 trained Wellington crews a month overseas, mainly to the Mediterranean Allied Air Forces, and this was in addition to some trained Halifax crews. At first the demand was met entirely by posting crews from any O.T.U., or even by taking them from operational squadrons, but in April, 1942, we put all the crews intended for overseas into two special O.T.U.s where they could have some specialised training in such matters as overseas intelligence, though otherwise there was little difference between this and the normal course at other O.T.U.s. It would obviously have been a good idea to have these crews trained by instructors with operational experience overseas. We repeatedly asked for crews who had had this experience to be sent home from the Middle East, but for a long time we could not get them.

No proper record of the whereabouts of air-crews trained in Bomber Command O.T.U.s was kept by the Air Ministry and no arrangement was made to ensure that these indispensable men were properly employed. In the Middle East and elsewhere there was at times a great surplus of air-crew, amounting to hundreds of men, which we had trained in Bomber Command O.T.U.s; they were either kept in idleness or misemployed in one fashion or another, at a time when the O.T.U.s themselves were short of several hundred air-crew and instructor pilots. We made great efforts to get this put right, and in this we were supported by the Inspector-General, Air Chief Marshal Sir Edgar Ludlow-Hewitt; eventually we got some of them back. In the end the obvious solution of the whole problem was adopted and Wellington O.T.U.s were formed in Palestine and elsewhere in the Middle East. The demands from overseas and Coastal Command were the main reason why Bomber Command failed to expand during 1943. Another hindrance to beginning the offensive at once was that the Command itself was in process of converting from medium two-engined to heavy four-engined bombers throughout the year. This, of course, was indispensable. As I have said elsewhere, the original decision to equip the R.A.F.'s bomber force with four-engined bombers of the type we eventually had was taken long ago, and the first specifications were drawn up in 1935, but the wisdom of this decision was frequently discussed at a later date. We had in England those who took the same view as the leaders of the German air force, that bombers should be light and rely on their speed and manœuvrability to evade the enemy's air defence. The Mosquito, was, in fact, the direct outcome of this controversy between supporters of the light and supporters of the heavy bomber; when rearmament was being planned there seemed to be no reason why we should not have the best of both worlds and add something like a thousand or so light bombers to the four thousand heavies. Unlike the Germans we grasped the point that any ordinary bomber is cold meat to any ordinary fighter, and so a light bomber, the Mosquito, was designed which should be at least as fast, and probably faster, than the average fighter. But in the end the wisdom of concentrating on the heavy bomber was conclusively proved. The decisive factor was the supply of pilots; the heavy bomber carries about three times the load of the medium type, but both aircraft only need one pilot. It is certain that even with the whole resources of the Empire Training Scheme we should never have got enough pilots to fly enough medium and light bombers to drop the bomb load that was dropped by the heavies. And, of course, the problem of concentrating the bomb load, if it had been carried by many light bombers instead of by a comparatively few heavies, would have been insoluble.

In January, 1942, we had an average of only forty-two heavy bombers available, and in December of that year we had an average of 261 heavies. In terms of squadrons, we had 36 heavy bomber squadrons at the end of the year as against 15 the year before. In February we were operating with Hampdens, Whitleys, Wellingtons, Manchesters, Stirlings, and Halifaxes, and we had two Lancaster squadrons non-operational while re-equipping with this new type. This list excludes the light bombers of No. 2 Group. At the end of 1942 the Hampdens and Whitleys had gone, the Whitleys during the summer, and the Hampdens in September. The Manchesters had also proved a failure and were withdrawn from operations in June. Halifaxes formed the bulk of the heavy bomber force, Stirlings, the first of the four-engined bombers to become operational, were falling behind in number, and there were ten Lancaster squadrons. operational, together with one temporarily non-operational. We also had half a Mosquito squadron.

It was therefore a much better-equipped and better balanced force at the end of the year than at the beginning, but the re-equipment could not be carried out without taking many squadrons off operations for the time being. In February, 1942, one-third of the whole front line strength was actually non-operational, either because new squadrons were in process of forming, or because old squadrons were in process in re-equipping with better aircraft. The introduction of the heavy bomber did, in fact, very considerably increase the period of training for each crew, and this lasted until the end of the war. At first it was thought that it would be a comparatively simple matter to introduce crews to the new aircraft, no longer a process than converting a crew from Whitleys to Wellingtons. But it was soon learned that a complete and thorough course, often involving forty hours flying together with considerable training on the ground, was absolutely indispensable for the efficient handling of these more complicated aircraft. Further delay was caused by the fact that the new aircraft had to be modified to bring them up to the standard required for operations, and this took on an average 400 man-hours per aircraft. It became vital to carry out re-equipment and conversion as rapidly as possible. It may not appear a considerable loss of effort if one squadron loses a week while engaged in re-equipment, but if 50 squadrons lost a week, this would be equivalent to dropping 10,000 tons of bombs less on Germany. Every conceivable effort was made to cut down the time taken for re-equipment, but in 1942 it undoubtedly reduced our effort against the enemy and checked the expansion of the Command.

This, however, unlike the loss of squadrons to other Commands, was unavoidable. The effect of the introduction of heavy bombers in 1942 is shown by the fact that, although numerical expansion was negligible, over the whole year there was an increase of 44 per cent as compared with 1941 in the weight of bombs dropped. But it must be remembered that we lacked any proper target finding equipment throughout the whole year, and that there is not much difference between the load of a medium bomber which misses the target and the load of a heavy bomber which also misses it.

The failure of the Manchester inevitably added to the delay in expansion and at the time was a real disaster to us. Four whole squadrons had to re-equip when this aircraft was taken off operations in June, and of course, it had been an immense waste of man-hours in industry to produce an aircraft which could not be used. The Manchester itself was a fine aeroplane, but the twin engines with which it was fitted failed to produce the necessary power: they were also unreliable because overloaded. The Manchester therefore quickly proved itself to be virtually useless for operations. But this disaster proved a blessing in disguise. When the fault was first discovered, a considerable time before the Manchester actually ceased to operate, the aircraft was rapidly re-designed, as an emergency measure, to take four engines. It was then rechristened the Lancaster, and this emergency design turned out to be without exception the finest bomber of the war.

Its efficiency was almost incredible, both in performance and in the way in which it could be saddled with ever increasing loads without breaking the camel's back. It is astonishing that so small an aircraft as the Lancaster could so easily take the enormous 22,000 lb. "Grand Slam" bomb, a weapon which no other aircraft in the world could or yet can carry. The Lancaster far surpassed all the other types of heavy bomber. Not only could it take heavier bomb loads, not only was it easier to handle, and not only were there fewer accidents with this than with other types; throughout the war the casualty rate of Lancasters was also consistently below that of other types. It is true that in 1944 the wastage of Lancasters from casualties became equal to, and at times even greater than, the wastage of Halifaxes, but this was the exception that proved the rule; at that time I invariably used Lancasters alone for those attacks which involved the deepest penetration into Germany and were consequently the most dangerous.

The Lancaster was so far the best aircraft we had that I continually pressed for its production at the expense of other types; I was even willing to lose nearly a year's industrial production from the Halifax factories while these were being converted to produce Lancasters. I did not get my way in this, but by other means we succeeded in the later stages of the offensive in re-equipping many Halifax squadrons with Lancasters. The superiority of the Lancaster also had its effect on our policy in training and the conversion of crews to heavy bombers. I wanted all the Lancasters I could get in the front line, and this meant we had to use Halifaxes and Stirlings for the greater part of the training in the heavy conversion units, with only a brief course at a Lancaster finishing school, as it was called, at the end; in this way large numbers of Lancasters were saved for operations, though at the expense, which was well worth while, of some increase in the time taken to train Lancaster crews.

Besides the time lost in converting to heavy bombers in 1942 our expansion was limited, especially in the first half of that year, by trouble with our airfields. The need for runways of adequate length for heavy bombers was not understood, except by those who knew something about heavy bombers and had seen and handled them.

As early as October, 1941, the Air Ministry had agreed to allow airfields of the size that became normal towards the end of the war, but it was more than a year before this policy was made effective. And just when shortage of airfields was causing the greatest difficulty—we needed the largest airfields not only for actual operations but also for the work of the heavy conversion units—we had to hand over a considerable number of those which had been scheduled for Bomber Command to the United States Army Air Force. It was, of course, entirely necessary that the Americans should have airfields in Britain—no one had anticipated or could have anticipated this need before Pearl Harbour—and drastic action had to be taken; in May, 1942, we disbanded a whole Bomber group, No. 8 Group, which was then forming but had not yet become operational, and handed over all its stations to the U.S.A.A.F.

It had been confidently expected that 1942 would see a great increase in the strength of the Command because aircraft and formed squadrons had been promised from America. In the event we gained nothing from this source. All the United States heavy bombers allotted to Britain went to Coastal Command and nearly all the United States medium and light bombers were sent either to Russia or to the Mediterranean. No. 2 Group, a purely tactical force which was scarcely concerned with the offensive against Germany, did get Bostons in place of Blenheims, which were taken off operations in the summer of 1942.

So during 1942 Bomber Command remained the smallest and weakest of the Commands and was likely to remain so unless something was done about it and done quickly. Even if I could succeed in convincing those in charge of the war that we could achieve something with adequate strength and equipment, there was bound to be a time lag between the decision to give us a little of what we wanted and the actual fulfilment of that decision; there was clearly no time to spare. I had to regard the operations of the next few months not only as training or trial runs from which, and only from which, we could learn many essential lessons, but also as commercial travellers' samples which I could show to the War Cabinet.

It is somewhat ironic that the first completely successful operation carried out after I took over the Command should have been not only a diversion from the main offensive against Germany but also a precision attack on a keypoint factory. This was the attack on the Renault works, near Paris, one of the French factories most actively engaged in producing war equipment for the enemy. This was a very short range target and it was almost undefended, which meant that we could attack it in clear weather and brilliant moonlight and that aircraft could come down very low to identify the factory. The attack was therefore no sort of test of our capacity to destroy heavily-defended targets at much greater range within Germany itself. But the bright moonlight in which the attack was carried out enabled us to plan a concentrated raid without having to rely on the small quantity of Gee equipment we then had; it was, in fact, the first attack in which the principle of concentration in time and space was effectively employed. The Renault factory was high in the list of collaborating French factories which had been given to me and this extremely destructive raid not only deprived the enemy of a considerable quantity of equipment, but was also of some value in discouraging the production of war material for the enemy elsewhere in France.

On the night of March 28th-29th the first German city went up in flames. This was Lübeck, a rather distant target on the Baltic coast, but not difficult to identify because of its position on the River Trave, by no means so well defended as the Ruhr, and from the nature of its buildings easier than most cities to set on fire. It was a city of moderate size, of some importance as a port, and with some submarine building yards of moderate size not far from it. It was not a vital target, but it seemed to me better to destroy an industrial town of moderate importance that to fail to destroy a large industrial city. However, the main object of the attack was to learn to what extent a first wave of aircraft could guide a second wave to the aiming point by starting a conflagration: I ordered a half an hour interval between the two waves in order to allow the fires to get a good hold before the second wave arrived. In all, 234 aircraft were dispatched and dropped 144 tons of incendiaries and 160 tons of high explosives. At least half of the town was destroyed, mainly by fire. It was conclusively proved that even the small force I had then could destroy the greater part of a town of secondary importance.

In the attack on Lübeck 13 aircraft were missing, most of them being shot down along the route, a loss rate of 5½ per cent, and no more than could be expected on a moonlight night and with the target at so great a distance from base. However, if this casualty rate had continued as an average for any length of time it would largely, if not entirely, have prevented the expansion of the Command, or as an alternative, would have prevented the Command from operating at the fullest intensity of which it was capable. There were two occasions during the later offensive when the losses were for a considerable period more than 5 per cent of the total operational sorties of the Command, and on each occasion expansion was extremely small, while operational intensity was comparatively low—if it had not been, the Command would have contracted instead of expanding. At the height of the offensive we were getting not much more than 200 aircraft a month from production, and it was only by unremitting effort and ingenuity that we kept our monthly casualty rate below that figure. We were working throughout the war with an extremely small margin for error and unless this is clearly realised it will be impossible to understand the nature of the prolonged battle we had to fight.

At times, as the offensive continued, I found impinging upon my consciousness, the fact that whereas in England both the public and the politicians expected our fighter and anti-aircraft defences, infinitesimally small by comparison with what the Germans had, to put a stop to the blitzes—which they and the Germans themselves did within a few months—both the public and the Government were equally convinced that Bomber Command ought not at any time to incur any really serious casualties. Though Bomber Command had on the average four or five times as far to fly over enemy territory as the Germans had to fly over England, and though this enemy territory had vastly better anti-aircraft defences than any part of England in 1940-1941, we were expected to get on with our job with ever-increasing success, at ever-increasing tempo, regardless of the weather, and if we ever suffered losses in any way comparable with those of the enemy there was immediate indignation and surprise. I naturally find these two attitudes of mind, the attitude to the enemy and the attitude to ourselves, not only quite incompatible but also quite incomprehensible. The two attitudes were nevertheless to be found in the minds alike of the highest and lowest of the land. Though the Prime Minister would vehemently complain (but invariably in a highly encouraging and heartening manner) if our defences seemed to be getting somewhat meagre results or building up rather slowly, yet he would at the same time be the first to express distress if our own casualties, the casualties we incurred on the offensive, were occasionally above the average— and if they had not sometimes been above the average we could not even have begun to strike an average. But I want to make it quite clear that I was never pressed by Mr. Churchill to do anything at his dictation, or anything with which I was not personally satisfied. If he ever expressed some impatience, very natural in the circumstances, when things were not going too well elsewhere and the bomber offensive had been held up for two or three nights in succession by the weather, he immediately qualified his expression by saying with deep concern, and clearly as a direct warning, that in no circumstances was he pressing me to fight the weather as well as the enemy. As a matter of fact, that was precisely what we always had to do, to fight the weather as well as the enemy. There was no conceivable way of avoiding this unfortunate fact, though in the end the skill of the air-crews, and the forethought of our meteorologists and scientists, made both the enemy and the weather, our two enemies, largely ineffective; they were less and less able to stop us from doing what we wanted to do.

Our losses were lower in an attack on Rostock, a rather more important target than Lübeck and at greater distance from base, but still in no sense a major industrial city; once again it was clearly proved that we had the force and equipment to tackle secondary targets, however completely we failed against major targets like the cities of the Ruhr. Rostock was another Baltic port, of some importance, and it had a large Heinkel aircraft factory on the outskirts. It took four attacks, on four consecutive nights of moon and clear weather, to wreck the town, and only 12 aircraft were missing out of a total of 521 sorties. The Lancaster operated on this attack for the first time, but as far as I can remember, only one of them. An interesting point about this attack was that it was a combination of area and precision bombing; the Heinkel factory was the aiming point for aircraft from No. 5 Group, and was seriously damaged. Picked crews from this Group, which throughout the war specialised in accurate bombing either of large or small areas by visual means, succeeded in identifying the factory and even the large assembly shed which was the most important part of it. But they had, of course, a burning town to guide them to within a short distance of their objective; there was also no similar factory outside the town which could be mistaken for the target, the defences were very light, and there were no decoys. These two attacks, against Lübeck and Rostock, brought the total acreage of devastation by bombing in Germany up to 780 acres, and in regard to bombing about squared our account with Germany. There is also no doubt that these two successes had a marked effect on the general morale of Bomber Command itself; throughout 1941 both air-crew and ground staff had been getting more and more depressed by the obvious failure of their attacks, and they, as well as the country at large, needed the stimulus of some definite achievement. And there is the possibility that the destruction of two towns of considerable size, and the mass evacuation which followed, gave the enemy a jolt which he badly needed.

There remained the problem of the first-class target, the major industrial town round which the enemy was bound to concentrate effective and heavy defences. So far all that the Lübeck and Rostock attacks had proved was that we could saturate the passive defences of a town by concentration of attack; it remained to be seen whether the active and passive defences of a vital industrial area could be similarly overcome. I was convinced that a force of 250-300 aircraft was wholly inadequate to saturate the then existing defences of a major industrial town of half a million or more inhabitants. But if we attacked with a larger force, supposing that we could get one, should we be able to organise it in such a way as to get a really high concentration over the target? It was becoming obvious that the degree of concentration we had achieved so far was not going to be good enough, but there was no previous experience to show whether it would be practical to put many hundreds of aircraft over a target at the rate of, say, ten a minute; in the past such a conception would have been thought as absurd as it was dangerous, for this was six times as high a concentration as had been aimed at towards the end of 1941. At that time, as it happened, I did have a force of well over 1000 aircraft in my Command; if the crews and aircraft at the O.T.U.s and conversion units were added to the front-line squadrons we could easily raise our strength to that figure. They were half-trained crews, of course, but the O.T.U.s had already undertaken the task of dropping propaganda leaflets over France, often on a large scale; it was useful training for them, it relieved the front-line squadrons of this task, and they gained some knowledge of what it was like to be shot at by flak or even intercepted by night fighters. If there were great risks involved in a high concentration of aircraft, then these risks would be increased by sending out large numbers of new crews; but if, on the other hand, this high concentration was a definite protection against fighters and flak then I should not be calling on new crews to run so grave a risk as the front line squadrons had habitually taken.

The dangers were many and obvious. If anything went

seriously wrong—and this was to be in many ways a wholly new type of operation—then I should be committing not only the whole of my front line strength but absolutely all my reserves in a single battle. Our whole programme of training and expansion might conceivably be wrecked, and in any case I had very seriously to consider the inevitable interference with normal training that would occur while the force was being organised for this special purpose.

As against the dangers, the advantages of a successful operation on such a scale would be very great. If we succeeded we should have before us a definite and attainable goal, a measure of what could be achieved as soon as our expansion really began. The result of using an adequate bomber force against Germany would be there for all the world to see, and I should be able to press for the aircraft, crews, and equipment we needed with far more effect than by putting forward theoretical arguments, however convincing, in favour of hitting the enemy where it would hurt him most. Such a demonstration was, in fact, the only argument I could see which was at all likely to prevent our squadrons from being snatched away and our effort diverted to subsidiary targets, or to extract the equipment we so desperately needed, the radar navigational aids and the target indicators, from the torpid departments which withheld them for so long. But it was not only, of course, a question of convincing those in power that bombing could be a decisive weapon; from such an operation we should also learn a number of tactical lessons of the greatest possible value, lessons which could not be learned in any other way and without which we could not prepare for the main offensive. As to the harm such an attack might do to the enemy, this would no doubt be considerable, even though it was obvious that Germany, with the industries of the Reich undamaged and the resources of all Europe at her disposal, would be able to restore any lost production in a comparatively short space of time. Not one or two such strokes, but the cumulative effect of hundreds of them, would be needed before the enemy felt the pinch. On the other hand there was a good chance that morale would be affected by the first really heavy blow to get through the main defences of Germany.

I got Winston Churchill to agree to the thousand bomber plan late on a Sunday at Chequers. He was prepared for a loss of 100 bombers on this operation. As I drove home from there in my Bentley at 3 a.m.—it was only ten minutes from my home at

Springfield—I found myself humming "Malbrouck s'en va-t'en guerre." I suddenly realised that that tune always came into my head whenever I had just left him. The spirit of Marlborough did indeed breathe in his descendant and most emphatically was he going to war. Whether it was coincidence at first and habit thereafter I do not know. Whatever it was, the mixture of Chequers moonlight, Winston's inspiring courage, and my knowledge of the desperate state of the war always sent me home whistling or singing that oldest, or one of the oldest, of war songs.

We made our preparations for the thousand, bomber attack during May; it had the code word "Millenium" although I believe there was some trouble about this because there was an idea that the army wanted this to be the code word, a very appropriate code word as it seemed then, for the second front. The organisation of the force involved a tremendous amount of work throughout the Command. The training units put up 366 aircraft. No. 3 Group, with its conversion units put up about 250 aircraft, which was at that time regarded as a strong force in itself. Apart from four aircraft of Flying Training Command, the whole force of 1047 aircraft was provided by Bomber Command, but Army Co-operation Command lent us fifteen light aircraft to join with the Blenheims of No. 2 Group in a diversionary attack on enemy airfields. Fighter Command supplied 39 aircraft to attack airfields along the route. By the time of the moon period, at the end of the month, the whole force was standing by.

The moon was full on the night of May 30th and that morning we were promised good weather over the home bases. On the other hand thundery cloud was known to cover much of Germany; the weather often helped the enemy throughout the war, and at this time it was much to his advantage that the winds which brought good weather over our bases tended to produce cloud over Germany. If I waited, I might have to keep this very large force standing idle for some time, and I might lose the good weather over England; to land such a force in difficult weather would at that time have been to court disaster and for so many aircraft it was necessary to have a large number of bases free from cloud. But if I sent the force that night, the target might be cloud-covered, and the whole operation reduced to naught and our plan disclosed. From among a number of suitable targets only Cologne was at all likely to have reasonably good weather during the night, and there was no certainty about the weather over Cologne.

I chose Cologne and dispatched the force. It was by no means the greatest risk that a commander in the field has had to take in war, but it was a considerable risk.

The weather in those days had absolute power to make or mar an operation. In this instance, as I saw it, the weather had the power to make or mar the future of the bomber offensive; it would have been of no use whatever to argue what might have happened if the weather had been different, if thundery clouds had not covered the city, and if we had therefore been able to hit Cologne. And at that time there was much greater uncertainty about the weather than towards the end of the war, when the meteorological service had a considerably larger staff and when several important discoveries had been made. Moreover the meteorological reconnaissance flight, which sent aircraft over enemy territory to make observations just before an operation, had only recently been formed, in January, 1942. Most important of all, when the first essential for a successful attack was that the sky should be clear, we were up against a special difficulty which made accurate forecasting almost impossible. The meteorological conditions favourable to clear skies are also, most unfortunately, about equally favourable to the development of strato-cumulus cloud, either broken or continouus.

Let me here go back to a point I made before; Bomber Command was expected—even, to some extent, by Winston Churchill—to succeed in the face of every conceivable difficulty and opposition, but the enemy was expected to fail if we could arrange for him to encounter a tenth or twentieth of the opposition that we normally encountered over Germany. And while it seemed wholly natural and proper that the enemy should be repeatedly defeated by the weather—the Spanish Armada had its difficulties—any idea that we might be similarly affected by such an act of God seemed as monstrous as that we should be in any way diverted by the machinations of the King's enemies. Such a state of mind is no doubt the natural if sometimes unfortunate result of the almost unbroken record of victory in all major wars, which the British have for so long enjoyed. I can only say that while the thousand bombers were on their way across the North Sea I did not share the average Englishman's confidence that if such a thing had to be done at all it was bound to be a complete success.

Over the North Sea there was, in point of fact, extremely dirty weather, but when the force reached Holland it cleared, and continued clear all the way to the target. Nearly 900 aircraft attacked out of the total of 1047, and within an hour and a half dropped 1455 tons of bombs, two-thirds of the whole load being incendiaries. The casualty rate was 3.3 per cent, with 39 aircraft missing, and, in spite of the fact that a large part of the force consisted of semi-trained crews and that many more fighters were airborne than usual, this was considerably less than the average 4.6 per cent for operations in similar weather during the previous twelve months. The medium bomber, mostly flown by crews from the O.T.U.s had a casualty rate of 4.5 per cent, which was remarkable, but it was still more remarkable that we lost scarcely any of the 300 heavy bombers that took part in this operation; the casualty rate for the heavies was only 1.9 per cent. These had attacked after the medium bombers, when the defences had been to some extent beaten down, and in greater concentration than was possible for the new crews in the medium bombers. The figures proved conclusively that the enemy's fighters and flak had been effectively saturated; an analysis of all reports on the attack showed that the enemy's radar location devices had been able to pick up single aircraft and follow them throughout the attack, but that the guns had been unable to engage more than a small proportion of the large concentration of aircraft.

Reconnaissance after the attack showed that 600 acres of Cologne had been devastated and this in turn conclusively proved that the passive defences of Cologne had been saturated in just the same way as its guns and searchlights had been, together with the air defence of the whole of Western Germany, by concentration of attack. The damage had increased out of all proportion to the increase of bomb tonnage; in fact, this single attack had caused very nearly as much damage in Germany—600 acres as against 780—as all Bomber Command's previous attacks, including the very successful attacks on Lübeck and Rostock, taken together.

I rang up Winston Churchill, who had just alighted from Washington, and told him that the operation had been successful, and that only 39 aircraft were missing, one less than my estimate of 40. I always knew from the tone and quality of Churchill's voice, quite so much as from what he actually said, whether or no he was satisfied. I knew at once that he was satisfied then. At a time when there was no other conceivable offensive weapon we could use against the Germans, and when on every front and theatre of war we were confined to purely defensive action, Churchill now knew that we had an immensely powerful weapon which would give us that initiative that only comes from taking the offensive. Churchill was all out to wage war. He certainly did not want the destruction of German cities in and for itself, or in any spirit of revenge, but he wanted above all to get on with the war and no one understood better than he the vast strategic consequences of this single operation, which proved that a serious bombing offensive against Germany itself was a real possibility. The dominating offensive weapon of the war was at last being used, nearly three years after the Germans had invaded Poland. My own opinion is that we should never have had a real bomber offensive if it had not been for the 1000 bomber attack on Cologne, an irrefutable demonstration of the power of what was to all intents and purposes a new and untried weapon.

The enemy understood the implications of the attack on Cologne as well as anyone in England and it had an immediate effect on their whole air strategy; this effect was enormously more important than the actual damage to war production, or the effect on the morale of industrial workers, which resulted from the attack on Cologne. It was not long after the attack on Cologne that there began those changes in the order of battle of the German air force, and that drastic modification of the enemy's aircraft production plan, which eventually stripped the German army of all air cover and of all close support from the air. An air force whose whole purpose was army co-operation had now, from the summer of 1942 onwards, to concentrate more and more on the defence of Germany and to leave the German army more and more to its own devices on the ground. In other words, we were already beginning to give that help to the Russians and to our armies in the Mediterranean which I had foreseen would be the first result of a bomber offensive. The strategic consequences of bombing Germany may be summed up in a few simple figures; in 1941, when the Germans invaded Russia the German army had the support of well over 50 per cent of the whole German air force. At the end of 1943, the German army had the support of less than 20 per cent of the whole German air force. And this change was the result of decisions made by the enemy in the summer of 1942; the decisions were forced upon him by Cologne and by the new threat of daylight operations over Germany by American heavy bombers.

A high proportion of the 3300 aircraft which supported the army when Germany first invaded Russia were bombers and dive bombers; the dive bombers rapidly became obsolete, and the twin-engined bombers, Messerschmitt 110s, Junker 88s, and Heinkel 217s, became the main weapon for close support of the army. But it was precisely these types of bombers that the enemy used for night fighters, just as in 1941 we used Blenheims, before we had anything else, for an improvised defence during the Blitz; the modification was easily made and at first the enemy naturally used the least successful type of bomber, the Messerschmitt 110, as his main night fighter. Thus in 1941 a force of about 250 Messerschmitt 110s was formed for defence against night attacks on Germany. In June of 1942 this force was not substantially altered in numbers or character, though the ground control stations and searchlights with which it co-operated had become far more numerous and efficient.

Within the next year, as a result of decisions made after the Cologne attack, the force had increased to 530 twin-engined night fighters, with a corresponding decrease in the front line strength of the bomber force; the more efficient type of army co-operation bombers were now being turned into night fighters. But the front line strength on paper of the two forces which used the same type of aircraft, the bomber and the night fighter forces, was deceptive. Actual production of night fighters was given priority over production of bombers, and the bomber force only maintained its large front line strength, 1300 aircraft in June of 1943, by a policy of conservation which inevitably prevented any sustained offensive in the air. Thus from 1944 onwards the bomber and twin-engined night fighter strength remained roughly equal, on paper about 800 each, but the bomber strength would have been very rapidly reduced if the enemy had made any serious use of this force. It was also in 1942 that the enemy, with an eye to American daylight operations and Anglo-American aircraft production, decided on a great increase in the production of single-engined fighters. The German Chief of Air Staff in 1942, General Jeschonneck, said that he would not know what to do with a production of more than 360 fighters a month, but General Milch, in charge of aircraft procurement from November, 1941, asked for an eventual production of 1000 fighters a month, and plans for increased fighter production were eventually decided on in September of 1942, after much controversy. From then on the diversion for the defence of Germany of single-engined fighters and twin-engined converted bombers was of increasing strategic importance and had a profound effect on all fronts. The growing strength of the enemy night fighter, from

1942 onwards, naturally had a marked and almost immediate effect on Bomber Command's casualty rate, and if we had not been able to change and improve our own tactics either the expansion of the Command would have been stopped or a policy of conservation of effort would have been as necessary for us as it was for the German bomber force.

Some little time after the 1000 bomber attack on Cologne, there was some astonishment, and even a considerable amount of irritation, in certain quarters, when a report was published in the newspapers and by the B.B.C. that I had broadcast to Germany. The broadcast itself was printed and re-broadcast in translation; it threatened the Germans with dire pains and penalties to be inflicted upon them by the bombers, though in point of fact with far less than was actually meted out to them in the event. Much ink was spilled and there was considerable discussion for and against the broadcast in the newspapers. There was no little indignation expressed by certain people, and this found outlet in Parliament. In particular, I was, I recall, attacked by Lord Addison in the House of Lords. But however much surprise the broadcast caused elsewhere, it was as nothing to what I myself felt when I learned that I had addressed the enemy as a Commander-in-Chief in the field, and what is more, in fluent German, of which I know not a word.

The fact is that I never made the broadcast at all. The whole thing was a typical muddle by some of the enthusiastic amateurs who were over frequently allowed to play at war with parts of our war machine; in this instance I believe it was mainly the concern of the Political Warfare Executive. It appears that they thought they would take advantage of the alarm and despondency which the attack on Cologne had undoubtedly brought about in Germany by threatening the Germans, in my name, with a continuous succession of such attacks, of increasing weight and for an indefinite period. To that end they wrote and printed a pamphlet, alleged to be a speech by me, to be dropped over the enemy's country. As is usual in such cases they had asked the Air Ministry for their permission, and the Air Ministry then asked me whether I objected to my name being used on such a pamphlet. I have given my views on the utility, or rather the futility, of pamphleteering in an earlier chapter; I told the Air Ministry that as long as they thought that warfare by pamphleteering was any good I had no objection to the use of my name. I was entirely uninterested in the whole thing; I have consistently regarded such methods of warfare as wholly ridiculous and a complete waste of time. In spite of the fact that the alleged speech was intended as a leaflet to be dropped over Germany, it was then broadcast in a propaganda programme to the enemy, a use of it which I believe had never been intended, and certainly had never been contemplated or authorised by me. After that, the newspapers and the B.B.C. naturally got hold of the speech and used it; there was a rule against printing pamphlets dropped on Germany because they were officially secret documents, but no one could stop the Press from reprinting broadcasts of this kind when they got hold of them. A word or two from the Air Minister and the Air Ministry behind the scenes would have stopped the whole affair before it developed, but, not for the first or last time I was left holding the baby.

The text of this spurious broadcast may be of some interest; it was as follows:

"We in Britain know quite enough about air raids. For ten months your Luftwaffe bombed us. First you bombed us by day. When we made this impossible, they came by night. Then you had a big fleet of bombers. Your airmen fought well. They bombed London for ninety-two nights running. They made heavy raids on Coventry, Plymouth, Liverpool, and other British cities. They did a lot of damage. Forty-three thousand British men, women and children lost their lives. Many of our most cherished historical buildings were destroyed.

"You thought, and Goering promised you, that you would be safe from bombs. And indeed, during all that time we could only send over a small number of aircraft in return. But now it is just the other way. Now you send only a few aircraft against us. And we are bombing Germany heavily.

"Why are we doing so? It is not revenge—though we do not forget Warsaw, Belgrade, Rotterdam, London, Plymouth and Coventry. We are bombing Germany, city by city, and even more terribly, in order to make it impossible for you to go on with the war. That is our object. We shall pursue it remorselessly. City by city; Lübeck, Rostock, Cologne, Emden, Bremen, Wilhelmshaven, Duisburg, Hamburg—and the list will grow longer and longer. Let the Nazis drag you down to disaster with them if you will. That is for you to decide.

"In fine weather we bomb you by night. Already 1000 bombers go to one town, like Cologne, and destroy a third of it in an hour's bombing. We know; we have the photographs. In cloudy weather we bomb your factories and shipyards by day. We have done that as far away as Danzig. We are coming by day and by night. No part of the Reich is safe.

"In Cologne, on the Ruhr, or at Rostock, Lübeck, or Emden, you may think that already our bombing amounts to something. But we do not think so. In comparison with what it will be like as soon as our own production of bombers comes to a flood and as American production doubles and then redoubles, all that has happened to you so far will seem very little.

"I will speak frankly about whether we bomb single military targets or whole cities. Obviously we prefer to hit factories, shipyards, and railways. It damages Hitler's war machine most. But those people who work in these plants live close to them. Therefore, we hit your houses and you. We regret the necessity for this. The workers of the Humboldt-Deutz, the Diesel-engine plant in Cologne, for instance—some of whom were killed on the night of May 30 last—must inevitably take the risk of war. Just as our merchant seamen who man ships which the U-boats (equipped with Humboldt-Deutz engines) would have tried to torpedo. Were not the aircraft workers, their wives and children, at Coventry just as much ' civilians ' as the aircraft workers at Rostock and their families? But Hitler wanted it that way.

"It is true that your defences inflict losses on our bombers. Your leaders try to comfort you by telling you that our losses are so heavy that we shall not be able to go on bombing you very much longer. Whoever believes that will be bitterly disappointed. I, who command the British bombers, will tell you what our losses are. Less than 5 per cent of the bombers which we send over Germany are lost. Such a percentage does very little even to check the constant increase ensured by the ever-increasing output of our own and the American factories.

"America has only just entered the fight in Europe. The squadrons, forerunners of a whole air fleet, have arrived in England from the United States of America. Do you realise what it will ¬ean to you when they bomb Germany also? In one American factory alone, the new Ford plant at Willow Run, Detroit, they are already turning out one four-engined bomber able to carry four tons of bombs to any part of the Reich every two hours. There are scores of other such factories in the United States of America. You cannot bomb those factories.

Your submarines cannot even try to prevent those Atlantic bombers from getting here; for they fly across the Atlantic.

"Soon we shall be coming every night and every day, rain, blow or snow—we and the Americans. I have just spent eight months in America, so I know exactly what is coming. We are going to scourge the Third Reich from end to end, if you make it necessary for us to do so. You cannot stop it, and you know it.

"You have no chance. You could not defeat us in 1940, when we were almost unarmed and stood alone. Your leaders were crazy to attack Russia as well as America (but then your leaders are crazy; the whole world thinks so except Italy).

"How can you hope to win now that we are getting even stronger, having both Russia and America as allies, while you are getting more and more exhausted?

"Remember this: no matter how far your armies march they can never get to England. They could not get here when we were unarmed. Whatever their victories, you will still have to settle the air war with us and America. You can never win that. But we are doing so already now.

"One final thing: it is up to you to end the war and the bombing. You can overthrow the Nazis and make peace. It is not true that we plan a peace of revenge. That is a German propaganda lie. But we shall certainly make it impossible for any German Government to start a total war again. And is not that as necessary in your own interests as in ours?"

The storm which the issue of this raised did not particularly worry me, but I must say that I very much resented the fact that the attacks in Parliament were allowed to develop and to continue for some time. It would have been perfectly easy—parliamentary customs being what they are—for those who brought the matter up by asking questions in the House to be tipped off beforehand; it only had to be privately explained that it was all a departmental mistake and that I had had nothing to do with the broadcast.

I went to dinner with the Prime Minister at Chequers soon afterwards and he said: "I hear you have been getting into trouble in the House about your broadcast, which I understand you never made." I said that it was quite true that I never made the broadcast, but for myself I should hardly have described being attacked by Lord Addison in the Lords or anywhere else as "getting into trouble." The Prime Minister laughed.

The *Economist*, which in this was duly, not to say dutifully, followed by the *Daily Worker*, has attacked me for having organised and initiated the whole bomber offensive, and has even gone so far as to say that I got my proposals adopted by making grossly exaggerated claims about what was being accomplished. Unless these newspapers had access to the secret files of the ministries, which I very much doubt, they must have been basing their statements on this broadcast; there can be no other published evidence of any claims made by me.

I never made any broadcasts, apart from an innocuous speech at a Wings for Victory Week. I once said a few words on a newsreel in 1941, but there the only definite suggestion I made was that we should wait and see what bombing could achieve. Some people, I remarked, thought that bombing could never win a war. "Well," I said, "we shall see. It hasn't been tried yet, and Germany, more and more desperately clinging to her widespread conquests and still foolishly striving for more, will make a most interesting subject for the initial experiment. Japan can be used to provide the confirmation. But don't expect too much yet . . ." That was in 1942 and Hiroshima heard the last word.

As a matter of fact I did my utmost during the war to avoid any sort of publicity for remarks by myself; in fact I considerably annoyed many representatives of the Press by refusing to see them or hold Press conferences. I do not claim to be diffident—far from it—but I had two very good reasons for my refusal. I consider that no Press interview with a Commander-in-Chief in the field can be published without incurring some extra military danger to the success of operations and to the safety of the men under his command. In this respect I am entirely at variance with one or two other commanders of this last war. Secondly—and this reason came up during the last part of the war—the Air Ministry issued an order that no Commander-in-Chief should give an interview for publication in the Press without first submitting to the Air Ministry an account of exactly what he was going to say. This order completely mystified me. If an interview means anything at all it means a series of questions and answers and I cannot imagine how you are to answer a number of unrehearsed questions and at the same time know, and have prior approval for precisely what you are going to say before you start! In the circumstances, I suggested that the Air Ministry should give the interviews themselves. As the Press well knows, they did.

Chapter Six

GETTING THE WEAPONS

Failure of an attack on Essen. The enemy defences increase. New radar devices. Oboe and H2S. Experiments and modifications. The Pathfinder Force. Arguments against its formation. Jamming the enemy's radar. The use of "Window" forbidden. The expansion of the force. First attacks on Berlin. Attacks on U-boat bases. The minelaying campaign. Attacks on North Italy.

THE RUHR TOWNS, and especially Essen, remained first priority targets for the Command, which meant that I was bound to attack them whenever the weather and other circumstances permitted. The fact that the 1000 bomber attack on Cologne had been a complete success was no guarantee that a similar attack on a target in the Ruhr would not fail; on the contrary, we had every reason to fear that concentration would be very difficult to achieve in this area, where the force would not have the easily recognisable shape of the Rhine to guide it, and where the industrial haze always made an effective smoke-screen. On the other hand, the Cologne attack showed that the enemy's defences were comparatively ineffective against so large a force, which meant that there might be less difficulty in identifying the target by Gee than when a small force was required to penetrate the defences in depth of the Ruhr. The attack on Cologne had also shown that dummy fires were of little use when a really large area was set alight, since the decoy could readily be distinguished from the much larger conflagration in the target area. Since I had 1000 bombers mobilised and intact, I decided to send the whole force to Essen two nights later, and so continue the campaign against the Ruhr which I had been instructed to begin with such inadequate forces in the spring. On the night of June 1st-2nd the weather was expected to be suitable, and there was still, of course, a bright moon. I did not expect that the attack would be as great a success as the raid on Cologne, but there seemed a good chance of doing serious damage to Essen, and possibly to Krupps.

I have little doubt that this would have happened had not a sudden and unforeseen change in the weather given almost complete protection to Essen that night; when the force got to the target area it was found that the whole town was covered with low stratus cloud. In several parts of the Ruhr, and especially in Oberhausen, the attack did a fair amount of damage. But, though the attack on the objective itself failed, losses were no heavier than in the raid on Cologne, which showed that concentration of the bomber stream was an effective protection even over the most heavily defended area in Germany.

We tried one more attack on the same scale in the next moon period, a month later. I had originally intended to make Hamburg the target, since the Battle of the Atlantic was then at its height and Hamburg was the largest centre for the production of U-boats in Germany. But the weather compelled me to choose Bremen, another U-boat centre, and once again we were let down by the unexpected arrival of cloud. However, the damage to Bremen, though not concentrated, was by no means negligible; among other things, a very important Focke-Wulf aircraft factory was largely destroyed. Once again, during 1942, I used crews from the O.T.U.s to reinforce our front line strength; this was on the night of July 31st-August 1st, when a very successful attack was made on Dusseldorf, a town on the outskirts of the Ruhr and just as important as Essen, but not so difficult to identify as Essen because it lies on the Rhine. This and a subsequent attack on September 10th-11th did so much damage that Dusseldorf was, in proportion to its size, as extensively devastated as Cologne.

We were always told, by the organisation which gave us information about targets, that Dusseldorf was not only a most important industrial town in itself, as it undoubtedly was, but also the site of the head offices of nearly all the industrial concerns of the Ruhr; it was believed that the destruction of these head offices and of the records in them would cause a lot of muddle and loss of production. After the war, Albert Speer, Reichminister for Armaments and War Production, was asked to what extent the loss of records affected efficiency in production. He replied: "On the contrary, the loss of records led to a temporary loosening of the ties of bureaucracy. We very often received the message ' Administrative building burnt out, production continues at full pressure.'" Perhaps our own problems could have been solved as expeditiously by a few bombs on the appropriate Government departments.

This was the last attack in which I could safely use the O.T.U.s without seriously interfering with training, and for the rest of the year, as in the intervening periods of June, July, and August between the full moon, attacks were carried out only by the front-line squadrons. These, it will be remembered, did not appreciably expand during the year, but the German defences did, with the result that we had to work with a force which was consistently too small to saturate the enemy's flak, searchlight and night fighter defences. Our casualty rate continually increased, to the point where, in the later months of 1942, the enemy appeared to have gained a serious degree of tactical superiority. And, as we were without any effective aid to navigation, the damage we did was very far from being enough to compensate for our losses. I repeatedly dispatched the force to coastal targets, which could be more easily identified than any target inland, and serious damage was done to the port of Emden. But as all major operations had to be carried out in moonlight the defences had it all their own way with our small force and continually prevented any real concentration of attack; though the force went again and again to Hamburg, Bremen, and Kiel, the damage was always scattered, save at Emden, where we succeeded in causing a quite large area of devastation. We also attacked some minor industrial cities, where the defences were naturally less heavy, and did considerable damage to Saarbrucken, Mainz, and Karlsruhe. To make a successful attack on a minor industrial objective was, of course, more useful than to fail against a major objective, but in the long run such a policy would have been almost as much an admission of defeat as the later German attacks on towns like Bath, Canterbury and Norwich, which were undefended and of only historical importance. Nevertheless the increasing diversion of Germany's material war potential and manpower to the air defence of the Reich made the offensive more than worthwhile even at that stage.

The success of the enemy defences in 1942 was not the result of any radically new tactics, and we knew, of course, that once we could operate on dark nights and in bad weather our casualties would decline, or at all events would not increase at the same rate that they otherwise would. The enemy's ground control stations were increased in number throughout 1942, and the night fighter squadrons were also reinforced to the point where they became of much greater importance for the defence of Germany than anti-aircraft guns even though these were now radar assisted and were becoming increasingly efficient. The one significant change that was made during the year was the removal of all searchlights previously arranged in a belt along the frontier; they were now set up in the actual target areas, where the searchlights were so dazzling that it became difficult to identify the aiming point visually even on moonlight nights. The searchlights were no longer needed to assist fighter-interception because an increasing number of fighters were being equipped with airborne radar.

A new and deadly tactic of the enemy fighters was first observed in March, 1942. The fighter climbed steeply until it got under the tail of the bomber, opened fire at close range, and continued to fire and to climb yet more steeply until it stalled. It is extremely difficult to spot another aircraft against the dark background below the tail of a bomber, and gunners were repeatedly taken by surprise; it often happened that crews reported that their aircraft had been hit by anti-aircraft fire when, in fact, as expert examination of the damage proved, they had been shot at from below, by a fighter. Instead of searching the sky for enemy fighters in the normal fashion it was now necessary for the bomber to be repeatedly banked while the area below was searched, and a corkscrewing flight was developed as a means of taking evasive action, but the radar assisted fighter using these tactics continued to be a serious menace. In June and July of 1942 we were losing aircraft, from all causes, at the rate of 5.6 per cent of all sorties, a rate, which, if continued, would put a stop to any considerable expansion of the Command.

To regain tactical superiority over the enemy much would have to be done. It would be necessary to find some means of identifying the target on moonless nights, and if possible in cloudy weather. It would be necessary to find means of breaking the extremely efficient control of the night fighters by the ground stations. And it would be necessary for the force to be doubled or trebled in size, in order that the enemy defences might be effectively saturated.

By this time the scientists had already devised the answers to the majority of our problems; it was a question either of getting the equipment we needed into full production or of getting permission to use it; such permission was apt to be withheld if the authorities feared that the Germans would be able to use a new weapon as effectively against the defences of Great Britain as we could use it against the defences of Germany.

The most important of all the new devices were the two radar aids to navigation which were known by the code names of Oboe and H2S; either of these, it was claimed by the designers, would make the bomber force largely independent of the weather and would greatly increase the accuracy of our attacks. The introduction of these radar aids became all the more important when the enemy started jamming Gee, as we knew he was bound to do before long. This jamming was first suspected on the night of August 6th-7th, 1942, and became obvious on the night of August 9th-10th when we attacked Osnabruck. The effect of the jamming was not to stop the use of Gee altogether, but it reduced the effective range of this aid by about 100 miles, so that all targets in Germany were outside the range of ground stations in Great Britain though Gee was still an extremely useful aid to navigation along the greater part of the bombers' route. New ground stations were built in England and the frequency range of the Gee transmission was enlarged and varied; these methods were successful from time to time, but there was always the risk of interference.

Oboe developed out of the methods used by the R.A.F. to "bend" and interfere with the beams used as navigational aids by the German bombers during the blitz. It was then discovered that an aircraft could fly along a certain beam and that its position on that beam could be calculated by measuring the distance of the aircraft, by means of radar, from a given point. A primitive version of the Oboe system was actually used during the Command's attacks on the *Scharnhorst* and *Gneisenau* in Brest, but it proved unreliable; the equipment was liable to break down and we had not yet got the right aircraft to use it. But it seemed likely that when these difficulties were overcome, Oboe would be far more accurate than any other then existing navigational aid; later tests showed that this was in fact the case. The system depended on the re-radiation from the aircraft of radar signals sent out to it, and use was made of the fact that it is far more easy to find the distance than the precise bearing of an object by radar. There are two ground stations. One controls the aircraft by signalling to it by a system of dots and dashes whenever it deviates from a given course; this course is a part of the circumference of a circle passing through the target, the centre of the circle being the ground station itself. Meanwhile a second ground station measures at intervals how far the aircraft has got along this arc of a circle; from these measurements the position and speed of the aircraft is calculated at the ground station and not in the aircraft—an important advantage. When the aircraft is in the exact position at which the bombs should be dropped a signal is sent, and the bombs are released. For the bomber's crew, the whole thing is pretty well automatic.

The main drawback to this system is that the aircraft must follow a steady course, without deviation, for a considerable distance until it reaches the target. This makes the aircraft extremely vulnerable. At the same time the range of the system is limited by the height at which the aircraft can fly, because the Oboe transmissions follow a straight line and therefore, owing to the curvature of the earth, must be received at an increasingly greater height above the ground as the aircraft's distance from the ground station increases.

In the first attempts to use this system, during the attacks on Brest, the Stirling, the least efficient of the four-engined bombers, was unfortunately chosen to be fitted with this equipment. Its altitude performance was, however, hopeless even when its bomb load was reduced or omitted. It was also slow, and when it flew on a steady course was in great danger from the defences. But in 1942 we had the Mosquito, an aircraft with a ceiling more than twice that of the Stirling, and an extremely fast bomber; it could fly with reasonable safety on a steady course through fighter-defended and gun-defended areas where any other bomber flying on a straight course would probably be destroyed. The Mosquito could not then carry a heavy bomb-load but in any case there could be no question, as with Gee, of equipping the whole force with this device; only a few aircraft could use the Oboe system in any one attack, for the two Oboe ground stations could only control one aircraft at a time and only a few in the course of an hour.

When the first tests were carried out in 1941 and early in 1942 Oboe was being considered simply as a blind bombing device, and if it was to be used as such the fact that only a handful of aircraft could be guided by it in any one attack seemed a fatal objection. But in the summer of 1942 Bomber Command suggested to the Air Ministry that Oboe should be used as a target-marking device; we asked for six aircraft to be equipped with Oboe and two ground stations to be set up, and for this we asked the highest priority. The Mosquito's then small bomb-load did not matter; the Oboe-Mosquito's main work was to mark the target for the main force, though it might occasionally engage in a small scale blind bombing.

In 1940, when it was decided to proceed with the development, or rather the re-development of Gee—it was an invention which had been known but neglected before the war—there was in existence another navigational aid, then known as "H," which promised to be a good deal more accurate than Gee. But "H" was rejected for the time being because only a comparatively small force, about 100 aircraft, could use it at a time. In 1942 the position was so different, and our ideas were so much less ambitious, that a navigational and bombing aid which could be used by no more than a single squadron of aircraft seemed likely to change the whole course of the bomber offensive, which, indeed, it most certainly did. In the two years between 1940 and 1942 there had been so great an alteration of strategy and tactics that we were no longer thinking in terms of thousands of bombers, the crews of which were each capable of finding the target by themselves, but of a much smaller force directed to an area which had been marked by a very few aircraft. "H" had to wait for development until a much later stage of the war, when its use made all the difference between the success and failure of the offensive against oil.

It is of some interest that the Stirlings which used the primitive version of Oboe hit by accident on much the same plan of marking by Oboe. If they were to fly at the required height they could only carry a small bomb-load, so the crews used to fill up with flares; these they dropped with the idea of lighting up the target for the other aircraft attacking it.

If Mosquitoes were used with Oboe, targets in the Ruhr would be well within range, but the range did not go much beyond this area. The theoretical margin of error was about 300 yards, and if this did not in practice prove very much greater any fairly large industrial town could be marked and accurately bombed. Oboe could certainly be jammed, but it was proposed to have ready a new mark of Oboe, working on a shorter wavelength and therefore less susceptible to jamming, to be used as soon as there was interference with Oboe Mark I.

H2S was an entirely different device from Oboe. This was contained wholly within the aircraft and required no transmission from ground stations; its range was therefore unlimited and it was most improbable that its use could be seriously interfered with in any way. There was no limit to the number of aircraft that could use this aid at one and the same time. H2S was under development throughout 1942; it was a modification of the equipment used for detecting submarines or other vessels at sea. It was discovered that objects on the ground, or on the surface of the sea, would return a distinctive radar echo to an aircraft, and after U-boats had been successfully made out in this way it was found that large buildings such as hangars and steel factory buildings would also return a distinguishable echo. Coast lines, estuaries and built-up areas could be detected through unbroken cloud or in total darkness. Nobody doubted that the principle of using this equipment as a navigational aid was sound, but at first there was a good deal of scepticism about whether it could ever be developed to such a point, as the enthusiasts thought it would be, that the navigator would be able to map-read by means of H2S in any weather or in any conditions of light.

The difficulty was that to make the instrument effective it was necessary, as Air Commodore Bennett discovered during tests which he made in July, 1942, to use the Magnetron valve.

In May of 1942, after our experience with Gee and the exaggerated claims that had been made for it, we decided to investigate the H2S equipment of the type that was then being projected and we pointed out that its range with the valve it then had, the Klystron valve, was not good enough for operational use. However, in July, Bennett tried out the version of the H2S equipment with the Magnetron valve and got promising results. The Magnetron valve was one of the most brilliant inventions of British science and indispensable for many forms of airborne radar; it enabled a powerful transmission to be made from a piece of equipment small enough to be easily carried in an aircraft, and without it we could scarcely have won the Battle of the Atlantic. There was much alarm at the prospect of it getting into enemy hands, as it almost certainly would do after any considerable number of aircraft had carried it over Germany; you can and we did attach detonators to secret equipment which will blow it up when the aircraft crashes, but you cannot guarantee that this will invariably work and sooner or later the enemy is bound to get a specimen of the equipment more or less intact. I understood the objections, but it seemed to me that it would take the Germans a considerable time to get any similar equipment into production, that is, if one could judge by the time it was taking us to produce it. Moreover the defences of Great Britain were rapidly improving, the German Air Force was deeply engaged either in Russia or in the air defence of Germany, and in general we should never get on with the offensive at all if everybody spent their time taking every conceivable precaution against the enemy retaliating in time. After weeks of argument I got permission for the Magnetron version of H2S to be produced and for two squadrons to be equipped with it by the end of the year.

As soon as Gee was introduced it became evident that the aircraft used to find the target and mark it in one way or another should be manned by specially trained and experienced crews, and particularly by highly skilled navigators and air-bombers. As far as possible, this was always done. But in the later spring of 1942 the Air Ministry began to ask us to set up an independent target finding force of picked crews. I was entirely opposed to the idea of taking the best men from each Group; the very men who were most needed to raise the general level by their example and precept and who were required as Squadron and Flight Commanders in their own units; the formation of a *corps-d'élite* seemed likely to lead to a good deal of trouble and might be thoroughly bad for morale. In this I was supported by all my Group Commanders. My own plan was to train and form target-marking squadrons in each Group; this would lead to a good deal of healthy competition and new ideas could be more easily tried out in this way. Eventually we were able to supplement the Air Ministry's plan of an independent target-finding force with the system of forming target-finding squadrons in an ordinary, unspecialised Group, No. 5 Group; not only were these squadrons as successful as those of the specialised target-finding force, but we were able to get the benefit of two opposed and distinct approaches to the problem being worked out at the same time. Some marking was also done on occasions by aircraft of No. 1 Group, and later on No. 3 Group did its own target-finding. However, though I opposed the formation of the special target-finding force for some months, preferring with my Group Commanders our own plan, I was overruled by the Air Ministry. In other circumstances I should not have accepted the position, but we were now faced with the fact that Gee had failed as a bombing aid and that the new radar aids, Oboe and H2S, which had been promised for the autumn of 1942, were not to be forth-coming until the end of the year. For the time being it was essential to improve our methods of finding the target visually and marking it, and this seemed to require the whole-time activities of a specialised force, not only for leading but for practical experiments. Accordingly the Pathfinder Force, as I christened it, was formed on August 15th, under the command of then Air Commodore D. C. T. Bennett. It seemed likely that the squadrons which were required to find and mark the target visually would have to stay longer in the target area, while they searched for distinguishing features, than aircraft of the main force; the enemy might also be expected to concentrate all his defences on the Pathfinder squadrons who got to the target first, in the hope of preventing the target from being marked. As the Pathfinder squadrons were to be asked to run even greater risks than the squadrons of the main force, to work longer tours and probably to miss promotion in their parent squadrons, I proposed that the men in them should get quicker promotion and wear some sort of distinguishing badge; as we were compelled by events to have a *corps d'élite* it seemed to me necessary to carry the principle through to its logical conclusion. It was also desirable for recruitment to arrange for the Pathfinder squadrons to be given adequate publicity in the Press and by the B.B.C., but this was prevented by the security aspect of the matter; men of the Pathfinder Force would necessarily know all about our latest equipment and tactics and it was feared that the enemy would go to particular pains to interrogate the Pathfinder crews who fell into their hands. No doubt it was best to be on the safe side and avoid publishing the names of any Pathfinder personnel, since the enemy made a card index of all the names and details about air-crew they could get from our newspapers and found this very useful in the interrogation of prisoners.

Don Bennett, whom I had known since 1931, was the obvious man at that time available for the job of head of the Pathfinder Force. He was in his early thirties, very young indeed to become a Group Commander, but his technical knowledge and his personal operational ability was altogether exceptional. I first met him, as I have described in an earlier chapter, when I was commanding a flying-boat base in 1930, and when his short term commission expired I got him a job in civil flying. He was a profound student of navigation, and in the early part of the war he took the major part in opening the transatlantic ferry. I then got him back into the Air Force as a Wing Commander. He commanded a Halifax squadron and in 1941 was shot down in flames over Norway when attacking the *Tirpitz* in his usual gallant manner; he escaped to Sweden after many adventures and was returned to England. His courage, both moral and physical, is outstanding, and as a technician he is unrivalled. He will forgive me if I say that his consciousness of his own intellectual powers sometimes made him impatient with slower or differently constituted minds, so that some people found him difficult to work with. He could not suffer fools gladly, and by his own high standards there were many fools. From my point of view the essential thing was that he tackled the complex and technical problems of our intricate bombing tactics with as much energy as ability. He has a most unusual memory and can pick up a book on some highly technical subject and in a very short time get the whole thing off by heart; he is, in fact, very much an intellectual and, being still a young man, had at times the young intellectual's habit of underrating experience and over-rating knowledge. All this is, of course, rather unusual in a fighting man and we were lucky to get a man of such attainments to lead and form the Pathfinders.

The formation of the Pathfinder Force coincided with the jamming of Gee by the enemy, and for the rest of 1942 the force was hampered by the lack of any special equipment for target-finding as well as by the lack of any proper target indicator; in spite of all our efforts this simple requirement, which I had urgently asked for in March, 1942, and the development of which I had suggested many years before, was not yet in production. No obvious and immediate successes could therefore be expected to follow the formation of the Pathfinder Force, but the Force did discover much that was important and useful about marking and illuminating targets.

The basis of Pathfinder tactics at this time was visual marking of the aiming point, either in the light of flares—these were still of an unsatisfactory type—or occasionally in moonlight. Flares were dropped with the help of Gee in the few instances where a target still remained within range of Gee, but the usual method was to make a timed run from a visually identified landmark. In September a new technique was used and proved effective. The flare dropping aircraft were divided into two groups, one of which, called the finders, dropped long sticks of flares right across the target area, and the other, called the illuminators, were detailed to search for the aiming point itself and, when they had found it to illuminate it with much shorter sticks of flares; the visual markers then marked this aiming point with incendiary bombs, in default of target indicators. Because of the difficulty of distinguishing incendiaries, salvoes of 30 lb. and 250 lb. incendiaries were dropped on the aiming point or as near to it as could be managed. Even these were not easy to see in the early stages of the attack, when the target was brightly lit up by flares, while in the later stages it was difficult to distinguish them from other incendiaries and flares. 4000 lb. special incendiaries, which went by the name of "pink pansies," were also tried, but these, though easily distinguishable when they burst, burnt out too soon to be of much use as a mark.

The bombing results after the formation of the Pathfinder Force were investigated by the Operational Research Section—a body of brilliant young civilian scientists and technicians at Bomber Command headquarters who did work of inestimable value in subjecting all aspects of our operations to an impartial scrutiny—and it was discovered that bombing concentration had undoubtedly increased, but at the same time another factor made the attacks as a whole hardly more accurate than they had been before. The bombing was certainly more closely concentrated round the marker bombs than it had previously been round the aiming point, but there was no advantage in this unless the marker bombs had in fact been dropped on the aiming point, which was not always the case. Any error in placing the marker bombs led the whole attack astray. This problem was always before us, but was never entirely solved even by the end of the war.

Towards the end of the year we began to get Mosquitoes equipped with Oboe and these, of course, were attached to the Pathfinder Force. The same squadron which had been used in connection with the work of bending the navigational beams used by German raiders during the Blitz and had thereafter been concerned with the development of Oboe was incorporated in the Pathfinder Force and was ready for operations in December. Aircraft equipped with H2S were also allotted to the Pathfinders and they had twelve Stirlings and twelve Halifaxes so equipped in December of 1942. But in spite of the fact that we had got permission in July for H2S to be produced with the Magnetron valve and for two squadrons to be equipped with it, we still had not got permission to fly the equipment over enemy territory and this permission was withheld for another month.

I knew that there were other ways, besides operating on dark nights and in bad weather, of counteracting the enemy's defences, which were steadily increasing as the Germans ruthlessly stripped their armies of their air cover and air support. By the beginning of 1942 we had a good idea of the menace that the enemy's system of ground-controlled night fighters was going to be, and during the next six months we learnt a great deal about how the system worked in detail. In getting information about the enemy's night fighter force we were, of course, continually hampered by the fact that their aircraft never operated over any except German occupied territory; it was most unlikely that we should ever take prisoner any night fighter crews or get hold of any of the equipment in the night fighter aircraft. There were, however, other methods. The Monitoring service kept a careful watch on all the enemy's radar transmissions, which gave us much useful information. Air photographs showed us the position of the enemy's radar apparatus and from its appearance it was possible to get some idea of its function and capacities. And on February 27th, 1942, parachute troops made a brilliant raid on Bruneval to capture a small example of the apparatus, to which the Germans gave the code word "Wurzburg," used for plotting the bomber and the night fighter which was trying to intercept it. By May of 1942 we had a very complete and exact idea of how the ground control of the German night fighter force was operated and we knew the wavelengths on which transmissions were made. We also knew a good deal about the enemy's radar early warning system, which operated in close connection with the Wurzburgs and so made it possible to get the fighters up in time to intercept the bombers. And we knew a good deal about the radio-telephone system by which instructions were transmitted to the night-fighter pilots from the ground.

We knew that any or all of these transmissions, on which the whole ground control of the enemy's night fighters depended, could be jammed, and possibly also the airborne radar carried by night fighters for interception in the dark. For example, jamming apparatus which could be carried in an aircraft was under development in 1941 and it had been known for some time that strips of metal, or paper with a thin coating of metal, would produce radar echoes if dropped from aircraft. The difficulty was that while Great Britain was wholly on the defensive it was thought injudicious to use measures which the Germans could use with effect against our own defences. It would have been idiotic to drop metallised paper over Germany in August of 1940, but in 1942 I was certain that the time had come to take such risks, which did not seem to be very serious, for the sake of the offensive. During the summer of 1942 I continually pressed for the development and, where possible, immediate use of equipment and measures to jam and interfere with the enemy's radar and radio transmissions. But the authorities considered that we were still too vulnerable to air attack for us to start too much in the way of a jamming war. We now know that the Germans also knew all about the effect of metallised paper on radar long before it was used, but did not initiate its use because they were afraid—in their case with good reason—of its effect on their own defences.

Under brilliant young Dr. Dickens, Bomber Command's Operational Research Section's investigations always enabled us to know exactly where we stood. In August they reported that in the previous two months between a third and two-thirds of all our losses—our total losses amounted to 5.6 per cent of all sorties—were caused by radar-assisted enemy defences, which included radar-assisted guns as well as ground-controlled fighters. They also estimated that effective countermeasures against radar transmissions would probably cut our losses by about a third, and, because bombing accuracy was seriously diminished by the strength of the enemy defences in the target area, would increase the efficiency of our attacks. In fact, there was so strong a case for the immediate use of Radio countermeasures that we made another application to the Air Ministry asking for them to be provided at once; we said this was a matter of the greatest importance and urgency. Countermeasures were already well developed; all we wanted was to be allowed to use them. After long discussion and many conferences we got permission to use some countermeasures, but not metallised paper, or "Window" as it was named. The jamming of the enemy's Wurzburgs, early warning system, and radio telephonic communication between ground and night fighter began on a serious scale in December. The jamming was done both by ground and by airborne equipment; air losses fell off appreciably after it was begun, but as this came at a time when wintry weather might be expected to reduce the efficiency of the enemy's defences it was difficult to estimate precisely how much good the jamming did. In any case, the jamming war at this time was a minor affair by comparison with what was done later. This wholly new kind of warfare, which had been begun by Bomber Command, was eventually to develop to such a point that it became a major factor in deceiving the enemy about our intentions and action by air, sea and land on D-day.

The main objection to the use of "Window" (the strips of metallised paper) which proved to be the most important and effective of all the weapons used against enemy radar, continued to be the fear of its effect on our own defences. It was hoped that our own radar would be developed to the point where the strips of paper would not cause any very serious interference, but even so, defensive radar might never be quite so effective after its introduction as before. When I continually pressed for the introduction of this weapon, other objections were also made. It appeared that we were short of suitable plant for the manufacture of the strips in quantity, and that it would be very difficult to get priority for the supply of aluminium needed. There can be little doubt that if we had been able and allowed to use this weapon in the first months of 1943 we should have saved hundreds of aircraft and thousands of lives and would have much increased the accuracy of our bombing.

In December of 1942 we had, as a daily average, 78 medium and 261 heavy bombers available in the front-line squadrons. The number of heavy bombers had therefore increased by 219 during the year, and the number of medium bombers decreased in proportion. Thus we were now able, at the end of 1942, to drop a much greater bomb load than at the beginning of the year, although there had been no significant increase in numbers of aircraft. But real expansion was now imminent, and our squadrons were not going to be taken away from us as fast as we had trained them, although O.T.U. aircraft were still being lent to Coastal Command for anti-submarine patrols. Our expansion was greatly helped by the Royal Canadian Air Force, which provided a whole group, No. 6 Group of Bomber Command, on January 1st, 1943, as well as other squadrons outside its own Group. The Canadian Government paid the whole cost of this Group and of all the R.C.A.F.'s operational squadrons, including the cost of the fuel and ammunition they used, out of Canadian taxes and domestic loans. In January, 1943, 37 per cent of the pilots in Bomber Command belonged to the Dominion and Colonial Air Forces, and of these 60 per cent were Canadian, 40 per cent coming from other parts of the Empire—mainly from the Australian and New Zealand air forces.

By the beginning of the year 1943, with the long deferred expansion of strength at last becoming effective, I was ready to start the real offensive, with Oboe and H2S for target finding, though as yet only a few aircraft were equipped with H2S, and with permission to use some of the available countermeasures against the enemy's air defences. We had also at last induced the authorities to supply the essential Target Indicators for which I had asked in the previous March.

In the autumn of 1942 I was being continually pressed to attack Berlin as soon as the nights were long enough to bring this objective within range. Indeed, throughout the year Berlin had been high on the priority list of targets allotted to me outside the Ruhr. But in 1942 I refused, however much I was urged, to attack Berlin; I knew that at this time we could do little damage there and declined to risk the very heavy casualties that could be expected, even though the news of an attack on Berlin might have a heartening effect on the Russians and also on our own people. The last attack on Berlin had been in December of 1941, at a time when such an attack could only have had a political effect, and our losses on that occasion were 10 per cent of the force dispatched. From whatever direction the force approached Berlin, it would have at the very least 4 hours of flying over very heavily defended areas. Berlin was the target which the night fighter force was bound at all costs to defend, and its ground defences were as heavy as anywhere in Germany. And the mere size of the target—this was not only a town of 4,000,000 inhabitants but it was also far from densely built up—meant that only a substantial force of heavy bombers could produce any concentrated or serious damage. Moreover it was my opinion that not only were heavy bombers needed for any successful attack on the capital, but also that only Lancasters could be sent there with any reasonable degree of safety and economy of force. In the autumn of 1942 I had only from 70 to 80 Lancasters available and these were having teething troubles with their fuel installation and were for the time being unable to fly at their full height. The Halifaxes and Stirlings would have to operate at between 10,000 and 18,000 feet, whereas the normal operational height of the Lancaster was considerably greater. The Halifaxes and Stirlings would therefore attract all the flak, while the Lancasters would go comparatively free, or the Lancasters would have to come down to the same level, in the hope of increasing the concentration of aircraft in space, and so saturating the flak; this would proportionately increase the Lancasters' casualties. At the same time, at that range the Halifaxes and Stirlings could only carry half or less of the bomb-load of the Lancaster.

In January 1943, the trouble with the Lancasters' fuel installation had been put right and several Lancaster squadrons which had been non-operational in the autumn were now ready. It would be possible, with some effort, to raise a force of 150-200 of them. This was also the right time of year to attack Berlin, when winter weather reduced the efficiency of the fighter defences and when, because bombing efficiency was also reduced by the weather, it was more profitable to attack a huge area like Berlin than a much smaller city like Essen.

Berlin was far beyond the range of Oboe or Gee and the target finding would either have to be done visually or by H2S. But it was only in January that we had got permission to use H2S and as yet we knew very little about its operational use; you can tell whether an instrument is likely to be a failure in tests at home but you can seldom know that it is going to be a success until it has been used in actual operations. We therefore decided that the Pathfinder force should mark the aiming point visually, not with incendiaries, but for the first time in any operation with readily distinguishable target indicators. On two consecutive nights about the middle of the month we attacked Berlin with all the Lancasters we could raise—there were 388 aircraft in the two attacks. Unfortunately haze and snow, which always make it more difficult to see the outlines of a built-up area, prevented the Pathfinders from identifying the aiming point and the damage was scattered, though a few important factories were hit. On the first night the enemy's fighters made scarcely any interceptions and, though the flak was heavy and the force too small to saturate it, only one aircraft was missing. On the next night the weather and the light proved favourable to the enemy; night fighters operated in strength and twenty-two bombers were lost. With the force then available Berlin was really too big a job for us, but any damage or dislocation caused in Berlin had much more effect on the enemy's war effort than a similar amount of damage elsewhere.

H2S was first used in an operation on the night of January 30th-31st, the target being Hamburg. Unlike Oboe, it was some time before H2S was effectively used; its tactical development was a slow process, marked by many disappointments during 1943.

Oboe was tested in a few very small scale experimental attacks during December, 1942, and January, 1943. The weather was usually bad, so that it was not easy to get good photographs by day to show whether the attacks had been successful. But from what evidence we could get, the Operational Research Station estimated that over enemy territory Oboe was likely to be accurate within 650 yards, with some possibility of a larger error on occasion. As 650 yards was scarcely more than the theoretical estimate of error, this was very promising indeed. Towards the end of January we were just about ready to use Oboe in full-scale operations against Germany when there occurred one of the most infuriating episodes in the whole course of the offensive. We were instructed, at the instigation of the Admiralty, to devastate the two French towns of Lorient and St. Nazaire. These ports on the Atlantic coast of France were the two main U-boat bases used in the Battle of the Atlantic; admittedly the German occupation of them constituted an extremely serious menace to our sea communications, so if bombing could have deprived the enemy of their use there would have been every reason to direct a good deal of our effort against them. But the Germans knew the facts as well as we did, and had taken due precautions. The U-boat shelters, the only worth-while targets in the two ports, were covered with many feet of reinforced concrete and were without question proof against any bomb we had at that time; when the bombs exploded on the roofs of these shelters they made no more than a slight indentation in the surface. The most we could hope to do was to cause universal devastation round the pens and in the town and in the process destroy a few outside machine shops and other worskshops of the kind that are useful in a naval base; we could also give U-boat crews on shore a disturbed night, if they were foolish enough to stay in the area, but of course they did not. The Admiralty may or may not have thought that this would exert a worthwhile influence on the Battle of the Atlantic, but there was no getting out of the job, though before we began on it I protested repeatedly against this hopeless misuse of air power on an operation which could not possibly achieve the object that was intended.

In January and February the Command made about 2000 sorties against Lorient, and in February and early March three attacks, the first of them by 400 aircraft, were carried out against St. Nazaire. We did, in fact, uselessly devastate two perfectly good French towns—the attacks were usually well concentrated —but the only effect that they had on the course of the war was to delay the opening of the Battle of the Ruhr and the main bomber offensive against Germany by nearly two months. Until the beginning of March we were able to use only a small part of our effort against Germany, for though expansion was beginning, we could at that time only raise about 400 aircraft for the average major operation. In the event, the strategic consequences of the delay were of considerable importance, and of course, wholly advantageous to the enemy. As Bomber Command's main offensive against the German industrial cities was only to last for about twelve months, the loss of two months, which may have seemed a small affair to the authorities at the time, may now be seen in its proper perspective. It was only after bitter argument, in which I received support from Winston Churchill in his capacity as Minister of Defence, that the Admiralty failed to get accepted their demand for Brest and Bordeaux to be similarly wiped out.

During the first year of my command we had been able, in point of fact, to exert a very considerable influence on the war at sea without in any way reducing the weight of the offensive against Germany. In February of 1942 all the minelaying of the Command, which had been made responsible for all air-sea mine-laying in Northern and Western Europe, was still being done by the aircraft of my old Group, No. 5 Group. I at once decided that minelaying from then on should be done by all Groups. I proposed that we should lay on an average 1000 mines a month, which would be perfectly feasible if all Groups did the work and a considerable number of four-engined bombers were engaged on it, although in 1941 the average was less than 90 a month. This proposal was welcomed by the Admiralty, and allowed by the Air Ministry on condition that it did not interfere with the bombing of Germany. There were many occasions when the weather did not permit of an operation in Germany, but would allow us to operate somewhere off the European coast between the South of the Bay of Biscay and the Baltic. Moreover, mines were then laid from between 600 and 1000 feet and aircraft could come safely below cloud to find their targets area at a time when this would have been fatal almost anywhere in Germany, with the result that weather suitable for minelaying was very different from that needed for bombing. So that by dispatching aircraft on mine-laying sorties on nights when there was no chance of operating over Germany we were able to conduct the whole campaign with little or not effect on the main offensive.

The necessary modifications to enable the mines to be carried by several different types of aircraft were quickly undertaken. The mines themselves were improved. The magnetic mines we used in the early days of the war were not absolutely safe to handle, and there were two bad explosions on airfields in the period 1940-1941, but this was put right, and we had no such accidents for the remainder of the war. In 1942 we dropped the first airborne acoustic mine, operated by the sound waves sent through the water by ships, and thereafter many ingenious mixtures of the magnetic-acoustic firing gear were devised. In March of 1942 there had, of course, to be an immediate and more than tenfold increase in the production of mines, but this was managed without any difficulty. Indeed, the whole minelaying campaign was marked by a total absence of all those production problems and difficulties in getting priorities which in everything else was our normal lot. Whenever anything was wanted in a great hurry, because we learned that the enemy had found out how to cope with the mines we were laying at that time, it was designed by a small factory largely staffed by Wrens and produced with a rapidity which would have been inconceivable if we had gone through the usual channels or if we had not had the Admiralty at our back. The workshops of the Navy's research establishment were at our disposal and everything went like clockwork. It was a lesson in how to get what you want, a lesson which the Navy learned long ago. On the other hand, if the Navy had had to struggle for anything and everything in the same way as the R.A.F. had, they might have lost some of their liking for obsolete and enormously expensive weapons. Our relations with the Naval mining authorities were always excellent and in Captain de Mowbray and his staff, Bomber Command had a wonderfully efficient mining team.

The minelaying campaign had considerably more effect than the destruction of Lorient and St. Nazaire on the U-boats using these other bases on the west coast of France. The soundings off that coast were by no means ideal for minelaying, but even so we managed to cause the enemy much trouble and repeatedly delayed the operation of his U-boats; channels had to be continually swept before they gave safe passage to submarines and this not only interrupted operations but also put a great strain on the enemy's local naval resources. Some U-boats were sunk or damaged, but this was of no greater importance than the widespread dislocation caused by minelaying. The most important minelaying operation of the year against these U-boat bases, was in November. Operation "Torch," the landing in North Africa, was imminent and large convoys were on their way from England to Gibraltar. At that time many U-boats were being held in the French bases, and they would have had only a short way to go to

intercept our convoys. We laid many more than the usual number
of mines in the approaches to the U-boat bases, and these held
up U-boat sailings at a most critical time. It was also our practice
to lay mines in the U-boat's exercising grounds in the Baltic,
which we knew then and have since confirmed caused great delays
and complications in U-boat crew training and working up trials.

A good deal of the minelaying was directed against German
merchant shipping and supply ships, particularly the shipping
used to bring iron ore for the Ruhr from Scandinavia to Rotterdam and from Bilbao to Bayonne; the same vessels used to
transport troops and warlike stores from the Western to the
Eastern Baltic and thence on to the Eastern Front. During the
whole period of the war one vessel is known to have been sunk
or damaged for every 50 mines that were laid.

By the end of 1942 minelaying operations were becoming
dangerous. Light flak is an extremely effective defence against
aircraft flying at a height of 1000 feet or less and the enemy had
disposed large numbers of light anti-aircraft guns near the most
important minefields, a clear proof that the minelaying was
hurting him. For a short time we had to direct our minelaying
to more open areas, where the only guns could be on ships, but
this was only while we were experimenting with new methods
of minelaying from a greater height. If this was to be done, it
would, of course, be more difficult to find the area where the
mines were to be laid, and we therefore experimented with laying
mines by radar fixes.

We kept up and indeed exceeded the promised monthly average
of 1000 a month. During the whole year the Command laid
9573 mines and, of course, it was only in the spring that all the
Groups began to do this work and the programme commenced.
This work required 14.7 per cent of all sorties for the year. Minelaying, by the way, had the code-word "Gardening," the mines
were called "vegetables," and the various minefields were given
the names of vegetables or other plants, artichokes, onions,
deodars, and so forth.

In the late autumn of 1942 there began the offensive which
was to throw the Germans out of Africa. To support this the
Command was required to attack the industrial cities of North
Italy. There were six night attacks against Genoa, seven night
attacks against Turin, and one daylight attack against Milan.
The fact that we were able to operate by day shows how weak
were the defences of Italy; almost the only difficulties were the

barrier of the Alps and the distance of the target, and these were easily surmounted. Against such weak defences and with the excellent visibility that was usual in the Italian climate it was easy to get a good concentration of attack without any navigational aids; the Pathfinders' tactics almost invariably went according to plan. The attacks were far lighter than those directed against Germany at that time; not only were a similar number of aircraft sent, but at this great range a small bomb load had to be carried. Nevertheless the effect on Italian morale was enormous and out of all proportion to the weight of the attack and to the extent of the damage. Three hundred thousand people, half the population, fled from Turin after our second attack on the city that autumn and there was as great, and probably greater, panic after the daylight attack on Milan by less than one hundred Lancasters. After this series of attacks Mussolini declared in public that it was necessary to organise a nightly evacuation of all civilians in the industrial cities of North Italy, where only the military would remain by night.

The attack on Milan was not the only daylight attack of the year. Indeed, I laid on, very soon after I had taken over, a daylight attack on an objective far within Germany. On April 17th, twelve Lancasters were dispatched to bomb the M.A.N. works at Augsburg, which produced a large proportion of the enemy's U-boat engines; the Diesel-engine shed in the midst of the very large factory was the precise target. The attack was very carefully planned; Augsburg was far beyond the then range of fighter cover, but Fighter Command laid on diversionary sweeps, which, however, did not go altogether according to plan. The Lancasters also flew at a very low level, because it was at that time difficult to detect very low flying aircraft by radar and also because this gave some protection against fighters and flak. Seven out of the twelve Lancasters were missing, a loss which was not excessive in proportion to the importance of the objective and the serious damage that was done to it, but which did demonstrate beyond all question that daylight attacks on Germany could at that time only be carried out by Bomber Command at a prohibitive casualty rate. Dusk attacks on coastal targets were still possible, but proved inaccurate. The U-boat building yards at Flensburg, Lübeck and Danzig were attacked in this way, but only those at Flensburg were hit.

In France and elsewhere in the occupied West the enemy's defences were still so weak that we could afford to attack several of the collaborating factories which were on my list by daylight. But this was no great advantage, because, against few or no defences, we were often able to attack by night with equal precision. I was therefore able to fulfil to the letter my instructions to discourage production of war material for the enemy, not only in the Renault works, but also in a good many other factories, including the Gnome et Rhone works at Gennevilliers, the Ford works at Poissy, and the Philips works at Eindhoven. The Philips works were attacked by the light bombers of No. 2 Group, which during 1942 rearmed, first with Bostons, and then with Mosquitoes. The Mosquitoes carried out a number of dashing attacks with hitherto unexampled precision on a series of small targets in the occupied countries, including a molybdenum mine at Knaben in Norway without which material, according to the Ministry of Economic Warfare, the enemy would be most gravely embarrassed in his special steel production. The first daylight attack on Berlin in the war was made by these Mosquitoes: it was simply a nuisance raid, by three aircraft, designed to set the sirens going at the precise moment when Goering was due to make a ceremonial appearance and an important speech. Possibly the Germans thought that the Americans were coming to Berlin in force—they had so far never attempted this objective—but at any rate Goering did not perform until an hour after the scheduled time at which his speech was to be broadcast. Excitement and even panic was heard through the microphone as the attack went in. Meanwhile another broadcasting station had already broadcast an eye-witness account of the ceremony which had not then taken place. But No. 2 Group's aircraft and operation were so different from those of the main force that it was decided in the spring of 1942 to transfer the whole Group to the Air Defence of Great Britain, the name which, for some inexplicable reason, was at that time given to Fighter Command. It was indeed extraordinary of the Air Ministry, when they had in Fighter Command a name of world wide fame unalterably connected with the greatest victory in the annals of the R.A.F., a victory even more important than Trafalgar, and one which in fact saved the world from Nazidom, that they should proceed to change that name for another which was as inevitably associated with the most depressing period in the history of the Air Force, the period of starvation between the two wars when what few bombers and fighters there were were lumped together in a formation misleadingly called the Air Defence of Great Britain;

moreover this was at a time when both the fighters and the light bombers were training for the invasion of Europe. Amongst others, I protested vigorously against this change and I am glad to say that the old name of Fighter Command was eventually restored.

So ended a year of preparation, in which very little material damage had been done to the enemy which he could not repair from his resources, but in which we had obtained or had in near prospect what was required to strike him to the ground, and learned how to use it.

Chapter Seven

THE OFFENSIVE UNDER WAY

The main offensive begins. A successful attack on Essen. The Battle of the Ruhr. Showing the results to the world. Field Marshal Smuts sees the bomb-damage. Winston Churchill and the offensive. Propaganda in the R.A.F. The Mohne and Eder dams. More new equipment. The Civil Service.

A T LONG LAST we were ready and equipped. Bomber Command's main offensive began at a precise moment, the moment of the first major attack on an objective in Germany by means of Oboe. This was on the night of March 5-6th, 1943, when I was at last able to undertake with real hope of success the task which had been given to me when I first took over the Command a little more than a year before, the task of destroying the main cities of the Ruhr. In the interval, however, the scope of my instructions had been enlarged, as a result of the Casablanca Conference, when it was decided to proceed with a joint Anglo-American bomber offensive against German war industry. The subject of morale had been dropped, and I was now required to proceed with the general "disorganisation" of German industry, giving priority to certain aspects of it such as U-boat building, aircraft production, oil production, transportation and so forth, which gave me a very wide range of choice and allowed me to attack pretty well any German industrial city of 100,000 inhabitants and above. But the Ruhr remained a principle objective because it was the most important industrial area in the whole of Germany, which was why it had been originally chosen for morale-breaking attacks; the new instructions therefore made no difference. Essen had been named as the first town for destruction a year before, as it was the largest and most important manufacturing centre in the Ruhr, and Essen was the target on the night of March 5-6th.

A force of 442 aircraft was dispatched. In the main force there were 140 Lancasters, 69 Halifaxes, 52 Stirlings, and 131 Wellingtons, while the Pathfinder marking force consisted of 22 heavy bombers and 8 Oboe-Mosquitoes, on which and on the equipment they carried everything in the last resort depended.

The force flew to Egmong on the Dutch coast, and thence directly to a point 15 miles north of Essen, which point Pathfinder heavies had marked with yellow markers on the ground as a guide to the main force. From there the bombers began the run-up to the target, which they were to reach at the rate of eleven a minute, the whole attack lasting thirty-eight minutes. The Mosquitoes dropped red target indicators, not visually but by means of Oboe on the aiming point before the bombing began, and thereafter at intervals alternately of three and seven minutes. These intervals were dictated by the fact that the Mosquitoes could only be guided to the target at the rate of one every ten minutes for each pair of ground stations with which they were in communication. We now had two pairs of ground stations instead of the single pair with which we had made our first experimental attacks by Oboe, which meant that we could get twelve Mosquitoes over the target in an hour instead of six as before, but there was always the risk, especially as the Mosquitoes could carry no great number of target indicators, that there would be intervals when no target indicators were burning on the ground. This was what the 22 heavy bombers of the Pathfinder force were for; they were to drop a large number of green target indicators, aimed at the red target indicators which the Mosquitoes had dropped, at intervals of one to two minutes throughout the attack. If the bomb-aimers of the main force could see the few but more accurately placed red target indicators they were to aim at these, but if not, at the green target indicators. In this way, though the ground might be quite invisible through haze or low cloud, it was hoped that the main force would have a clearly distinguishable mark at which to aim at every moment throughout the attack. The weather on this occasion was clear, but there was the usual industrial haze of the Ruhr, and this in itself made the use of target indicators and a blind-bombing aid absolutely essential.

In the event the red target indicators proved to have fallen very close to the aiming point if not on it, the green target indicators were most accurately aimed by the highly trained bomb-aimers of the Pathfinder force, and the main force bombing was equally good. A conflagration which seemed to cover, almost without a break, a circular area some two miles in diameter surrounded the target indicators. The municipal archives of Essen afterwards revealed that the greater part of the bomb-load had in fact fallen within the built-up area under attack. The concentration of the bomber force had been so great that only 14 aircraft were lost, just over 3 per cent of the whole, a casualty rate much below the average for that period.

This was easily the most important attack so far carried out by Bomber Command. It was not only that a hitherto invulnerable target had for the first time been seriously damaged, but also that there was no reason why the success should not be indefinitely repeated in attacks on any targets within Oboe range. This had never been the case before, every previous success had been dependent on the caprice of the weather and had usually been won by seizing some opportunity that might never recur. But now the whole Ruhr was evidently at our mercy. Five more attacks were made on Essen in the next few months, the last of them being made by 700 aircraft; by this time, the end of July, there had at long last been an impressive expansion in the strength of the Command. All six attacks were extremely successful and after the last of them both Krupps and Essen were largely in ruins; even in the first three attacks of this series about half of the 300 separate buildings of Krupps were damaged, and the last attack, on July 25th-26th did as much damage to Krupps as in all the previous· attacks put together. The largest building in the plant, the Hindenburg Hall in which locomotives were built, was so badly damaged that the Germans never attempted to repair it, though the enemy was then giving as high priority to the production of locomotives ás to the production of aircraft, tanks, and U-boats, and though Krupps was, next to the locomotive works at Kassel, the largest locomotive building plant in Europe. From then on the production by Krupps of large shells, previously made at the rate of four hundred a month, and of fuses, previously made there at the rate of two hundred thousand a month, altogether ceased. The output of guns was cut by half and the production of aero-engine crankshafts—most important to the enemy at this stage of the air war—was seriously reduced.

In all 3261 sorties were made against Essen between March and July of 1943. This should be compared with the 3724 sorties made against Essen in 1942 which did no significant damage to Krupps and very little damage to the town of Essen. And in 1942 201 aircraft were missing from the 3724 sorties dispatched against Essen, a casualty rate of 5.4 per cent, but in 1943, 138 aircraft were missing from the 3261 sorties dispatched against Essen, a casualty rate of 4.2 per cent, although between 1942 and 1943 the Germans had strongly reinforced their night fighter force, to the great detriment of the German armies in Russia and the Mediterranean, and had also in this interval brought their radar-assisted night fighters and anti-aircraft guns to a point of extreme efficiency.

As an objective Essen differed from a number of Ruhr towns in that the huge Krupps works, covering several hundred acres, was right in the heart of the city. Elsewhere very large and important factories might be on the outskirts of the town, where they could not easily be destroyed in the course of area attack, though there was no general rule; the Rheinmetall Borsig plant at Dusseldorf, an armament works of about equal importance to Krupps though not so well known, was not so far from the centre of the city as to be outside the target area for a general attack on the place. But it must be emphasised that in no instance, except in Essen, were we aiming specifically at any one factory during the Battle of the Ruhr; the destruction of factories, which was nevertheless on an enormous scale, could be regarded as a bonus. The aiming points were usually right in the centre of the town; the average German city had spread outwards from an old centre, which was naturally more densely built-up than the newer and well-planned suburbs; it was this densely built-up centre which was most susceptible to area attack with incendiary bombs. The objective of the campaign was to reduce production in the industries of the Ruhr at least as much by the indirect effect of damage to services, housing, and amenities, as by any direct damage to the factories or railways themselves. At this stage of the war there was no alternative method or means of attacking German industry, but at the same time I had good reason to believe that the indirect effects of this general damage would be extremely important in the long run.

During the first five months of the Battle of the Ruhr, Essen was by no means the only target. Dortmund, one of the most important centres of heavy industry in Germany, Duisburg, Bochum, Gelsenkirchen, Oberhausen, Mulheim, Wuppertal, Remscheid, Munchen-Gladbach, Krefeld, Munster, Aachen, Dusseldorf, and Cologne were all heavily attacked and in most instances heavily damaged, the devastated areas amounting to hundreds and in some instances to thousands of acres, usually right in the centre of the city. Several of these towns were not, of course, strictly within the Ruhr area, but belonged to the same industrial complex; all were within Oboe range.

The two towns which had been most heavily damaged in 1942, Cologne and Dusseldorf, were attacked again in 1943 and far more extensive damage was done than in the previous year. There was, I believe, some surprise when the general public learned that we were attacking Cologne again, after damaging the city so severely in the 1000 bomber attack. But, of course, the 600 acres previously damaged left a good deal of Cologne still standing and in the interval the enemy had made the most strenuous efforts to repair the place; in 1942 the Germans had been able to carry out repairs on a scale that was never possible afterwards. In the first years of the war the German policy was to conceal air-raid damage with hoardings behind which the repairs were carried out at high speed. There could be no concealment of the damage at Cologne, but every attempt was made to convince the inhabitants that no irreparable disaster had occurred. All important factories were, of course, repaired, but small industrial plants were also restored to their original condition. Completely wrecked houses were demolished or left alone, but any houses that could be mended were put to rights by December of 1942. And even buildings which were apparently of no use to the war effort in any way, like churches and exhibition halls, were restored.

Two attacks were made on Dusseldorf during this first Battle of the Ruhr, each by about 700 bombers. The first, on the night of May 25th-26th, was a failure because cloud rising to a great height hid the target indicators; the second, on the night of June 11th-12th was made in good weather and raised a vast conflagration which wrecked the greater part of the city. There was so great a concentration of attack that the fire brigades lost all control of the situation and some buildings were still smouldering a week later. The industrial damage was heavy.

Nothing like the whole succession of catastrophes which overcame the cities of the Ruhr and North-West Germany in the first half of 1943 had ever occurred before, either in Germany or elsewhere. It was an impressive victory, but I knew that it could be only the beginning of a serious bomber offensive; not before a very much larger number of cities elsewhere in Germany had been reduced to the same condition, and not before the wrecked cities of the Ruhr and elsewhere had been attacked once or even twice again to prevent recovery, could there be any decisive effect. The possession of Oboe and an average striking force of seven to eight hundred bombers had done a great deal, but we had by no means solved the problem of attacking cities outside Oboe range, and Germany still had vast industrial resources out of the Ruhr.

I therefore needed much more than I had got in the way of priorities, industrial resources, equipment, reinforcements of personnel, and aircraft, if I was to complete the task which I had only just begun. It was still as necessary as it had been in 1942 to convince those in charge of the war and, indeed, the general public, that if given the weapons the bomber force could do the work.

The results so far achieved were spectacular enough to have aroused a great deal of interest in the work of Bomber Command and this I naturally welcomed. I wanted everyone to see for themselves what the bomber offensive was doing to Germany, and to this end I took pains to get the facts properly illustrated in photographs, charts, and so forth. I had a large book prepared, which we called the blue book, in which after each attack on a German city the area of devastation was progressively marked with blue paint over an air photograph, or rather a mosaic of air photographs, of the city a as whole. This book eventually extended to two or three enormous volumes which could be sent anywhere about the Command or elsewhere. But I also wanted people to see the damage for themselves, not in diagrammatic form, and to get any real idea of the damage in an air photograph taken from a great height it is necessary to look at it through a stereoscope; this is the method always used in the interpretation of photographs taken by reconnaissance aircraft because it brings out details which might be easily overlooked in ordinary photographs. In particular, air raid damage shows up to an extent that would hardly be believed by those who have only seen ordinary photographs. But the stereoscopes used in the photographic interpretation section are not easy for the average untrained person to use, and I wanted something better. I remembered those stereoscopes with which the Victorians used to amuse themselves; it was another production problem, but I made inquiries and found that a relative of mine had one of these instruments—it was called a stereopticon. I got hold of this, and later had some others made to the same pattern. With this equipment and also with enlargements of ordinary air photographs of particularly clear and significant damage I did my best to convince the people who mattered. These records were shown to thousands of official visitors, at my house or at Command Headquarters, during the course of the war.

On the first occasion on which Smuts came to England during the time I was at Bomber Command I tried to get hold of him but failed—most unfortunately. On a second visit of his I was determined to have a go at explaining the bomber offensive to him personally, so I wrote to him and reminded him of the fact that we were brothers in arms in German West Africa in 1914; actually he was then Chief of Staff to General Louis Botha, the C.-in-C., and I was the junior bugler in the 1st Rhodesian Regiment. I also told him that as a citizen of his country I had, after all, more right to demand his presence than a good many other people in England.

At last we managed to get him down to Springfield. After dinner, and very soon after, because I remembered his South African Veldt habit of going to bed and getting up with the sun, I steered him into what we called the "conversion room" next door and got his nose into one of the stereopticons which showed some of the damage we had already done in Germany; it was small enough at that time by comparison with what came later. At first he had not been remarkably keen on listening to my exposition of bombing theory, but by the time he had seen two or three of the photographs he was fumbling for a focus, pulling up his chair, and obviously sitting down to absorb things. Finally he examined with the greatest care everything we had in the place both in the stereopticons and in the blue books. Beyond a few ejaculations, he made no comment, but when he had finished, he walked back into the drawing-room, turned to me, and said: "It is extraordinary, it's fantastic, it is something entirely new, something which I never even suspected; it's tremendous."

There are many outstanding things about Smuts, the brilliance of his intellect, his immense physical hardiness and toughness so that you cannot believe you are looking, not at a man of forty, but of seventy, his great personal bravery, and his delightful sense of humour. Speaking in a clear, high-pitched voice, he will give you the answer to almost any proposition that you put before him. A practical answer, and a better one than most.

Smuts of course puts the welfare of his country first. But he undoubtedly believes that the best thing for the world is the extension of the ideas that have produced the British Commonwealth. The most brilliant, if not the most bitter opponent of ours during the Boer War, he has never forgotten the aftermath, when the Transvaal and the Orange Free State were handed back, and indeed the whole of "South" Africa including such predominantly "British" places as Natal and the Cape, and the Union of South Africa at last brought into being. He regards that as a most extraordinary example of far-sighted statesmanship, as indeed it was; not only because it brought into the Commonwealth such great Boer patriots as Smuts and Botha, but it healed also to a large extent the spiritual wounds of Boer and British in South Africa, and not the least those of the "dear irreconcilable" Deneys Rietz.

Though Smuts had predicted how the air war would develop as long ago as 1917, I could see that he was astounded by what I showed him at Bomber Command; it was then that he realised in full for the first time what our bomber offensive meant to the war as a whole. I knew I was assured of his support in military affairs if I should require it. He told me that he would talk to Winston about what we had done, but I do not know whether he in fact got the opportunity to do so. I did not worry much about that, because I knew that Winston himself always wanted to know first hand about everything.

I was frequently bidden to Chequers, especially during the week-ends when Winston was normally there. I never failed to return from these visits invigorated and full of renewed hope and enthusiasm, in spite of the appalling hours that Winston habitually kept. If it was a mixed party—which was not very often—and I could take my wife, I knew that we might get home somewhere between midnight and one in the morning, but when I was asked alone, it would be anywhere between three and four before I got back. Not that I minded.

After dinner Winston would talk; he was really thinking aloud about how things were going. He would get repeated reminders that a film show was waiting for him, and eventually we would all go up to the gallery—the household staff, and the rest of the family, and even the military guard from outside—to see the picture. There the Prime Minister would sit, occasionally making amusing comments about the drama. One realised, of course, that he was really resting himself in this atmosphere and that this thoughts were often far away. Sometimes one could hear him rehearse a phrase for a telegram he would send later. Well after midnight we would go back down to the hall and he would get down to another batch of work, sending signals, dictating to his secretaries, and so on, while at intervals one of his family, and sometimes his naval A.D.C. would attempt to steer him off to bed, as his doctors had advised, but invariably without the least success. He went to bed when he wanted to. The only man who stood up to Winston about his late hours was Smuts. I have heard him come out of dinner and say: "Well, Winston, I suppose you are going on with the argument all night. I am going to bed, good night."

I think the first thing that impresses one about Winston is the extraordinary mixture in him of real human kindness and of sometimes impish mischief, all overlaid with an immense, thrusting, purposeful determination to reach the goal which he so clearly sees. The affection which the whole Churchill family feel for one another is very obvious and most refreshing.

The worse the state of the war was, the greater was the support, enthusiasm, encouragement and constructive criticism that one got from this extraordinary man; it was all done with the utmost kindness, though not without a mischievous dig now and again just for the fun of it. He did not mind your expressing views contrary to his own, but he was difficult to argue with for the simple reason that he seldom seemed to listen long to sides of a question other than his own. He has, in fact, developed to a perhaps extreme degree this rather unfortunate trait of the man who has almost absolute power, knows his own mind, and really does not want to be bothered with everybody else's ideas. He is a bad listener, and frequently interrupts anyone who is expressing views, whether they are opposed to his own or not, halfway through a sentence; then he is off at a tangent, holding forth, always with interest and generally on sound lines, on some other aspect of the subject under discussion, or even on some entirely different subject. Consequently I found it much more satisfactory to listen than to argue, only sticking in a word here and there with the intention of steering the conversation round to the subject in which I was interested, or on which I wanted his opinion and guidance.

If I wanted to get anything across or to give any complicated explanation I found it much better to send him a paper than to talk to him. If the paper was long he would not read it, but if it ran to no more than two or three pages—and everything was put tersely and crystallised into snappy sentences, so that he could get the meaning quickly and would not have to wade through a mass of detail—then I always found him very willing to investigate one's point of view and do all that he could to help.

He was always at his best when things were worst, which, of course, is the mark of real leadership, especially in wartime. When things were really desperate, as indeed they were on many occasions, it was a tonic to watch him prowling up and down, bent in thought, rehearsing half aloud the wording of some urgent telegram he was about to dispatch to some corner of the globe where something had gone badly wrong. His extraordinary mastery of the simple, clear, unambiguous phrase was obviously a source of great delight, and, indeed, of strength to him. When he had to give some final decision which it had taken a long time to reach nothing seemed to confirm him in his resolution more than the discovery of the apt phrase in which to express it.

I well remember such an occasion when there had been much doubt and argument between the services whether to hold on to Tobruk; it was by then a foregone conclusion that the rest of our forces would have to retire a long way farther East. I have never known Churchill at a loss on any question of pure strategy; naturally enough, the service representatives would often have to press him to reject or alter a solution he proposed when the right decision on grounds of pure strategy was unacceptable for lack of resources or for reasons of time and space—which were perhaps not Winston's strongest suit. On grounds of pure strategy Winston was therefore arguing passionately—I never knew him overrule—for the retention of Tobruk. When Winston asked for my opinion, I supported his desire to hold on, not because it was his idea but because it seemed to me to offer absolutely the only hope of stopping the rot. I pointed out that though there would indeed be difficulties for the Navy and Air Force in supplying and supporting Tobruk, these difficulties on our side, even though our forces were inadequate, would be as nothing to the fears and uncertainties of the enemy when he came to advance far beyond a by-passed Tobruk, with our forces there threatening his communications while they were at extreme stretch across hundreds of miles of desert. The alternative for Rommel would be to devote so large a part of his force to the investment and capture of Tobruk that with what was left he would find it impossible to advance farther into Egypt. To leave a force in Tobruk, on that first occasion, to threaten Rommel's tenuous communications seemed the one chance left of giving pause to an otherwise victorious enemy who at that time looked like stopping nowhere short of Alexandria or Cairo.

Winston greeted this support for his own ideas with unfeigned delight. And at once he found the right phrase for Tobruk; "a sally port," he said, pronouncing this with his slight lisp between the "s" and the "a." He rolled the phrase round his mouth and repeated it. "Yes, a sally port, a sally port; that is what we want, that is the thing to do with them. The farther he advances the more you threaten, the more he has to fear. That is the answer, a sally port . . ." Having found his phrase, the Prime Minister was off into the charge at once, and no holding him; he harangued until he had everyone round to his way of thinking. That was why we came to stop in Tobruk on the first occasion, and, as I think can be fairly claimed, why the enemy never got to Alexandria. I had nothing to do with the decision to stay in Tobruk on the second occasion, but I am sure that this decision was as right as the first one had been. Why we failed to hold the place on the second occasion will probably come out in the history of the campaign.

I do not remember a single occasion of the many on which I appealed to Winston for help or advice when either or both were not forthcoming, no matter how overwhelmed he might be by other weighty affairs. He never failed in encouragement, just as he never failed to apply the spur. When a week or two of bad weather prevented us from doing anything much to get on with the offensive he would express his disappointment, but then—and it was amazing to watch this—his better judgment would at once prevail and he would always conclude his harangue by saying: "I am not pressing you to fight the weather as well as the Germans; never forget that." Always what he had to say was both a comfort and an inspiration, and I doubt if any nation has ever had such a leader in war. I like to think that science will some day give us the means of recalling past scenes, so that our descendants may be able to visit Chequers, switch on the set, and see anew this Prime Minister of England on the prowl—siren suit, embroidered slippers, dressing-gown, all complete—disposing with sonorous phrase and valiant gesture of each of the many desperate crises that arose during the time of his leadership.

I am certain that Winston is no more of a politician in the accepted sense of the word than I am, which is probably why he has spent so much of his political life out of office. By this I mean that he is not a trimmer, a man who sets his sails to any and every breeze that may take him to some or any harbour. On the contrary, having chosen his course he would stick to it through thick and thin if he thought it was the right one, and would let nothing, least of all personal or party considerations, divert him from his course; it did not matter how long this would keep him from the comfortable political career that would have been his if he had trimmed his sails to suit each fitful gust.

He had to have all or nothing, he was always statesman rather than politician, and this very fact brought him to the fore twice in wartime, as a man determined at all costs to hold the course that he knew would carry us, however sorely beset, to victory.

The last occasion when I went to Chequers to see Winston was on the day after it had been decided to break up the National Government; I remember feeling horrified by the certainty with which Winston asserted that the coming election would go in his favour. I was equally certain that this showed a complete blindness to political realities, and when I left that night, or rather in the small hours of the next morning, I knew that I should never again go to Chequers as the guest of Winston Churchill. I counted that my darkest hour. But I knew the war was won. At Chequers I had seen three years of history, and the greatest of England's valiants give it shape.

Winston was, of course, delighted by the way the offensive was developing during the Battle of the Ruhr. He was also distressed, as I was, by the slowness with which the Command had gathered strength, its expansion having been continually checked by the loss of squadrons to other Commands as soon as we had trained them.

I once remarked to Portal that, although hundreds of very important people had gone to all the trouble of coming to Bomber Command to see the results of bombing, the other two Chiefs of Staff had entirely ignored the manner, which seemed to me quite extraordinary. So it was arranged that I should take the blue books and some of the stereopticans to the Chiefs of Staff and explain the bomb damage in Germany to them after one of their committee meetings. This experiment rather failed in its object. The Chief of the Naval Staff did not attend, but sent a deputy, and the reaction of the C.I.G.S. when the Blue Book was put in front of him did not convince me that he had grasped the significance of the bombing offensive.

Among my many visitors I must especially recall Lord Camrose of the *Daily Telegraph*. He came to see me one summer evening and stayed to supper. This was in the early days when there was much opposition to the whole idea of a bomber offensive, and he wanted to know for himself. He was far from being already converted when he arrived, rather the reverse, but he had an open mind. He spent hours going into the pros and cons of the whole matter with me and minutely studying what evidence was then available. Just before he left we strolled through the garden in the dusk; he finally turned to me and said: "I believe you, and I will support you to the finish." He certainly did as he said, and without his support and that of the *Daily Telegraph* life would have been much more difficult than it was; and it was difficult and wearing enough.

Though I wanted no publicity for myself and did not wish anything I said to be quoted, mainly on grounds of security, I was far from overlooking the importance of getting support in the Press. It was the greatest help to get the facts fairly presented and, on occasion, to have something published to set against the nonsense which gets written in wartime when correspondents do not know the facts and, "for reasons of security," are not told them. I have had a good deal of experience of correspondents both in America and England. In America I found that correspondents never let you down and that you could give them "off the record" stuff straight away. It was just the same with the best of the English correspondents, only more so, because the best of the English correspondents were more intelligent. But it was obvious to me that the Press was being treated in such an extraordinarily cautious manner by the Air Ministry that it was by no means easy to get journalists of repute to visit Bomber Command and its stations.

The Air Ministry had certainly had the idea that it would be a good thing to get the support of the Press and to have the operations of the Air Force reported as fully as possible. No doubt it was hoped to compensate in this way for the obvious inability of the Air Ministry, by comparison with the ministries of other services, to get the attention and the favour of those who matter; public support was to be called in to redress the balance. For this purpose a huge Public Relation Department was set up, too large to do the work without everybody interfering with everybody else, usually with people at the top who knew very little about the Press and even less about air matters, and who were also unwilling to take any responsibility; consequently the Press got a mass of useless propaganda material and few solid facts or even reasonable arguments. Correspondents of reputable papers were not treated as they should have been if they were to do any good; their questions were answered by slick evasions and they were not given much opportunity to see things for themselves. As to our own operations, I know that there was often the greatest difficulty in getting a fair report of them through the Air Ministry and out to the Press. There was also the Air Ministry's apparently inevitable fear of hurting someone's feelings, especially the feelings of the other services, by putting forward its own case. The fact that the Air Force was sinking more submarines than the Navy never seemed to get published at all, just as the fact that Bomber Command sank more German naval ships has never got out, and it should most definitely have been the Air Ministry's business to see that these facts got out; as it was, the Navy was able to hush everything up on the grounds of security. The activities of the departments responsible for censorship and security were often wholly inexplicable; for example, we were not allowed to have some facts about the Pathfinder Force published at a time when these same facts had already been given in a propaganda broadcast directed to listeners in the Luftwaffe.

However we did, by hook and by crook, get a good deal of support for the bomber offensive in the Press. Arthur Salzberger of the *New York Times*, a man of intelligence, was as firm a support, once convinced, as a foundation of rock. So also were Ogden-Reed of the *New York Herald Tribune*, Colin Bedneall of the *Daily Mail*, and Allan Michie of the *Reader's Digest*.

The breaching of the Möhne dam on the night of May 16th-17th was one incident in the Battle of the Ruhr. This was carried out by a new squadron, No. 617 squadron of No. 5 Group, which was formed and trained expressly for this operation, though it continued to engage in precision-bombing attacks of diverse kinds until the end of the war. On the same night as the attack on the Möhne dam, which was designed to supply water for the Ruhr, the Eder dam farther east was also successfully attacked. There could never have been any attempt on a concrete structure one hundred and forty feet thick if it had not been for an extraordinary weapon invented by B. N. Wallis of Vickers Armstrong, a kind of mine, the principle and construction of which must for some obscure reason still be considered secret. It was one of the weapons designed for the Command outside the official Ministry of Aircraft Production and Air Ministry organisation which produced the greater part of our armament; it could be taken almost as a rule that such weapons were successful, while those produced by the official organisation were too often failures. In designing such weapons Wallis was really working outside his own job which was mainly aircraft design; the Command certainly owed a very great deal to his brilliant inventions.

I cannot add much to the published account of the actual

operation against the dams, operation "Chastise," that was written by Wing Commander Guy Gibson before he was killed in action. Everyone who knew about the operation beforehand, including Winston Churchill, expected much from it and was in a considerable state of excitement on the night that it occurred. I myself went with Wallis and Cochrane, who was then A.O.C. of No. 5 Group, to Grantham, the Group Headquarters which 617 Squadron ran; this was only one of innumerable successful operations carried out by 5 Group when it was under the command of Cochrane, a most brilliant, enthusiastic, and hard working leader of men. We spent the night in the operations room waiting for the signals from Gibson which should tell us of the success or failure of the attack. When I learnt that the Möhne and Eder dams had been breached I rang up Washington, where Churchill and Portal were at the time, to give them the news. The telephone personnel seemed never to have heard of the White House, and there was some little difficulty. When I did get through I was intercepted and asked for an assurance that the person I was calling was reliable. I don't know whether she was eventually persuaded that Winston Churchill came into that category, but I got through to Portal in the end and told him that the two dams had gone. Another Ruhr dam, the Sorpe dam, was also attacked by two aircraft of the squadron, but this dam was of different construction from that of the other two. It was of earth with a watertight concrete blade as core, and could not be breached outright as the other two dams were, but it was hoped that the concrete core might be cracked and the water eventually seep through the earth. In the event, no serious damage was done to the Sorpe dam, though we continued to put reconnaissance aircraft over it for a while in the hope of detecting some damage. On the journey back from Grantham to my headquarters my chauffeur took the car over a bump in the road so that I hit my head on the roof; he said that when he heard no protest from me he knew that the attack must have been a success.

The nature of Wallis's weapon made it necessary to attack the targets from a height of sixty feet, and this being so, even a small amount of opposition made such an operation extremely hazardous. At the time of the attack the Möhne dam was well defended, but the others were not, and it was clear that such an operation could not be repeated against similar targets if the enemy were to defend his dams at all strongly as he was now perfectly certain to do; in particular, it was extremely doubtful whether the operation could have been carried out at all if there had been searchlights on or near the dams. In any case, it was only possible to attack the dams during a short period of a week or two in any given year, when the dams were at their fullest. For these reasons no further attacks on dams were made with Wallis's weapon, though the Sorpe dam was attacked with heavy bombs at a later stage in the war; this attack also failed to breach it.

Nineteen Lancasters took off for the attack. Three had to return early, and eight were missing. The Lancasters flew at a very low level the whole way, using a very carefully planned course; it is probable that most of the missing aircraft got slightly off course and ran into gun-defended areas. This risk had to be taken since the risk from enemy fighters on a moonlight night to a small and scattered bomber force would have been even greater if they had flown above one thousand feet. There would, of course, have been a better chance of breaching the Sorpe dam or other Ruhr dams—the Schwelme dam was also attacked without effect by one aircraft on the same night—if so many aircraft had not been lost on the way to the target, and if the whole squadron had been able to attack.

The breach of the Möhne Dam released a flood of one hundred and thirty million gallons, but the destruction caused by flooding was not, and was never expected to be, as serious as the subsequent shortage of water for industrial purposes. This shortage was most serious in the eastern districts of the Ruhr, but the enemy still had the water from other reservoirs whose dams were unbroken and from wells. The Eder dam was primarily intended not to provide water for industry, but to prevent flooding of agricultural land, to make the river Weser more navigable, and to supply some of the water for the Mittelland Canal. The dam held back 202,000,000 tons of water and the release of this flooded considerable areas in Kassel. Such a disaster, brought about by only nineteen aircraft, must undoubtedly have caused great alarm and despondency in Germany.

The greater number of our attacks during the Battle of the Ruhr were equally successful, but they did not always go according to plan. We were now very largely independent of the weather, and we had even made provision for the unexpected arrival over the target of clouds thick enough to hide the target indicators. The Oboe Mosquitoes carried not only the usual target indicators but also "sky-markers," as they were called, a kind of firework which floated slowly downwards and which made a point of aim above the clouds. Naturally the aim was not so accurate as when the target indicators could be seen, but the use of sky-markers did prevent the total failure of an operation and certainly produced enough damage to be worth while. It is an indication of the accuracy of Oboe that in one of the earliest experimental attacks in January, 1943, sixty per cent of a small force dispatched to Essen bombed within three miles of the aiming point by aiming at sky-markers; in all previous attacks on Essen without Oboe the highest percentage of aircraft attacking within three miles of the aiming point was twenty per cent. But there were occasions when even the use of sky-markers was not enough to save an operation from failure; this was when the clouds were so high that the sky-markers quickly fell into them and were lost to sight. This is what happened on the night of May 25th–26th, when there was cloud up to 20,000 feet over Dusseldorf.

Another difficulty, which led to the partial failure of some attacks, was the small number of Oboe Mosquitoes that could be got over the target during the period of attack, and this was made worse by the fact that the Oboe equipment was inclined to break down in the early stages of its use. We could count on the equipment going wrong in one out of three of all Oboe Mosquitoes, and as only twelve such Mosquitoes could be put over the target in an hour this was serious; in fact we were never able to maintain absolute continuity of marking during the first five months of Oboe. During the intervals when no ground markers could be seen by the main force, there was always a tendency for the bombing to drift away from the aiming point even though large fires might be burning in the target area at the time. It is true that the main force still had the target indicators dropped by Pathfinder heavies as an aiming point when the Oboe target indicators had burnt out, but these supplementary markers were also liable to drift gradually away from the true aiming point. Moreover the enemy soon began to use imitation target-indicators, an obvious expedient. These seldom attracted any bombs when the real target indicators could be seen at the same time; because the enemy was never able to get the imitation quite right. But when there were no real target indicators of the same colour to be seen, the forgery was not so easily detected and the bombing went astray.

In July, 1943, things got much better because we were able to get a third pair of Oboe ground stations working, which meant that we could bring eighteen Oboe-Mosquitoes over the target within an hour. The most successful attack on Essen up till then, the attack on the night of July 25th-26th, was the first to be made after the third pair of Oboe ground stations had been set up, and the Oboe marking was almost continuous during the fifty minutes of this attack. Five days later, in an attack on Remscheid, continuous Oboe marking was achieved for the first time, and the greater part of the city was destroyed. This was particularly significant because Remscheid was a good deal smaller than most of the towns attacked during the Battle of the Ruhr, so that any drift away from the aiming point, such as was usual when the Oboe marking was not continuous, would have wasted a great many bombs.

By the spring of 1943 we had got a fair quantity of our aircraft equipped with a new and far more efficient bomb-sight, the "Mark XIV"; I had been asking for this "tactically free" sight for years. As soon as the enemy really took his defences in hand it became obvious, as it had long been, that the older bomb-sights would not do for the average operation, though they might still be useful in special precision attacks by highly trained crews. With the older types the aircraft had to be flown straight and level for much too long and the risk was altogether excessive; with the Mark XIV bomb-sight the aircraft can be flown in any reasonable way the pilot chooses up till the moment of releasing the bombs, and the bombs can even be accurately aimed while the aircraft is climbing, gliding, or making a correctly banked turn. At the same time with the Mark XIV bomb-sight the bomb-aimer had to make very few settings during flight, so that he could concentrate on releasing the bombs at the right moment.

The 4 lb. incendiary bomb, our main weapon in all attacks on cities, was too small to be aimed individually. The 4 lb. incendiary, and all other bombs up to 40 lb. in weight, were therefore carried in Small Bomb Containers—S.B.C.'s—which were apt to scatter bombs all over the place; a good number of incendiaries were always wasted and our own aircraft ran serious risks from incendiaries showering round them. The 4 lb. incendiary was also ballistically hopeless and no bomb-sight could compete with its vagaries and shortcomings. It was a slow and laborious business to fill the S.B.C.'s, an important matter now that our operations were on so large a scale. In the spring of 1943 I asked for a cluster projectile to be produced which would do away with these dangers and disadvantages; I asked for one weighing 1000 lb., but it was decided to go ahead with a 500 lb one first, because this could be carried by heavy bombers of every type. I went on asking for this very necessary and not very complicated requirement, but I only began to get a few of them at the end of 1943, and a few of the 1000 lb. type a whole year later. Production was always uncertain, the projectiles were not properly packed, and they were easily damaged by the weather or in handling. In fact almost everything went wrong, and in the event we failed to get a satisfactory projectile of this type for holding incendiaries before the end of the war. Our incendiary attacks would have been vastly more efficient and effective if the armament and production authorities had not bungled everything as they did.

Besides the 4 lb. incendiary we also used a 30 lb. phosphorous incendiary, which was not so good at raising fires as the four-pounder, but could at least be aimed; its use also had a marked effect on the morale of the enemy. Another incendiary, the "J" bomb, a kind of flamethrower, was under development early in 1943, and I may as well give the lamentable history of this bomb. I was told in the middle of April, 1943, that it was going to be produced in quantity. In August the enthusiasts for the bomb staged a demonstration of it at my headquarters, where a little wooden house was built and a sample "J" bomb applied to it. I was not impressed by the design or effects of the bomb, though it certainly produced a rather spectacular jet of flame. Our own unit fire brigade did not altogether cover itself with glory on that occasion; they were supposed to put out the remains of the fire, but their hose went wrong and they only succeeded in giving me and some others a good sprinkling. After this trial I said that I did not want to judge the issue in advance, but I wanted to be certain that production of the "J" bomb would not hold up production of the 30 lb. phosphorous bomb. Later I found that essential pyrotechnic bombs for the Pathfinders were being held up because the "J" bomb was getting priority. When a small number of "J" bombs arrived in December—a large quantity had previously been promised by October or even earlier—the first type was unsatisfactory; we got a new type in February, 1944. Next spring and summer we tried out the "J" bomb ten times on operations, and conclusively proved that ton for ton it was just half as effective as the 4 lb. incendiary. This was a weapon which looked well on paper and was put into production without regard for the opinions or needs of the people who were going to use it. In any case, we really had no need for another incendiary bomb;

what we wanted, and what we could not get was some means of preventing the 4 lb. incendiary from scattering and of making it possible to aim it.

By contrast with the way things too often happen in this country the Americans show what seems to us a perfectly astounding speed and efficiency in getting things done when there is an emergency. But I do not think we have very far to look for the reason for this. If, for instance, a drastic modification is required for operational reasons to a Flying Fortress, the general who runs the Flying Fortresses says "get on with it," and they get on with it. But in England the matter is argued about by all sorts of junior officers at the Ministries concerned and then once again by all sorts of irresponsible and very often operationally ignorant officials in places like the Ministry of Aircraft Production. After that the manufacturer, who may not want to be bothered to undertake the modification, is very naturally inclined to play one Ministry against another, and both Ministries against the fighting man in the field. This eases the pressure, and he probably gets away with it and never has to make the modification.

Besides the instances I have given, there is the fact that it took me more than three years of bitter dispute and argument to fail to get a serviceable and useful .5 inch gun-turret through the official channels. The only time we were ever supplied with .5 inch armament as standard equipment, was when we got some American light bombers equipped with these guns for operations by No. 2 Group, which, of course, had really nothing to do with our main striking force and the main offensive. Early in the war it became obvious that our normal gun, the .303 inch, was of far too light a calibre for defence against the German night fighters, which had thick protective armour as well as guns of heavier calibre than ours. The result was that the bombers were invariably outranged while at normal range the .303 bullets would not penetrate the fighter's armour. Our turrets were also not well designed to give the gunner a good field of view or to enable air-crew to abandon ship with necessary speed. Eventually, as I had done before with the Hampden's armament, I despaired of the official channels and went again to Rose Brothers of Gainsborough. They produced a first-class turret of revolutionary design equipped with .5 guns, with a large field of view from which the gunner could readily escape if he had to; we had this in less than a year, and one whole Group, E. B. Rice's Group, was equipped with it. Rose's and Bomber Command personnel, including the technically minded Rice himself, worked together on the turret, and, of course, we should never have got it if we had not ordered it on our own and in an entirely irregular way.

The Americans would certainly have got their turret in a matter of months, but that is because their commanders in the field have the say-so, and this is not liable to be disputed by everyone in any appropriate or inappropriate ministry who thinks he knows better. Nor is his order subject to interference by pseudo-technicians and civil servants in the Supply ministries.

In my mind there is no doubt whatsoever that the main reason for the speed and efficiency with which the Americans get things done in war is simply because America has no civil service that can interfere. In the American fighting services they ask for the money they want as a lump sum, or for the aircraft they want as a round number, and once they get either of these they can do what they please with them, equipping or modifying their aircraft according to their own ideas. In war no system that makes for delay is tolerable.

After thirty years experience of working under the dead hand of the Civil Service, I am persuaded that the progressive multiplication of government regulations and controls, operated by civil servants who themselves are multiplying fast, is leading the country to catastrophe, complete, and perhaps irreparable. I have the greatest admiration for the integrity, ability, and immense capacity for grinding and often monotonous work which is indeed the hall-mark of the British civil servant. I have none whatever for the results, which have to be experienced to be believed, that he achieves in times of urgent national emergency.

I can recall one civil servant whose whole-hearted devotion to the country and to his work, was worth at least a division to the enemy on every day of the war. But for the human limitations of even his devotion to duty and to an eighteen-hour day he would undoubtedly have been worth two divisions. Luckily he was far from being typical, else should we have perished. Not for nothing was it said in the fighting services that had they only the King's Enemies to deal with—how easy that would be.

Chapter Eight

LONG RANGE ATTACKS

Targets in Eastern Germany. The use of H2S. Tactics and marking. The destruction of Hamburg. The Ethics of bombing. The jamming war begins. Peenemunde and the V-weapons. The Battle of Berlin. A revolution in tactics. The invasion of Europe ends the campaign of strategic bombing.

IT WAS essential, for the whole progress of the offensive, to be able to attack targets east of the Ruhr and beyond Oboe range. In June of 1943 I was instructed to give first priority to centres of German aircraft production, because of the growing strength of the German air force, which threatened both the bomber offensive itself and the projected invasion of Europe. The 8th United States Army Air Force was to attack the principal airframe and other aircraft factories while my Command was to attack those industrial towns in which there was the largest number of aircraft component factories; most of these towns, as it happened, were farther east or south than the Ruhr. But it was not only because of the intrinsic importance of the targets themselves that it was advisable to attack objectives farther inside Germany; there was also the risk that if I concentrated exclusively on north-west Germany for too long a time the enemy would shift his defences to that area, thereby economising in men and material and at the same time increasing our losses. During the late spring and early summer the short nights would inevitably confine our attacks to the west of Germany and largely to targets within Oboe range, but I had to take the earliest opportunity to carry out operations at greater range.

On June 20th-21st, 1943, when the nights were shortest, I laid on an attack on the former Zeppelin works at Friedrichshafen on the shores of Lake Constance, a factory which was producing radar apparatus. The defences there were comparatively light and the target would not be difficult to find, especially as a picked force of Lancaster crews of No. 5 Group was to make the attack. On this occasion No. 5 Group initiated a new tactic which was to be of the greatest importance in the later stages of the war; the whole attack was directed by an experienced officer who was in touch with the rest of the force by radio-telephone. It would, of course, have been quite impossible for aircraft to attack a target so far south in June and get back to base in darkness, but on this occasion it was arranged that the bombers should fly on to North Africa after attacking the Zeppelin works, land there and refuel and reload, and then fly home again, attacking the Italian naval base at Spezia on the way back. The Zeppelin works were in themselves an important target, but a further reason for carrying out this rather elaborate operation was that it would help to spread the enemy defences; Friedrichshafen had every reason to consider itself safe from attack, especially in the summer months, and this unexpectedly deep penetration might well cause other places outside the more vulnerable areas to scream for defences, and it might prevent the defences from being removed from similar areas. A "shuttle service" attack was not an operation that could be at all frequently carried out because, as I knew very well, bases outside England would not have any adequate facilities for maintaining and servicing heavy bombers; as it was, the arrangements on the airfield in North Africa where the Lancasters landed were far from satisfactory. But it was well worth while on this occasion to keep some of our Lancasters inactive for a week or so. The attack on Friedrichshafen was successful; the Zeppelin works were heavily damaged—about half its equipment was probably destroyed—and a tank engine factory close to the Zeppelin works was also damaged.

The only possible navigational and bombing aid for use outside Oboe range was H2S. At the beginning of 1943 we had very few aircraft equipped with H2S, and very little idea of the best method of using it in operations. During the first two or three months of 1943 we only had an average of about 14 aircraft equipped with H2S for use in any one attack, and it was obvious that for the time being H2S, like Oboe, would have to be used as a Pathfinder device. Later on we might be able to take advantage of the fact that H2S, unlike Oboe, could be used by an unlimited number of aircraft at the same time, but for the moment we had to base our tactics on the use of H2S by a small number of aircraft of the Pathfinder Force. On the other hand we knew already that H2S would not be as precise as Oboe and it was expected that some of the markers dropped on H2S alone, with no visual identification of the target, would scatter. To counteract this we used a new method of marking. After the first target indicators had been dropped blind by H2S the main force was instructed to aim, not at the markers themselves, but at what was estimated to be the centre of them, or to put it more technically, their mean point of impact. This was obviously a pretty difficult thing for the average crew to attempt under operational conditions and in the face of heavy defences, so to help the main force we appointed a number of Pathfinder crews flying heavy bombers to estimate this mean point of impact and mark it with target indicators of a different colour from those dropped by the first H2S marker aircraft.

The forces used to mark the mean point of impact were called "backers-up" and later "visual centerers." In the first H2S operation, against Hamburg on the night of January 30th-31st, 1943, there were five backers-up, but this proved to be far too few to keep up continuous marking throughout an attack, and thereafter we used about 20 backers-up. When the weather was good enough, the backers-up were instructed to look for the aiming point in the light of flares dropped by the H2S markers.

This plan of attack, though rather elaborate, sounded all right at first. In practice it worked badly, and out of 15 major operations with H2S marking in the next two months, only three could be considered reasonably successful. The H2S apparatus was liable to get unserviceable even more often than the Oboe equipment in the early stages of its use; scarcely more than half the sets worked properly in the average operation. Two few aircraft were equipped with H2S—it was not until September, 1943, that all the heavy bombers of the Pathfinder Force were so equipped—and in consequence far too few target indicators were burning at any given moment during the attack; this meant that it was impossible for the backers-up to strike a fair average and make any correct estimate of the mean point of impact. It was also found that bomb-aimers had a tendency not to rely on the H2S equipment but to aim their target indicators at what they could see; sometimes they would merely aim at target indicators already burning on the ground, and this, of course, made it quite impossible for the backers-up to strike a genuine average. As soon as this was discovered Pathfinder crews were, of course, most strictly instructed not to aim visually and they were told that if their H2S equipment was not working satisfactorily they were not to drop any markers at all. Another cause of failure was even more easily removed. Special target maps for use with H2S had been prepared in which the built-up areas had been drawn to look as far as possible like the actual image of them that would appear in the

H2S screen or cathode-ray tube, but it was found that these maps were not always up-to-date. On the night of February 19th-20th, 1943, the Pathfinders mistook a new suburban area in Wilhelmshaven, which had not been marked on their maps, for the actual target area. We had all the H2S target maps revised at once to accord with the latest air photographs of the targets.

There had been a great deal of scepticism in the early days of the war about whether H2S could ever be developed beyond the point of being a mere scientific curiosity; the idea of being able to see what amounted to a complete map of a town in total darkness or through unbroken cloud, is indeed, so astonishing that there is no wonder that some too hard-headed people had their doubts about it. For myself in spite of my wide experience of lunatics and lunatic weapons, I have seen too many apparently mad ideas put into practice to reject one of them, provided it is backed by men who obviously knew their job. But it must be admitted that some of our first experiences with H2S did suggest that the scientists had been rather optimistic about it. In practice there was sometimes little or no relation between the real shape of a town and the image of it that appeared in the H2S apparatus; it seemed that much depended on the angle or direction from which the town was viewed. In fact, it was impossible without previous experience to predict exactly how any particular town was going to show up in the H2S apparatus, with the result that only the most skilful and experienced navigators could use H2S with any real accuracy; this meant that there were bound to be a good many failures while crews were still new to the job. It was found that the difference between land and water showed up far more clearly than the difference between buildings and open ground, which meant that costal targets could be more easily identified than targets inland. It was also found that small towns were more easily attacked by H2S than large built-up areas, because it was fairly easy to identify the town as a whole but extremely difficult, in most cases, to distinguish any particular area in the town from the town as a whole.

In the course of the preliminary and experimental phase in the operational use of H2S my Command carried out three attacks on Berlin. It may be remembered that I had been continually pressed to attack the German capital during 1942 and had resisted making any attack while my force was still too small to attack so well-defended a target; in January, 1943, when the force was just large enough to stand some chance against the defences of

Berlin, I had laid on two attacks in which the target was to be identified visually and without any navigational aids. By March of the same year we were getting very near the time when Berlin would be outside the range of heavy bombers in the hours of darkness, it was obviously of great importance not to prolong the immunity of the German capital, and H2S gave us a better chance than we had had before of getting some concentration of attack.

The first H2S attack on Berlin was on the night of March 1st-2nd. The target was so large that the responses from its buildings entirely filled the H2S screen and it was quite impossible to identify the aiming point. However, the attack caused serious damage in the south western suburbs, about six miles from the actual aiming point, destroying many factories, business premises and houses. Two further attacks on Berlin towards the end of March revealed a new difficulty in attacking the city by H2S marking. This time it was decided to make timed runs from landmarks on the outside of Berlin which would give a good response on the H2S screen, but it was difficult to find any landmark which fulfilled the condition. On the night of March 29th-30th, a lake, the Müggel See, was used as the landmark from which to begin a timed run, and this was in fact visually identified in the light of flares. Unfortunately, although everything went well with the marking, bad weather on the route prevented the main force from arriving in time to bomb before the target indicators had gone out. In another attack in March, the markers themselves were wrongly placed. For the two attacks in January and three of March of this year, our casualty rate was 4.6 per cent, which was remarkably low for so difficult, distant, and well-defended a target. Moreover, much heavier losses might have been expected owing to the fact that in these March attacks on Berlin I was compelled to include Halifaxes and Stirlings in the force. In the January attacks of the same year I had sent all-Lancaster forces, because of their greater bomb load and higher ceiling, but there were really not enough Lancasters then either to saturate the defences or do any serious damage to so large a target; by March I still did not have enough Lancasters for the task and so I reluctantly had to send Stirlings and Halifaxes in spite of the great risk they ran from flak.

In April and May of 1943, my Command made two attempts to destroy the Skoda Armament Works at Pilsen which had become of much greater importance to the enemy now that

Krupps at Essen had been so heavily damaged. Unfortunately both attacks were unsuccessful; the bombing concentrations were remarkably good for so distant a target, but the main force had aimed with great accuracy at markers placed a mile or two away from the aiming point.

By April we had developed a standard H2S marking technique which, with some small changes, we continued to use until the end of the war. The attack began with a wave of H2S aircraft, all of which at the same moment dropped target indicators and illuminating flares. These aircraft were called "Blind Marker Illuminators" and they were followed about two minutes later by a smaller number of aircraft called "visual markers" who were to identify the target visually in the light of the flares dropped by the blind marker illuminators, and, when they had done this, to mark the aiming point with target indicators of another colour. If for any reason they could not identify the aiming point, they were not to drop their target indicators. Last came the "Backers-up" who would either aim more target indicators, at intervals of one or two minutes throughout the attack, at the target indicators laid by the visual markers, or, if the visual markers had failed to identify the aiming point, would strike an average of the target indicators dropped on H2S by the blind marker illuminators and mark their mean point of impact. Improvements in this technique were made from time to time, but the principle remained the same. The great merit of this technique was that it made every possible allowance for changes in the weather, and the Pathfinder Force was ready either for visual or for non-visual marking of the aiming point. Moreover, if it seemed probable that there would be so much cloud over the target that the normal target indicators would be hidden, the H2S aircraft had an alternative load of sky-marking flares, red with green stars, or green with red stars. If these had to be used, the subsequent technique was rather different. These flares normally drifted so much in the wind that it would have been hopeless to drop them at the beginning of the attack and trust to backers-up to keep the target continuously marked by aiming new flares at those previously dropped.

It was therefore necessary, when the cloud was very thick, for the H2S aircraft to drop their sky-markers not altogether at the beginning of the attack but at intervals throughout it. The difficulty was to plan an attack in such a way as to arrange for the H2S aircraft either to mark the target altogether, or simply at intervals, according to the state of the weather; it was obviously very difficult to organise an attack in such a way that either of two entirely different systems of timing could be used at the last moment. We did our best to get over this by dividing the H2S blind marking force into two sections, one to mark the target at the beginning of the attack and the other to mark it at intervals throughout the attack. But this meant that we had, in fact, to double the blind marking force if either method of marking was to be carried out really effectively, and we never had enough crews who were fully experienced in blind H2S marking for this. As a result, there was seldom any very close concentration of attack when the target was marked entirely by sky markers, though occasionally we did achieve a remarkable success.

Even when the target indicators could be clearly seen on the ground and had been accurately dropped around the aiming point a curious and rather unexpected difficulty turned up. If H2S had been as accurate as Oboe there would have been no trouble, but it never was, and therefore a very great deal depended on finding the mean point of impact of a considerable number of target indicators distributed over a comparatively large area. It was found that even when everything was satisfactory at the beginning of an H2S attack there was a persistent tendency for the focus of the bombing to shift gradually away from the aiming point, so much so that the whole attack might by the end have gradually shifted as much as three or four miles away from the the aiming point. The shift was always in one direction, towards the point from which the bombers approached the target. After considerable trouble, the reason for this shift was discovered. As the bombers approached the group of target indicators the bomb-aimers naturally saw these in perspective, and it is very easy to make a mistake in finding the centre of a surface seen in perspective. The reason for this can be most easily shown in a diagram. The natural tendency is to put the centre too near to the point from which one is looking at it. The result was that a large proportion of the backers-up as well as of the main force persistently undershot the aiming point, and this explains why the whole attack gradually shifted in the direction from which the bombers approached. We made an attempt to put this right by directing the backers-up to aim at the far side of the concentration of all the markers that could be seen, but there still remained a tendency for the attack to creep back from the aiming point; the tendency was not cured until a year later, when attacks became so concentrated in time that there was no need for backers-up and all the bombs could be aimed at the first markers dropped by the H2S marking force.

The Battle of the Ruhr was drawing to its close in July of 1943, the nights were getting longer, and we had to be ready to carry the offensive deeper into Germany. This, of course, would normally mean heavier casualties than in attacks on north-west Germany and the Battle of the Ruhr had not been won without heavy losses. In spite of the fact that our navigational aids gave essential protection against the enemy's fighters by enabling us to operate on dark and cloudy nights, in spite of the fact that we had achieved a remarkable concentration of the bomber force in time and space and by this means had sometimes cut down our losses to as low as 3 per cent in individual attacks, and in spite of the fact that we seldom went deep into Germany in the spring and early summer of 1943, the enemy had so effectively reinforced his defences, especially the night fighter force, that the situation was almost as serious as in 1942. We were once again getting very near the danger line when expansion would be seriously affected unless the losses could be cut down, and this at a time when we should have to accept the added risk of operating much farther east and south if we were to continue the offensive. It is true that we had the satisfaction of knowing that the harm we were doing to the enemy's war industry was out of all proportion to our own losses and that the enemy was only inflicting these losses on us by leaving the German army in Russia disastrously short of aircraft. But even so, and however great might be the strategic effects of our operations, it would be impossible to maintain the offensive unless something was done to cut our losses down.

There was also the danger that if our loss rate increased, or even if it remained steady at somewhere between 5 and 6 per cent of all sorties, we should find it increasingly difficult to make any accurate attack beyond Oboe range; with anything less than a foolproof navigational and bombing aid, and not even Oboe was that, the accuracy of attack would always be in inverse proportion to the strength of the defence, and the complicated H2S marking technique was most liable to go wrong when crews were distracted by an energetic defence.

As I have explained before, we had known the main answer to the German defences for a long time; there was every reason to believe that if the authorities would only allow us to drop strips of metallised paper during our attacks we should hopelessly confuse the enemy's radar on which he relied for the control of his night fighters and the accuracy of his gunfire. Early in 1943 there had already been developed a suitable form of this weapon for jamming the enemy's ground control stations, radar-sighted guns, and airborne radar for interception. And we had already worked out the quantity of strips of paper that would be required, the rate at which it should be dropped, and the areas over which it should be released. It cannot be said that there was ever an occasion when we did not need to use this weapon, but we needed it as much as ever before at the end of July, 1943, and it was just at that time that the Air Ministry after I had urged the use of this weapon at repeated intervals for many months, decided that it was now possible to accept the risk of the enemy using the same weapon against our own defences. The strips of paper—they were given the code name "Window"—were dropped for the first time on the night of July 24th-25th. The target was Hamburg, beyond Oboe range and therefore attacked by means of the standard H2S marking technique described above. Like other coastal targets, Hamburg was particularly easy to identify by H2S, for the outline of water gave us a clear response on the H2S screen. Some 700 aircraft attacked, and the weather was in every way favourable.

A publication intended only for German official use describes what happened. On the night of July 24th-25th our attack caused gigantic fires which could not be put out even after 24 hours had elapsed.

> "Coal and coke supplies stored for the winter in many houses caught fire and could only be extinguished weeks later. Essential services were severely damaged and telephone services were cut early in the attack. Dockyards and industrial installations were severely hit. At mid-day next day there was still a gigantic, dense cloud of smoke and dust hovering over the city which, despite the clear sky, prevented the sun from penetrating through. . . . Despite employment of all available force, big fires could not be prevented from flaring up again and again."

This was the most successful operation so far carried out by H2S and it was one of the heaviest attacks which the Command had yet made. But the damage as yet was not much beyond what the Ruhr had already experienced. Two nights later, when the

Command again attacked with a force of about the same size, there occurred an event which in the words of a German secret document, went "beyond all human imagination." This was the fire-storm or fire typhoon, which to judge from the German descriptions of it must have been even more cataclysmic than the bursting of the two atom bombs over Japanese cities: To quote again from the German secret document:

"The alternative dropping of block busters (4000 lb. high capacity bombs) high explosives, and incendiaries, made fire-fighting impossible, small fires united into conflagrations in the shortest time and these in turn led to the fire storms. To comprehend these . . . one can only analyse them from a physical, meteorological angle. Through the union of a number of fires, the air gets so hot that on account of its decreasing specific weight, it receives a terrific momentum, which in its turn causes other surrounding air to be sucked towards the centre. By that suction, combined with the enormous difference in temperature (600-1000 degrees centigrade) tempests are caused which go beyond their meteorological counterparts (20-30 centigrades). In a built-up area the suction could not follow its shortest course, but the overheated air stormed through the street with immense force taking along not only sparks but burning timber and roof beams, so spreading the fire farther and farther, developing in a short time into a fire typhoon such as was never before witnessed, against which every human resistance was quite useless."

Another report says that the fire storms were so violent and the suction so strong that trees were pulled out of the ground. But this was not the end of the battle of Hamburg. On the night of July 29th-30th my Command attacked again in force, and the German impression was that this was the heaviest of all attacks in terms of the weight of bombs dropped. On this night most of the destruction was in areas that had not been hit before. The official German report described the attack as follows:

"The failure of the water system and the fires which still remained from earlier attacks severely hampered all work. The whole of Hamburg was on fire. Rescue . . . evacuation, clearing of vital roads, fire fighting, etc., asked the impossible from all available forces. Economically, Hamburg was knocked out, as even the undamaged parts had to stop work on account of the destruction of water, gas and electricity supplies."

After the attack on the night of July 27th-28th hundreds of thousands of the inhabitants of Hamburg were evacuated and only the defence forces were left behind.

A further heavy attack was made on the night of August 2nd-3rd, but weather proved unexpectedly bad, with thick icing clouds over the target. No real concentration of attack was achieved and we lost a number of aircraft because of the appalling weather. The U.S. Eighth Air Force made two small scale day attacks, dispatching 235 aircraft altogether, on July 25th and 26th, and on the nights when Bomber Command did not operate in force the attack was continued by small forces of Mosquitoes which made nuisance raids. Excluding the attack on the night of August 2nd-3rd, Bomber Command made 2353 sorties against Hamburg on three nights and dropped 7196 tons of bombs. It was some time before the smoke of the burning city cleared away and air photographs of the damage could be taken. When this was done there was at last revealed a scene of unimaginable devastation. 6200 acres in the most densely built-up district had been destroyed, 74 per cent of the mostly closely built-up parts of the city. All four of Hamburg's main shipbuildings yards, in which great numbers of U-boats had been built, were severely damaged, and it was clear that all work and transport in the city had been stopped.

The use of Window had an immediate effect. On the first night of the attack the night of July 24th-25th, the radar-controlled searchlights waved aimlessly in all directions, the gunfire was inaccurate, and in England the stations which intercepted the enemy's wireless traffic were immediately aware of hopeless confusion in the German ground control stations. In fact, the ground controllers gave the whole situation up, their instruments behaved as though the sky was filled with thousands of hostile aircraft, and they had to tell the night fighters they were controlling that they could do nothing to help them. A ground controller was overheard saying, "I cannot follow any of the hostiles—they are very cunning." In the three main night attacks of July the Command lost 57 aircraft, 2.4 per cent of all sorties; the average loss rate for all previous attacks on Hamburg, a rather distant and very well defended target, had been 6 per cent. It is true that in the unsuccessful attack on Hamburg on the night of August 2nd-3rd our casualties amounted to 4.1 per cent of all sorties dispatched, but this was almost entirely the result of the extremely bad weather, and especially of the icing conditions.

At that moment Germany was therefore faced with a double catastrophe. No air raid ever known before had been so terrible as that which Hamburg had endured; the second largest city in Germany, with a population of nearly 2,000,000, had been wiped out in three nights. And at the same time the whole system of air defence, carefully built up, at the expense of all the other battle fronts in which the Germans were fighting, over a period of years, had been thrown into utter confusion; the night fighters, it appeared, would in future be powerless to detect the bombers in the dark, and the guns and searchlights would be altogether inefficient. The first type of Window used by Bomber Command in the attacks on Hamburg was designed to confuse the enemy's Wurzburgs, used both for ground control of fighters and for gun laying, and we knew at once that it had been successful in this. But the enemy also knew what we discovered later, that Window seriously interfered with the night fighters' airborne radar as well.

It is not surprising that the disaster of Hamburg terrified the German war leaders. "We were of the opinion," Speer said in his interrogation in July, 1945, "that a rapid repetition of this type of attack upon another six German towns would inevitably cripple the will to sustain armament manufacture and war production. It was I who first verbally reported to the Fuehrer at that time that a continuation of these attacks might bring about a rapid end to the war."

In spite of all that happened at Hamburg, bombing proved a comparatively humane method. For one thing, it saved the flower of the youth of this country and of our allies from being mown down by the military in the field, as it was in Flanders in the war of 1914-1918. But the point is often made that bombing is specially wicked because it causes casualties among civilians. This is true, but then all wars have caused casualties among civilians. For instance, after the last war the British Government issued a White Paper in which it was estimated that our blockade of Germany had caused nearly 800,000 deaths—naturally these were mainly of women and children and old people because at all costs the enemy had had to keep his fighting men adequately fed, so that most of what food there was went to them. This was a death-rate much in excess of the ambition of even the most ruthless exponents of air frightfulness. It is not easy to estimate what in effect were the casualties caused by allied bombing in Germany because the German records were incomplete and often unreliable, but the Americans have put the number of deaths at 305,000. There is no estimate of how many of these were women and children, but there was no reason why bombing, like the blockade, should fall most heavily on women and children; on the contrary, the Germans carried out large schemes of evacuation, especially of children, from the main industrial cities.

Whenever the fact that our aircraft occasionally killed women and children is cast in my teeth I always produce this example of the blockade, although there are endless others to be got from the wars of the past. I never forget, as so many do, that in all normal warfare of the past, and of the not distant past, it was the common practice to besiege cities and, if they refused to surrender when called upon with due formality to do so, every living thing in them was in the end put to the sword. Even in the more civilised times of to-day the siege of cities, accompanied by the bombardment of the city as a whole, is still a normal practice; in no circumstances were women and children allowed to pass out of the city, because their presence in it and their consumption of food would inevitably hasten the end of the siege. And as to bombardment, what city in what war has ever failed to receive the maximum bombardment from all enemy artillery within range so long as it has continued resistance?

International law can always be argued pro and con, but in this matter of the use of aircraft in war there is, it so happens, no international law at all. There was never any agreement about it, with the single exception that about the time of the siege of Paris in the war of 1870 the French and Germans came to an agreement between themselves that neither side should drop explosives from free balloons.

Immediately after Hamburg the Germans found themselves almost defenceless against air attack, but they reacted to the situation with remarkable energy and promptness. Almost at once, they improvised a fighter defence system on altogether new lines. The Observer Corps plotted the main bomber stream and orders were broadcast to large numbers of fighters with a running commentary giving the height, direction and whereabouts of the bomber stream, and of the probable target for which it was making or the actual target which it was attacking. The fighters were not otherwise in touch with the ground, but until the bombers' target had been guessed they were kept circling round a number of beacons. Then, when the defence organisation had made up its mind about the target, the fighters were at once sent there, with the object of intercepting the bombers over the target or of following and intercepting them on the return flight. The fighters were now far more dependent than they had been before on visually intercepting the bombers by night, and to help them the enemy used great numbers of searchlights in the target area; the searchlights were used either to catch the bombers in their cones or to light up the cloud base so that the bombers could be seen from above silhouetted against the clouds. At the same time some of the enemy fighters were detailed to drop large numbers of illuminating flares over the targets or to lay these in lanes along the bomber's probable route as they ran up to the target or left it. A considerable number of single-engined fighters were also thrown into the battle, and used to intercept the bombers over the target.

This method of defence did achieve some success, even in the first few weeks of its use, but it had great disadvantages and could not compare in efficiency with the old method which Window had destroyed. The main drawback was that it was extremely difficult to get the fighters to the target in time; often they arrived there too late and consequently made no interceptions at all. We took advantage of the enemy's disadvantage in two ways. We decided to cut down the length of every attack, sending the bombers over the target at the rate of 30 a minute, instead of 10 a minute as before. Ten a minute had been considered about the greatest concentration compatible with a reasonable degree of immunity from collision or from falling bombs and there had previously been no reason to increase it; now we decided to accept the greater risk from collision and falling bombs because by escaping the enemy fighters we should save far more aircraft than we lost. This new tactic worked, and it became quite usual for the bombers to be well on their way home before the enemy controllers got the fighters over the target. At the same time it was realised that the ground controllers, who had to make rapid inferences about the direction and aim of the bomber stream from the reports of the Observer Corps, could be easily misled. At the first the enemy added to his own confusion by employing several controllers who were naturally apt to issue contradictory instructions to the patrolling fighters, but he gradually saw the folly of this and it became the usual practice for authority to be given to one controller who directed the whole available fighter force at the time. Even so, it was easy for us to add to the controller's problems. We worked out erratic routes for the bomber stream so that the controllers were being continually deceived about our probable target and we carried out small diversionary attacks, usually made by small forces of Mosquitoes which took the same route as the main force for most of the way to the target. The main force then suddenly altered course and attacked the real target.

The controller's running commentary was also susceptible to interference, and we used two methods to deal with it. A number of our aircraft were fitted with equipment for jamming the transmission of the commentary, and this worked very well until the enemy began using several frequencies at once. In turn, we divided the aircraft equipped with jamming apparatus into several sections, each of them jamming the enemy's broadcast on a different wave length. This, of course, meant that the jamming was not so intense as when all the aircraft were interfering with one frequency, but it forced the night fighter crews to waste time going from one frequency to another to find the one on which the controller's instructions could be clearly heard. Besides this, we set up ground stations in England to broadcast on the same frequencies that the enemy used for his running commentary, which was not in code—there would have been no time for the air-crew to decipher code messages of any length— but in straightforward German. There was an obvious temptation to broadcast misleading or contradictory instructions to the German night fighters; we could, for example, have sent the enemy fighters to Essen when the bombers were due to attack Berlin. But this, it was realised, would be far too dangerous. The night fighter crews would not be able to distinguish the false from the genuine instructions, but the ground controllers would, and would therefore be able to get useful imformation and make valuable deductions from what we were broadcasting; in the attempt to mislead, we might on occasion give the enemy a very good idea of the real target and lose a hundred or more aircraft. Our broadcasts therefore confined themselves to telling the enemy air-crew to land, warning them that weather at their bases was deteriorating, or making tuning transmissions. All this distracted the German crews, shook their confidence in the genuine running commentary, and wasted the very short time that they had in which to reach the real target. We had evidence of the effectiveness of this method when we began to hear the enemy controllers lose their tempers.

The enemy reacted by prefacing his messages with code numbers, but we were prepared for this and almost immediately used the same code numbers. On one occasion the enemy suddenly got a woman to broadcast the running commentary, but this had been expected and a German-speaking woman was already waiting at our broadcasting station to take over from our announcer. From time to time, while our announcers took a rest, we broadcast lively extracts from Hitler's speeches to the German air-crew. It was very satisfactory to imagine the irritation of the enemy crews as they flew aimlessly about in darkness, trying to pick up the instructions they knew were being broadcast to them but getting only the screams of their Fuehrer.

It was in point of fact a physical impossibility for Bomber Command, at this stage of its expansion and equipment, to do what, in Speer's opinion, would have brought the war quickly to an end. Even with all the luck in the world, we could not have hoped to destroy in a brief space of time six more great cities as effectively as Hamburg had been destroyed. There was no great city within Oboe range which had not already been effectively attacked, and to find new targets even half or a third the size of Hamburg, we should have had to go as far afield as Dresden or Breslau. Weather, the size of the force, and the limitations of H2S, stood in the way. It is true that there was Berlin which in a short time would come within range of night attack as the hours of darkness increased. To damage Berlin as Hamburg had been damaged would have been a shattering and possibly even a decisive blow to the enemy, and the Germans were waiting in horrified suspense for this to happen. But if other great cities were difficult targets for attack beyond Oboe range and by H2S alone, Berlin was the most difficult of them all.

At the earliest opportunity, a month after the destruction of Hamburg, we did in fact attack the German capital, but not with any hope of burning any very great proportion of it to the ground. The moment the nights were long enough and the weather reasonably favourable I dispatched 1647 aircraft against Berlin in three attacks within ten days. In the first of these attacks the Pathfinders attempted to get an H2S fix, from which to fly to the real aiming point in the centre of the city, on a feature which showed up very clearly on a map or air photograph of the town. This was a built-up area projecting outwards from the main part of the city in the shape of a hook; theoretically it ought to have come out very clearly on the H2S screen, but in practice it did not. In the second attack, the Pathfinders again tried to use this projecting bit of the city to get an H2S fix, but this time there was yet another cause of failure; the winds were wrongly predicted, and in consequence the main force came in to attack on the wrong track and at the wrong time. In the third attack, which was on the night of September 4th-5th, we reverted to the method of making a timed run from the same lake, the Müggel See, which had been used as a landmark in the attacks of the previous March. Once again, the attack was not made near the real aiming point, which escaped damage. But as against this, a large area in the suburbs was destroyed. In all, about 560 acres of Berlin had now been destroyed, and the last three attacks had also caused serious industrial damage in the Siemenstadt and Mariendorf districts.

Berlin is a city half the size of London, and 500 acres were therefore not at all a large area of devastation in proportion to the whole, especially as very little of this damage was in the most densely built-up areas of the city. Nevertheless it was enough with the Germans still under the influence of the catastrophe at Hamburg, to cause a panic evacuation; many observers said that the crowds leaving the city were as large and as terrified as those which had fled from Hamburg itself.

Meanwhile the enemy had for years been preparing an attack on England by wholly new weapons. Even before the war we had been warned of the possibility that the Germans were attempting to develop long-range projectiles such as rockets, and in the summer of 1943 the threat was obviously becoming serious and was taken very seriously by the British Government. The Germans had no bombers with which to attack our cities, largely because our area bombing had put the whole German air force on the defensive, but it looked very much as though the Germans were going to develop a very efficient substitute; in fact, their discoveries might well have made all bombers obsolete; there were, for example, quite substantial reports of a rocket weighing 80 tons with a warhead containing ten tons of explosive. In 1943, to raise morale at a time when terrific damage was being done to the German cities, the enemy were uttering a series of threats about new secret weapons to be used against the English; but we had much better information to go upon than this. It was known that these secret weapons were being developed at a particular place, a large research establishment and factory on the shores of the Baltic, at Peenemunde.

On July 7th I held a conference at my headquarters to consider the best method of attacking this objective. It must be remembered that at that time our only successful attacks on single factories in Germany had been made by small forces of exceptionally experienced crews, either in daylight, or, as in the attack on the Heinkel aircraft works at Rostock in the spring of 1942 or in the shuttle attack on the Zeppelin works at Friedrichshafen, when there was an unusually good chance of identifying the target by night. In the attack on Peenemunde, I knew that I should have to use the main force to ensure the destruction of a target of such great strategic importance; and that the attack would have to be made in moonlight; there could be no question of trusting only to H2S for the identification and marking of a target of this nature and Peenemunde was far beyond Oboe range. Even in moonlight, it would be an extremely difficult task to destroy the whole establishment. Its buildings lay scattered in a narrow strip along the coast line and there was obviously a great risk of wasting most of the bomb load unless some new method of attack was devised; there would clearly have to be several aiming points with different sections of the force assigned to each of them. It was also known that Peenemunde had a smoke screen and, though the target indicators would show through this and timed runs from a marked position outside the smoke screen would help, the marking itself would be a complicated business.

The tactics eventually adopted were a combination of the normal Pathfinder tactics and those worked out by No. 5 Group for attacks by specially experienced crews. There was, for example, a Master Bomber to assess the accuracy of marking and to give instructions by radio telephone to the whole force; it will be remembered that 5 Group had used this tactic in the previous June in an attack on Friedrichshaven. The main force bombed target indicators dropped by the Pathfinders and were guided by route markers laid by them, but a force of Lancasters from 5 Group were to attack separately in the later stages of the attack, when there was reason to fear that the markers would be obscured by smoke, by making a time and distance run from Rügen Island, a convenient landmark close to Peenemunde. If, when the crews had made their time and distance run, they found that the Pathfinders' target indicators coincided with the position they had reached, then they were to bomb there. If the target indicators were obscured, or obviously misplaced, the crews were to bomb on the time and distance run alone; in any case they were to be guided by the instructions of the Master Bomber provided by the Pathfinder Force. It was clear that such tactics could not be efficiently used without previous training, and exercises in tracking and timing were carried out for several days before the attack over country near one of our bombing ranges where the coastline and other landmarks bore some resemblance to the neighbourhood of Peenemunde. The value of such exercises was shown by the fact that in the first practice errors of 1000 yards and more were common, but in the last practice the margin of error was cut down to 300 yards. The important point was that the Island of Rügen, from which the time and distance runs were to be made, should be visible on the night of the operation.

It was obviously essential not to cause alarm and despondency in England by publishing the reason for this operation and the implied fact that the Government was treating the threat of the German secret weapons so seriously; it was even necessary to keep this fact from the bomber crews themselves because if not there would certainly have been an eventual leakage. At briefing the crews were therefore told that some highly specialised radar equipment was being made and developed at Peenemunde and that if this was not stopped the German night fighter defence would be greatly improved and our own bomber casualties would rapidly increase. The crews were also told that this was a matter of such extreme importance that if the operation failed of its object on the first night it would have to be repeated on the next night, and on all suitable nights thereafter, regardless of casualties and regardless of the fact that the enemy would obviously do everything possible to increase the defences of the place after the first attack. This warning would, it was hoped, ensure that the crews would make even greater efforts than usual to destroy the target in one attack. They were to bomb from 8000 feet, much below the usual operational height.

We had to accept the grave risk of operating in moonlight against a distant target close to many fighter defended areas, but everything possible was done to protect the bomber force. The route taken was almost the same as that used in previous attacks on Berlin, and in order to make the enemy think that Berlin was going to be the target, a small force of Mosquitoes was sent to attack it.

About 600 aircraft were dispatched on the night of August

17th-18th, the earliest occasion when there was bright moonlight, reasonably suitable weather, and sufficient hours of darkness to allow the flight over enemy territory to be made between nautical twilight in the evening and the morning. The weather close to the target was worse than had been expected, with a good deal of cloud about, so that it was difficult to find the required landmarks. But towards Rügen Island the weather cleared, and it was therefore possible for many crews to start their time and distance runs punctually from this island. Over the target there was again a good deal of cloud and the smoke screen was working, but the very careful planning of the attack ensured a good concentration of bombs on all the aiming points. The master bomber's instructions proved very helpful. It is clear that the enemy was at first deceived by the feint attack on Berlin, but not for long enough for the bomber force to get right away before the fighters came up; the last part of the force was intercepted and in bright moonlight 40 of them were shot down, a serious loss but by no means as serious as it might well have been. There was heavy damage to almost every section of the establishment and before long it was known that the enemy's casualties had been heavy and that many scientists and important members of the staff had been killed.

This was the first counter-attack delivered by the allies against the enemy's V-weapon offensive. A year later the Eighth United States Army Air Force carried out three attacks on Peenemunde, where the research station had been constructed, and of course, a vast bomb load was eventually dropped by allied bombers on the V-weapon launching sites, as will be described later. The "Overall Report" of the United States Strategic Bombing Survey, issued in September, 1945, says that Bomber Command's attack left the experimental work at Peenemunde unaffected, and suggests that the three later attacks by the American bombers, though they were made after the development of V.1 (flying bombs) had been completed, may possible have had some effect on the development of V.2 (rockets). In point of fact it was noticeable that after Bomber Command's attack on Peenemunde the enemy became much less definite in the threats he uttered about the secret weapons he was preparing for England: in particular he ceased to mention any specific dates when the V-weapons could be expected. There was never, of course, any question of putting a complete stop to the use of V-weapons by bombing Peenemunde; we knew very well by then that if the enemy chose to give first priority to the production of anything, a single attack on any plant could only cause a delay of a month or two at the most. But in the war of V-weapons time was everything and every delay we could cause the enemy, however brief, was thoroughly worth while.

The destruction of Hamburg was, and remained, the greatest success gained by the use of H2S; by itself, it would have more than justified the time and labour spent on developing equipment. But H2S continued to be an uncertain bombing aid, and not only when used against Berlin; it was the exception rather than the rule for an attack which depended on H2S marking to go completely according to plan. A new type of H2S was, however, expected before long, which it was hoped, would give a much clearer definition of landmarks; this was H2S Mark III, working on a shorter wave length. But in the meanwhile, in the autumn of 1943, the ordinary type of H2S did bring about a few remarkable successes. In a devastating attack on Kassel on the night of October 22nd-23rd, more than 90 per cent of the whole bomb load fell on the target and attacks on Mannheim on the night of September 5th-6th and on Hanover on October 8th-9th were extremely successful. Towns were now being chosen for attack because they were centres of German aircraft production and in these and later attacks on other large cities the direct damage to aircraft assembly and component factories was very heavy.

By the end of September, 1943, H2S was being supplied to the main force; all the heavy aircraft of the Pathfinder Force were by then equipped with it. A question of policy then had to be decided, whether H2S should continue to be used as a Pathfinding device, or whether it should be used as an instrument for blind bombing as had been originally intended. The fact that attacks were always more successful when the H2S marking could be checked by visual identification of the aiming point suggested that there was little to gain by experimenting with a new technique, but on the night of November 17th-18th 83 aircraft of the Pathfinder Force made an experimental blind bombing attack with H2S on Mannheim-Ludwigshafen, two cities only separated from each other by the Rhine. No markers were dropped and the crews were all instructed to bomb on H2S alone. The radar people were much excited by this experiment, and it did, in fact, achieve some success. Sixty per cent of the bombs were estimated to have dropped in the target area, and 50 per cent within a mile and a half of the aiming point. But these results were got by the highly trained crews of the Pathfinder Force, all of them experienced in the use of the H2S apparatus; it is very unlikely that crews of the main force would have done so well. H2S was, however, of great value to the main force as an aid to navigation on the route, and routes were often chosen which took the force over landmarks which showed up well on the screen. By the end of the year 12 squadrons of the main force were equipped with H2S.

By the middle of November a number of Pathfinder aircraft were equipped with H2S Mark III, and the Command had also got an instrument, the Ground Position Indicator, which made it possible to carry out accurate timed runs even in very heavily defended areas. This, then, was in my judgment the right moment to begin the really heavy attack on Berlin which was so long overdue. It was, of course, most unfortunate that we had not been able to begin the Battle of Berlin as soon after the destruction of Hamburg as the nights were long enough. We should then have been able to strike just when everybody in Berlin, and for that matter in Germany, had been thrown into a state of panic by the news of what happened to Hamburg. And we should also have been able to take advantage of the confusion into which the use of Window had thrown the defences; by November, the fighter defence had been reorganised and strongly reinforced, though even so it was not as effective as it had been just before the use of Window. But the three attacks on Berlin which we had carried out in September had altogether failed to hit the centre of the city and until we got the new type of H2S I considered it better to attack other cities which we had a much greater chance of destroying, especially as any attack on Berlin, even after the first disorganisation of the enemy's ground control system, was bound to be more costly than an attack on any other target within reasonable range. Moreover there was this advantage in attacking Berlin during the winter months that at this time of year bombing efficiency was invariably reduced, but not proportionately so much in attacks on Berlin, because of the great size of the target, as on any other town.

The Battle of Berlin, as it came to be called, began on the night of November 18th-19th and lasted until the middle of March, 1944; in all, my Command made sixteen major attacks on the German capital. The whole battle was fought in appalling weather and in conditions resembling those of no other campaign in the history of warfare. Scarcely a single crew caught a single glimpse of the objective they were attacking and for long periods we were wholly ignorant, except from such admissions as the enemy made from time to time, of how the battle was going. Thousands upon thousands of tons of bombs were aimed at the Pathfinders' pyrotechnic sky-markers and fell through unbroken cloud which concealed everything below it except the confused glare of fires. Scarcely any photographs taken during the bombing showed anything except clouds, and day after day reconnaissance aircraft flew over the capital to return with no information. We knew, of course, from what the Germans said, that we were hitting Berlin, but we had little idea of which attacks had been successful and which had gone astray. Then, after six attacks, a reconnaissance aircraft did bring back some not very clear photographs which showed that we had at last succeeded in hitting the enemy's capital hard; there were many hundreds of acres of devastation, particularly in the western half of the city and round the Tiergarten. Then the clouds closed again over Berlin and the Command made eight more attacks without any means of discovering whether all or any of them had been as successful as the first six raids. It was not until March was far advanced and the nights were too short for any but Mosquito attacks on Berlin that an aircraft brought back more photographs and it was possible to assess the results of the Battle of Berlin as a whole.

Judged by the standards of our attacks on Hamburg, the Battle of Berlin did not appear to be an overwhelming success. With many times as many sorties, a far greater bomb load, and ten times as many casualties, we appeared to have succeeded in destroying about a third of the acreage destroyed in the attack on Hamburg; the actual figure, as far as it could then be estimated from air photographs, was 2180 acres over and above the 500 or so acres destroyed before the main Battle of Berlin began. But by comparison with the results of all earlier attacks on Berlin it was a devastating blow, and the industrial damage, as often happened in rather scattered attacks, was particularly heavy; among the factories damaged were many of the largest and most important plants for the production of war material in Germany, and government offices of all kinds were very heavily damaged, so that a number of government departments had to be evacuated. Moreover, it seems that we underestimated the effects of our bombing at the time. When complete photographic cover of Berlin was obtained at the end of the war, it was found that 6340 acres of the main built-up areas had been destroyed. Of this total 1000 acres had been destroyed in American daylight attacks and subsequent Mosquito attacks also did considerable damage, but all the rest must have been done in the main Battle of Berlin.

The Battle of Berlin cost us 300 aircraft missing, which was a loss rate of 6.4 per cent. This could not be considered excessive for a prolonged assault on this distant, most difficult, and most heavily defended target; it was equivalent to the loss rate, before the use of Window, against Hamburg, which was less heavily defended than Berlin and could be attacked after only a short flight over enemy territory. But it did mean that the enemy had succeeded in reorganising his defences and finding new tactics.

In spite of our jamming and interference with the instructions broadcast to fighters, and although all routes were worked out whenever possible with the intention of deceiving the enemy, our losses began to rise soon after the beginning of the Battle of Berlin and the opposition was no longer mainly over the target and on the return flight, but on the outward journey. It was clear that the long flights over Germany to Berlin and other eastern targets gave the enemy controllers ample time in which to get the fighters together from all over Germany and then direct them to the area within which it was judged that the bombers would attack. Against this we devised a new kind of routeing; the bombers now took a course towards an important target and then turned at the last possible moment towards the real objective. But by the new year the enemy had given up directing the fighters to any particular area; they now were sent directly from the beacons they were orbiting into the bomber stream as it flew across Germany, or even when it was still on its way across the North Sea. These tactics were not invariably successful, but when the fighters did get into the bomber stream and the weather was reasonably favourable for interception, then our losses were much above the average; in some attacks in February, 1944, we lost between 70 and 80 aircraft, though on other nights the bombers were able to make as deep penetrations with a loss of only one or two per cent of the force. It was also discovered, towards the beginning of 1944, as we had always anticipated, that the enemy was using the route markers dropped by the Pathfinders as landmarks and turning points as a guide to the movements and whereabouts of the bomber stream. To counter this, Mosquitoes were sent out to drop misleading route-markers and also fighter flares similar to those used by the enemy, but before long it was decided that it would be best to abandon our route-markers altogether; the main force was now largely equipped with H2S, the standard of navigation was much improved by this and other measures, and route markers were no longer indispensable.

On the night of November 3rd-4th, 1943, the monitoring station in England heard the powerful broadcast station at Stuttgart interrupt its programme and issue brief instructions to fighters. This was clear proof that our jamming and interference had been highly effective against the special broadcasts to the fighter force, but by using such a powerful station as Stuttgart the enemy might have got away with it if we had not been fortunate enough to have an even more powerful broadcasting station in the country with which to jam the Stuttgart station. After a while our jamming made the enemy abandon this method, but he still used Stuttgart. After a careful watch on the ordinary broadcast programme it was suspected that the enemy was using it to convey messages in code to the fighters; one kind of music, or the playing of a particular musical instrument, meant a particular area in Germany and indicated that the target had already been attacked or conveyed an instruction to land. This was obviously a cumbrous and uncertain method of broadcasting orders, but it was the best the enemy could do.

The jamming war, against the enemy's early warning system, radar of all kinds, and communication with the night fighter force, had become so complicated that in December, 1943, we formed a new group, 100 Group, which did no bombing but was entirely concerned with this new and highly scientific kind of warfare. 100 Group's heavy bombers, which included a number of Fortresses because these could fly at a greater height than our own night bombers, carried the very large and complicated machines that were now being used for jamming, and some squadrons of the Group flew Mosquito fighters equipped with an instrument for homing on the enemy night fighters' airborne radar used for interception of bombers in the dark. These Mosquitoes were flown by a number of the most experienced night-fighter crews in England; they had gained their experience with Fighter Command, but now that German bombing attacks on this country were negligible, they were transferred to Bomber Command and so went over to the offensive. The formation of such a specialist group was put forward from Bomber Command in June, 1943, approved by the Air Ministry at the end of September, and ready to operate on a small scale in December.

In spite of all the various ways in which we hindered the enemy's defences, our casualties continued to increase until February, 1944, and in that month I decided that a complete revision of our ever-changing tactics was again necessary. The great thing was to avoid whenever possible a single stream of bombers making a deep penetration into Germany; such a stream could be easily plotted and intercepted before it reached the target. As an alternative, we could divide the striking force into two parts, and either send the two forces to two different targets or to the same target by different routes; this should effectively divide and confuse the enemy's air defence and the two shorter bomber streams should be more difficult to plot. Or again, two separate attacks could be made on the same target on the same night, with a long enough interval of time between them to ensure that the fighter force which had gone up to attack the first bomber force would have landed and dispersed itself when the second bomber force arrived. Diversionary attacks by Mosquitoes were by now having little effect and the enemy appeared to have no difficulty in distinguishing between those and the main assault; it was therefore decided in February that comparatively large forces of heavy bombers should in future be used for diversions. We therefore dispatched minelaying aircraft in considerable numbers by routes which would suggest to the enemy that they were coming to attack a town, and we also sent out forces of several hundred bombers from the operational training units and heavy conversion training units which flew across the North Sea until they were near the enemy coast and could be plotted, when they at once turned back and made for home.

As soon as possible, we abolished the use of route markers, because it was known that the enemy was using them for his own purposes; an obvious plan to use radio transmitters dropped at turning points on the route had to be reluctantly abandoned because of the difficulty of procuring such equipment. And we decided to use a southern route across France and Germany as often as possible, because we had learnt that the enemy's defences were much less efficiently organised there than in the north and west. The essence of the new tactics was variety; it was important to use as many different methods of confusing the enemy as possible and to see that no one of these methods was used too frequently or for too long a time.

The effect of these new tactics was almost immediate. In

attacks on targets in Germany our loss rate for the first two operations in February was 7.1 per cent, and for the last three attacks in February 3.3 per cent. At the end of March our casualties went up again because on two operations we ran into most abnormal weather and lost 10.5 per cent of sorties, so that the loss rate for the whole month's attacks on Germany was 5.1 per cent. But for the whole of April's attacks on German targets the loss rate was only 3.5 per cent and thereafter it was clear that we had at last got the measure of the German defences and had the enemy at our mercy. We had also, by this time, got together a striking force of formidable proportions, though it is true that it was still little more than a quarter of the size of the force originally projected. In 1943 we had throughout the year an average of 570 heavy, 106 medium, and 41 light bombers available with crews; in 1944 the average number of aircraft available with crews was 1119 heavy, no medium and 97 light bombers, figures which do not include the aircraft of 100 Group. But in April of 1944, as for much of the remaining year, there was little opportunity of using this force for the work for which it had been designed.

From April till September all strategic bomber forces, both R.A.F. and American, were placed under the direction of the Supreme Allied Commander, General Eisenhower, when these were engaged on operations connected either with the reduction of the German air force or with the invasion of Europe. All such commitments in preparation for, or support of, the invasion had absolute and overriding priority. Thus the strategic bombing of Germany had lasted for almost exactly a year, and for no longer. This is a point which I cannot emphasise too strongly. The average man considering the effects of the bombing of German industrial towns is apt to think of it as a campaign which went on for three years during which a force of 1000 bombers regularly hammered away at all the enemy's main industrial centres. Actually only 45 per cent of Bomber Command's effort during the whole of the war was directed against German cities and this 45 per cent includes a number of exceptionally heavy raids carried out towards the end of the war which were tactical rather than strategic in their aim and were designed to have a short term effect on the land campaign by blocking the communications of the Germany army. In April of 1944 I certainly had no illusion that the strategic bombers had done their work; it never occurred to me that we could reduce the largest and most efficient industrial power in Europe to impotence by a year's bombing with an average striking force of six or seven hundred bombers which were never certain to find the target if it lay east or south of the Ruhr. On the contrary, I expected that the damage we had done to German industry—and for the size of the force it was most impressive—would be repaired in five or six months if we gave the enemy any respite from strategic bombing, and so I informed all concerned. That respite we were now proposing to give him; there was no alternative if the most formidable military problem of this and possibly of any war was to be solved and Europe was to be invaded across the sea. Naturally I did not quarrel with the decision to put the bomber force at the disposal of the invading armies once the die had been cast; I knew that the armies could not succeed without them. The entry of America into the war and the time we had gained in which to build up large and well-equipped armies had made all the difference. In 1940 and for some time thereafter, it had seemed to me that the plans some people were making for the re-invasion of the continent were wildly optimistic and absurd. It was only quite late in the day, after America was in the war and not really until adequate forces had at last been built up, that the full magnitude of the proposed task was appreciated; the invasion of Europe was even seriously contemplated for 1943, at a time when any such attempt would inevitably have led to the greatest military disaster of all time; I remember that I had to argue strenuously against this premature invasion. As to the campaign for starting a second front in 1942 to oblige the Russians, a campaign which was waged with considerable energy in the Press and the House of Commons and even became an issue at by-elections, I can imagine no better example of that lack of realism which seems to affect whole sections of the community in wartime. But by 1944 it was clear that we had a good chance of success provided that all the armed forces of Britain and America available in the European theatre concentrated on this single task, the strategic bomber forces no less than any other. At the same time it seemed to me necessary to take a realistic view and to appreciate the fact that if Bomber Command was now to engage almost exclusively in army co-operation work, then all the work of our single year of strategic bombing could be undone in about five months. No one could tell how soon it would be before the armies could dispense with the heavy bombers but, as it seemed to me, the part that the destruction of German industries by the heavy bombers would play in the war as a whole would depend almost entirely on how soon they could get back to the offensive against German industrial cities.

Meanwhile the strategic bombers, both R.A.F. and American. had already done one service to the Army which was of incalculable importance in preparing the way for the invasion. Solely as a result of Allied bombing by day and night the German air force which had been used with exceptional efficiency to blast a path across Europe for the German armies, was now incapable of offensive action and hopelessly unbalanced. Early in 1944 the Order of Battle for the German air force was as follows: one-sixth in the Mediterranean, two-sixths on the eastern front and three-sixths on the western front, engaged almost exclusively in the defence of German cities and consisting almost wholly of fighters with the result that there was a great shortage of fighters on the eastern and Mediterranean fronts. The Germans, in fact, had already lost air superiority in Russia and this had already had a profound effect on the eastern campaign; it would have had a still greater effect if the Russians had had an air force capable of taking advantage of the situation. As far as a land campaign in the west was concerned, it was obvious that there was no hope of succeeding without complete air superiority, and the fact that the German air force was now largely engaged in the highly specialised task of defending German industry, and was largely designed and trained for that purpose, guaranteed air supremacy for the R.A.F. and the U.S.A.A.F. No one could say whether the German air force would be thrown into the invasion battle, but if it was, it would consist almost entirely of fighters; almost the whole German bomber force had by this time been converted to night fighters which could play no part whatever in any land battle. And if the German day-fighter force, which already tended to avoid battle except when faced with an attack on some vital target, should fight it out with the Allied air forces on and after D-Day, we were fully prepared for this engagement and would welcome it.

Since the previous June of 1943 when German centres of aircraft production had become first priority targets for both British and American bombers, many successful attacks had still further reduced the strength of the German air force. During the Battle of Berlin, Bomber Command continued to bomb many industrial cities associated with aircraft production, and in spite of the fact that winter weather could normally be expected to have a serious effect on bombing efficiency, very successful attacks were made on Leipzig, Augsburg, and Frankfurt between December, 1943 and March, 1944; Bomber Command also caused heavy damage to aircraft component works in Stuttgart. During the winter, and particularly in February, the Americans also made destructive attacks on a number of aircraft and airframe factories of critical importance. The general effect of these attacks was not so much to reduce the actual front line strength of the German air force as to prevent expansion and·at the same time to encourage the enemy's disastrous policy of conserving his forces, a policy towards which he was in any case being driven for lack of pilot and other air-crews; the Germans had never had the sense to organise a proper scheme of training air-crew in time, and now had to pay for this lack of foresight. All this did not, of course, benefit Bomber Command itself or cut down our losses, because whatever happened the night fighter force was unlikely to incur heavy casualties and did not have to fight any other fighters except an occasional Mosquito in the bomber stream. But the Allied forces as a whole were well prepared for the invasion of Europe now that strategic bombing had put the enemy so completely on the defensive and in addition done very considerable harm to the aircraft industry.

Chapter Nine

THE INVASION OF EUROPE

The Atlantic Wall. Appreciation of the situation. The heavy bomber made invasion possible. Attacks on French railways. Precision bombing and the Master Bomber. The Operational Research Section. The coastal guns. Other tactical targets. The feint attack on the Pas de Calais. The 12,000 lb. bomb. Daylight operations. Close support of the army. The capture of the Channel ports. The flying bombs. A night-fighter lands in England.

O N THE face of it, the invasion of Europe seemed to present the Western allies with an insoluble problem. The Germans evidently thought so, and took the risk of putting their optimistic appreciation of the situation before the German people. There was first the "Atlantic Wall," a ring of strong fortifications along all the accessible stretches of the coast, with very long range, very heavy, radar-sighted guns which could sink any warships before these could shoot back, and, of course, could smash any convoy to pieces. The beach obstacles and other constructional works were equally strong. For some time the enemy appears to have put his main trust in the Atlantic Wall, which had been constructed by the Todt organisation at vast expense of equipment and slave labour, but eventually he seems to have realised that no system of fortifications could be regarded as completely unbreakable; the German propagandists then put it about that the allies might be able to get a beachhead, but if so, that the German army would welcome the chance of getting to grips with them. For in this case the allies, after crossing the sea, would be in an appallingly dangerous situation.

In the West the enemy had a complete army, including many of his best divisions, with a mass of armour. These divisions, moving on interior lines of communication, could reach any part of the coast in a day or two, and thereafter they would be continuously supplied by excellent railways; the allies, on the other hand, would take many days to bring any equivalent army across the Channel and put it ashore, while that army's supplies would all have to come by sea and would almost certainly have to be put ashore with most inadequate landing facilities. For it was wildly improbable that the allies would capture any port intact, and, if not, it would be impossible to land anything like the quantity of supplies that the Germans could bring up by railway. In fact, if the issue of any battle could be regarded as mathematically certain, this would be so. But if by any chance the German army failed to wipe out the allies as they straggled ashore, then there would be the problem of breaking out of the beachhead, surrounded as it would be by an iron ring of Panzer divisions.

This appreciation of the situation was exact in all particulars except one—it overlooked the existence of a heavy bomber force, More particularly, it overlooked the existence of Bomber Command, which at this stage of the war could still drop a greater weight of bombs, and much heavier bombs, than the Flying Fortresses of the U.S.A.A.F.

It was perhaps natural that the Germans should make this mistake. The Allied bombers had so far confined themselves entirely to strategic bombing and had never yet been successfully employed on a large scale in a tactical rôle. If they were to be used in this way, the U.S.A.A.F. had certainly been trained in precision bombing, and most tactical bombing is aimed at small targets, but without Bomber Command it was most unlikely that the allies would be able to drop a large enough weight of bombs to have any decisive effect. Very occasionally, Bomber Command had attacked small targets like Peenemunde, but by far the greater part of its work had been against very large industrial cities, and there was little reason to think that the whole force could be rapidly switched to the destruction of small targets; on the contrary, all previous experience had gone to show that the R.A.F.'s heavy bombers, with their futile .303 defensive armament, could not operate by day in the face of any serious opposition, and could not hit small targets by night except when the opposition was negligible and the weather and light exceptionally good. Any sustained campaign against a large number of small tactical targets could not be carried out in any reasonable period of time if the bombers had to wait for such unusual conditions.

It was obvious to me that the heavy bomber offered the only conceivable means of breaching the Atlantic Wall, destroying the enemy's interior lines of communications, and thus enabling the army to break out of its beachhead when it had gathered sufficient strength. Of these three problems, the most complicated was that of disrupting the enemy's communications; it would certainly take much longer than the other tasks, and would therefore have to be the first to be undertaken—the date for this elaborate campaign to begin was March, 1944. The plan of the campaign was worked out by the competent authorities in Shaef—Supreme Headquarters Allied Expeditionary Force. It was entirely the conception of Tedder, who certainly has one of the most brilliant minds in any of the services, and it was forced through against continuous opposition, some of which was based on the fear that it would turn the French against us. There was, of course, no reason to believe that the bombing would be as accurate as it proved to be, and I myself doubted whether we could achieve the extraordinary precision needed if the project was to succeed. It was Tedder, and the men under him, who saved the British Army in the Middle East when Rommel was threatening Egypt, and then did so much to make El Alamein a victory. In the invasion of Italy, Eisenhower saw what a great commander he was. It was, of course, of the greatest importance that the Deputy Supreme Commander should come from the Air Force, since air power would be dominant in any combined campaign. It was at one time suggested that the Deputy should come from the British Army, but Eisenhower knew both Tedder's worth and the importance of the weapons he understood so well, and insisted on his appointment and his retention of it. In such matters there was often the difficulty that Air Ministry regulations were so contrived that R.A.F. Commanders-in-the-Field were invariably outranked by those who held similar positions in other services. To the working out of the plan of campaign for the disorganisation of the French railways, Tedder brought a genuinely scientific mind, with all the detachment of the scientist.

Railways are extraordinarily difficult and unrewarding targets for air attack. Main lines can be repaired in a few hours, and through lines in wrecked marshalling yards in a few days, provided that there is an efficient organisation to do the work; in this, as in everything of the kind, the Germans were extremely efficient and had unlimited slave labour. But what if the repair organisation should itself be attacked? That, in effect, was what it was decided to do. The problem was to paralyse the whole railway system of North-Western Europe, from the Rhine to Normandy, the area chosen for the landings. Seventy-nine railway centres were accordingly picked out, in each of which there were important repair shops, with depots containing the necessary materials for the work. Nearly all such shops and depots are situated in or beside railway marshalling yards, and the plan was to select one or more aiming points in the marshalling yards in such a way that a heavy and effective concentration of bombing round these aiming points would destroy or severely damage the repair centres. It was not the principal aim of this campaign to damage the marshalling yards or destroy rolling stock, but if this were done, as it inevitably would be, this would be all to the good; the enemy would then have more and more to repair at the very moment when our bombing was more and more depriving him of the means of doing so. Most of this work was to be done by the heavy bombers of the R.A.F. and U.S.A.A.F., but the Allied tactical air forces were also to take part in the campaign; heavy bombers in the Mediterranean area were to be used against suitable targets. Bomber Command was given the largest share of the targets.

In planning to move the whole Command over to precision bombing the first thing to be done was to study our attacks on small targets in the past. We did not have much to go on, but by March of 1944, there was a good deal more than there had been in the previous year.

In December of 1943, there began a most successful attack, in which Bomber Command played some part, on 56 sites for launching flying bombs in the Pas de Calais and another eight on the Cherbourg peninsula. These objectives were naturally very small, but they were well within Oboe range and both Bomber Command and the Americans were able to bomb them so accurately that the enemy was forced to abandon the whole system which he had originally worked out for the launching of flying bombs. These "permanent" sites were called "Ski-sites," because of the shape of their constructional works as seen from the air. They would have been able to launch a considerably greater number of flying bombs than those which were subsequently used, but they had the great disadvantage that they were easily detected from the air and vulnerable to air attack. By forcing the enemy to abandon this first method of launching flying bombs the Allied bombers gained about six months' vital respite for Southern England, and, when the flying bombs were eventually launched, the enemy was compelled to use a much less efficient form of temporary site.

Nor were these the only precision attacks which could provide us with data for an attack on the railways of North-Western

Europe. In the new year a considerable list of aircraft and associated factories in France was put down for attack in connection with the Allied campaign against the aircraft industry in Germany itself. I ordered No. 5 Group to undertake this task; the Group had already shown remarkable initiative and resource in several precision attacks in the past and by now it contained many crews who had been specially trained in this work, not only 617 Squadron, but enough to carry out a full scale attack on a single large factory. Most of the required attacks on French factories were, however, made by small forces of picked crews; in all twelve targets were attacked, from February 8th-9th until the end of March, and only 350 sorties were needed to destroy or very severely damage all but one of them. In the course of these attacks a new technique of low-level marking, with a Master Bomber to check its accuracy, was carefully worked out and proved extremely successful. A single marker was laid by an expert crew about a quarter of a mile upwind of the target. The Master Bomber then estimated the distance and direction of the target from this indicator. The crews of other aircraft were then instructed to measure the strength and direction of the wind; they gave the results by radio-telephone to the Master Bomber and he then struck an average. After this the Master Bomber then calculated a "false wind," as it was called, which meant that he altered the figures for the real wind strength and direction of the wind in such a way as to ensure that if the bomb-sights were set according to the altered figures, bombs aimed at the target indicator a quarter of a mile from the target would in fact hit the target itself. He then broadcast this "false wind" to the rest of the force, and the attack was made. The great advantage of this method was that every bomb-aimer was able to keep in his bomb-sight a target indicator quite clear of the target itself which could not be blown out by the explosion of the bombs or obscured by smoke.

By this, or by some similar method, there was obviously a good chance of making a whole series of successful attacks on the enemy's railways, especially as 5 Group's attacks on the French factories had often been carried out in bad weather. The weather was, for example, almost impossible when an attack was made on the needle-bearing works at St. Etienne-la-Ricamarie, a very small factory; it proved impossible to see the target except from immediately overhead; the clouds were at 6000 feet, and flares could not be used to light up the target. But the presence of a Master Bomber meant that tactics could be flexible and the plan of attack was changed at the last minute. The leader of the force decided to mark the boundaries of the target with 30lb. incendiaries and ordered the rest of the force, 15 Lancasters, to bomb these incendiaries through clouds. Although the factory buildings only covered an area of 70 by 90 yards, they were destroyed.

Before any new tactics for pre-invasion bombing were decided on it was advisable to discover, if possible, just how large a force should be detailed to attack each target. Experts on railways had advised us that unless we got a certain density of hits by bombs of at least 500 lb. weight we should not be likely to destroy or seriously damage the repair sheds and other essential buildings, and we had to work out what force would be required to get this density of attack. Previously we had had no precise idea of just how large a force was needed to destroy a given target, which was natural enough, because we had never had anything like as large a force as we wanted for the work that was assigned to us; it would have been a merely academic study to work out just how large a force would be needed to destroy Essen when all that we could do was to use every aircraft we could scrape up against this or any similar target. But now we certainly had a large enough force to attack a marshalling yard with a reasonable presumption of success, provided that we could make sure of a good concentration of bombing, and it was essential to destroy as many such targets as possible in the shortest time and therefore with the greatest economy of effort.

The necessary calculations were made by the Operational Research Section of my Command and, apart from the unfortunate but inevitable fact that the mathematicians had not much data to use because there had been so few precision attacks in the past, the work was done in a thoroughly scientific fashion. From this point dates a most important revolution in bombing tactics, the significance of which might well be overlooked. For in the last two years of the war it was possible to get from the Operational Research Section a very fair estimate of the weight of attack that would be required for the destruction of any given target. Naturally the estimates became more and more accurate as more operational data were accumulated, and as a result we were able to use our force with increasing economy of effort. Scarcely a month passed during these last two years when some new committment was not given to my Command, and as our strength in terms of numbers of aircraft scarcely increased it became ever more imperative to get the most out of our force.

An Operational Research Section is indispensable to every Command in modern war. The main work of such a section is statistical analysis, a method which in some sciences has largely taken the place of arranged experiments; it is used, for example, if it is desired, to find out what is the best fertiliser for a given crop in given circumstances. In war it is of enormous value to be able to substitute a statistical probe for an experimental operation, and the work of the large research section at my Command saved thousands of lives and hundreds of aircraft. I will give an instance of the sort of inquiry that was made. In 1944 we suspected that the enemy night fighters were "homing" on to the H2S transmissions of our bombers over Germany, that is to say, that they were using these transmissions, just as they might use any radar or radio transmission from an aircraft, as a guide to the bombers' whereabouts. An experimental method of deciding whether this suspicion was true, and, if so, what to do about it, would have been to dispatch a number of sorties several times over with instructions to use H2S, and as many with instructions not to do so; this would obviously be a risky and wasteful proceeding. But statistical analysis of pilots' raid reports over a considerable period gave the answer with much more certainty, because so many more factors could be taken into account than in an arranged experiment, and with no added risk at all. Thereafter we were able to base our instructions to crews on a rational compromise, using H2S where it was necessary but not where it was merely convenient. In the past, of course, statistics have often been viewed with suspicion and were believed capable of proving anything, but nowadays statistical techniques are so much more refined than in the past that there is little possibility of making seriously fallacious deductions from them. It is, of course, essential for the intelligence sections to see to it that the operational research sections get plentiful data, which they certainly would not have done at the beginning of the war before the importance of statistical analysis of operations was fully realised; admittedly it is often difficult to get really accurate and detailed reports from the fighting man, who has other things to think about, but as time went on very great improvements were made in this respect.

When we had our estimates of the tonnage required for each target we had to take into account the uncertainties of weather and the fact that we should be using new and experimental tactics; this meant that we had to be more lavish with our bombs than the strictly mathematical estimate required. Moreover we were working as never before against time. The date of D-Day had been many times changed at staff conferences, but now it was pretty well fixed for early June, which gave us just about three months, not only for the destruction of the railways but for all the rest of the pre-invasion bombing that would have to be done. As always, much depended on the weather, and with this in mind, I decided whenever we got reasonable weather, to carry out one heavy attack, even when it might appear an unnecessarily heavy attack, rather than a number of light ones.

The first attacks on the marshalling yards and railway centres, the greater number of which were in France, were made without anything very new in tactics; markers were laid by the Pathfinder Force by Oboe-equipped Mosquitoes flying at a great height, exactly as in attacks on German cities, but the crews were expressly forbidden to bomb if they could not clearly see the markers, a very necessary precaution in order to avoid casualties among French civilians. But before long a Master Bomber, with a deputy in case of accident or casualty, was dispatched in every attack; it was his business to check the position of the markers dropped by Oboe and to direct the main force to bomb the most accurately placed of these markers; the master bomber was also to mark the target himself after identifying it visually. Later still, markers were dropped by Oboe, some little time before the attack was due to begin, and these markers were intended only as a guide for a flare-dropping force which lit up the target for a number of experienced crews, "visual markers" to mark by sight. This technique closely resembled the standard H2S attack, as described in an earlier chapter, and at first we used the same method of dispatching a force of "backers-up" to keep up the marking after the first target-indicators had been dropped. But it was then found that backers-up were really unnecessary, because these attacks lasted a very short time and the first target-indicators lasted long enough. For some targets, No. 5 Group used its special method of low-level marking, the bombs being aimed at a target-indicator placed about a quarter of a mile from the target by the "false-wind" method. Some targets were also marked by No. 1 Group, which developed a variant of the Pathfinder Forces' technique for precision bombing. It will be seen that at this stage of the war we were getting towards that state of affairs which I had recommended when the formation of a Pathfinder Force was first under discussion, for we now had the benefit of several different techniques, developed by different Groups, which were suitable for a variety of targets or conditions of weather. But I do not mean in any way to suggest that the Pathfinder Force, as the force which was mainly responsible for identifying the target, had in any way been superseded or lost its commanding position; on the contrary, I continued to entrust the Pathfinder Force with the identification of the target in nearly all our principal attacks until the end of the war, and, under the leadership of Bennett, the force did brilliant work and continually improved its tactics.

Most of the railway centres in France were defended by few anti-aircraft guns, and as a result we were often able to bomb from much below the usual operational height, and sometimes from well below the cloud level. This, of course, made for increased accuracy of attack. Our attacks on the marshalling yards proved to be astonishingly accurate; never before had there been such concentrated bombing, with the bomb craters over-lapping each other in the target which was churned up into a landscape of fantastic desolation. In fact I may as well say out-right that Bomber Command's night bombing, from this point onwards, proved to be rather more accurate, much heavier in weight, and more concentrated, than the American daylight attacks, a fact which was afterwards clearly recognised by Shaef when the time came for the bombing of German troop concentrations within a mile or so of our own troops. Some instances of the outstanding results of these attacks were the railway centres of Juvisy and La Chapelle near Paris; each was attacked once, and afterwards not only the primary objectives, the engine round-houses and repair depots, but also the permanent way of the whole marshalling yard and nearly all the rolling stock in it, had disappeared.

The first attack of the campaign was on the night of March 6th-7th, when the railway yards at Trappes were bombed. Thirty-seven such railway centres were allotted to Bomber Command out of a total of 79. The remaining 42 were allotted to the Eighth U.S.A.A.F., the Allied Expeditionary Air Force of medium and light bombers and fighter bombers, and the Mediterranean based 15th Air Force, but this last was only able to operate on three days at the end of May. All 37 of the targets allotted to Bomber Command were judged to have been so severely damaged that no further attacks by heavy bombers were considered necessary, though in some few instances attacks by lighter bombers were thought advisable to destroy some particular small building which was not so severely damaged, and might still be of some use to the enemy for repair work. Of the remainder of the 79 targets allotted to all other Commands 38 out of 42 were considered to have been as severely damaged as the 37 targets attacked by Bomber Command.

At the end of May the comparatively long-term campaign against railway repair facilities was so near completion that the Command was able to begin attacking railway targets which formed direct links with the proposed battlefield in Normandy; these attacks were, of course, designed to have the short term effect of isolating the battlefield for a period of days or weeks. This campaign against short-term railway objectives was naturally continued after the allies had landed. Up till the end of June, Bomber Command carried out 13,349 sorties against the railways of North-West Europe, dropping 52,347 tons of bombs, with a casualty rate of 2.6 per cent. This 2.6 per cent is the average for 4 months of operations: casualties were low at first, but steadily increased as the enemy began to appreciate what we were up to and what it would mean to him.

In March and early April our attacks on the French railways were seldom opposed by any considerable number of night-fighters, but it was not long before the enemy took measures to protect what he soon realised were vitally important objectives. He began to extend the network of beacons, which already covered most of Germany and served as an assembly point for night-fighters, into France and Belgium, often using airfield beacons for this purpose; the night-fighters themselves were also brought up in large numbers to bases in this area, until there was a large force which could be used against bomber forces making short-range attacks; this force was for the most part locally controlled and did not operate far from its base. Before long our casualty rate began to rise; whatever happened, we had to go on attacking targets in the same comparatively small area, without much chance of confusing the night-fighter force by widely separated attacks, and in many instances the target indicators dropped by the Pathfinders must have been visible from the enemys airfields. It was also easier for the enemy to intercept the bombers, even when these were only attacking coastal targets, during the light summer nights. Moreover the enemy had begun to use some new airborne radar equipment, which was much more efficient than anything he had had before, and about this we knew scarcely little, though we suspected much, at the time. It is no wonder that by June of 1944 our loss-rate had risen to the critical five per cent for inland targets in France and Belgium. For the moment the only effective counter-measure that could be devised was to make the attacks extremely short; a number of seperate forces, each usually consisting of a single bomber Group, were sent to attack different targets simultaneously.

After the long-term campaign against railway centres, Bomber Command, while simultaneously attacking a number of railway targets near the battlefield, had to concentrate on silencing the coastal fortifications. Here the main problem was how to give no indication to the enemy of where the actual landing was to be made. The only way of doing this was by the wildly extravagant method of bombing at least two coastal batteries or defences elsewhere for every one that was attacked on the invasion coast of Normandy. The guns were, of course, extremely small objectives, and the only chance of putting them out of action was by covering a quite considerable area round them with bomb craters. Many of these guns were enclosed in thick concrete casemates, though the casemates for some were still under construction. It was at first thought impossible that where the building of casemates was complete we could do any real harm to the guns by bombing, but this quite reasonable opinion proved to be wrong. On the night of May 28th-29th, 64 Lancasters, guided by seven Oboe-equipped Mosquitoes, attacked the coastal battery at St. Martin de Varreville, and a captured German report said that, after several direct hits on one of the casemates there, it "apparently burst open and then collapsed." In any case, even when the casemate itself was undamaged, the command posts, fire director gear, and signal equipment were often smashed and the batteries thus made ineffective.

On the night of the invasion ten batteries in the actual area of the landing had to be attacked, and this took more than 5000 tons of bombs, by far the greatest weight of bombs dropped by Bomber Command in any single attack up till then. In all 14,000 tons of bombs had to be dropped on the defences of the Atlantic Wall.

Besides railways and fortifications, a number of other military objectives were put on the list of priority targets. During May Bomber Command wrecked the military depots at Bourg Leopold and Mailly-le-Camp. Mailly-le-Camp was the more important of the two, as it was a large tank training centre as well as the headquarters of the 21st Panzer Division. The report of the officer commanding this depot later came into our hands and it gives an impressive account of the attack. "The main concentration," he wrote, "was accurately aimed at the most important buildings. ... In that part of the camp which was destroyed, the concentration of bombs was so great that not only did the splinter-proof trenches receive direct hits, but even the bombs which missed choked them up and made the sides cave in." Five of the largest ammunition dumps used by the German army and air force were also blown up during May, and in April we destroyed a large explosive works at St. Medard-en-Jalles.

Just before the invasion we were required to put out of action three wireless stations and a radar station, which was successfully done. On the night of the invasion itself besides dispatching 1136 aircraft to attack coastal batteries, we sent over 100 aircraft to take part in a very elaborate radar deception which was designed to make the enemy believe that a large scale landing by sea and air was about to be made near Boulogne and Cap d'Antifer. Two squadrons of Lancasters, one of them 617 squadron, the squadron of outstanding airmen who had breached the Möhne and Eder dams, were to simulate the reactions which a large convoy would produce in the enemy's coastal radar stations by dropping a special type of "Window" designed for this occasion. The bundles of "Window" had to be dropped from exactly the right height to give the same reaction as a number of large ships would do, and, what was far more difficult to contrive, the "Window" had to be dropped in such a way as to suggest the steady approach of a convoy at seven knots. This was done by the Lancasters circling with great accuracy in a long series of overlapping orbits for about five hours; in this way, as each orbit came a little closer to the enemy coast, the bundles of metallised paper seemed to be approaching equally slowly. To do this so accurately that the enemy did not suspect that aircraft and not ships were producing the reactions was, of course, a remarkable feat of navigation.

At the same time Stirlings, reinforced by American Fortresses, carried jamming equipment to limit the range of the enemy's early warning radar—but not, of course, to the detriment of the feint by the Window-dropping Lancasters. This was a method of jamming which Bomber Command had not been able to use before, but everything to do with the invasion had such high priority that we were at last able to get and use the equipment;

it proved to be very a valuable weapon against the enemy's early warning system in the future.

A third force of Bomber Command aircraft, Lancasters of No. 1 Group, patrolled in the direction from which enemy fighters might be expected to approach if they disputed the invasion in Normandy; they carried equipment for jamming the night fighters' radio-telephone communications with their ground control stations. Curiously enough, although this was only designed to protect the Window-dropping aircraft and the airborne forces landing in Normandy, the enemy was actually the more inclined to believe that the invasion was taking place in the Pas de Calais because they believed that airborne forces approaching that area were being protected by this Lancaster force. Finally Stirlings of No. 3 Group, dropping bundles of "Window" to simulate a much larger force, dropped dummy parachutists, together with machines which made noises like rifle fire and other sounds of battle, in order to make a diversion and cover the real airborne landings in the Normandy area.

Within a few hours of the bombing of the ten coastal batteries we knew how successful the operation had been; only one of these batteries was able to open fire at all, and that ineffectively as the convoys approached the coast of Normandy. It was not until much later that we learnt of the success of our jamming and diversionary operations. The enemy, it appears, was completely taken in by the bogus convoys and convinced that the main assault was to be in the Pas de Calais. This, it is now known, caused a definite and vital delay in bringing up strategic reserves to Normandy.

The success of the three months' campaign against the railways of North-Western Europe was seen as the two opposing armies began to build up their strength in the battlefield. In this the allies were always well ahead of the enemy, and if the railways had been working normally the artificial port which the allies had constructed and their lavish use of ingenious equipment for landing supplies on to the beaches would never have compensated for the immense advantage the enemy would have had from an efficient railway system and interior lines of communication.

Even to move troops and supplies through and round Paris took the enemy several days, and while still far from the battlefield they found the lines blocked as a result of our subsequent bombing of the railways behind the invasion area.

One of the most effective attacks on these approaches to the battlefield was made by Lancasters of No. 5 Group using a new weapon, Wallis's 12,000 lb. medium capacity bomb, which became available at this time, though in very short supply. This remarkable bomb was a contradiction in terms; it could penetrate 12 feet of concrete or pierce any ship's armour, but, whereas most armour-piercing bombs have so thick a case that they contain little explosive, this one carried terrific power. It was ballistically perfect and had a very high terminal velocity; it could therefore be aimed with great accuracy. It was an entirely different weapon from the 12,000 lb. high capacity and blast bomb which we had now been using for some months against special targets; this blast bomb was less effective than three 4000 lb. blast bombs when used in attacks on large areas but was useful in precision attacks on single factories, where the object was to concentrate the destruction into a very small area, even at the cost of losing some explosive power.

The Lancasters of No. 5 Group dropped a few of these bombs on the tunnel at Saumur, which was on a main line leading northward to Normandy, on the night of June 8th-9th. The bombs broke in the roof of the tunnel and also blocked the line by making enormous craters in the deep cutting leading to the tunnel.

After the war almost every German officer who knew anything about the subject said that the bombing of the railways of North-West Europe was the main cause of the success of the invasion. Here is one such opinion on the subject:

"Your strategic bombing of our lines of communication and transportation resulted in our being unable to move our reserves in time and prevented our troops from ever coming into effective tactical deployment against your forces. . . . Without this strategic bombing of our lines of communication and transportation, without your gigantic aerial coverage of the landings of your troops, your invasion ships and barges would have been sunk or driven out to sea, and the invasion would have been a dismal failure."

Another opinion:

"We had forty (not all motorised) reserve divisions in strategic positions, in readiness in France. Your effective bombing of the road nets, transportation and lines of supply made it impossible for us to move our troops rapidly, if at all."

Yet another:

"You could undoubtedly have landed on the Continent, but it is highly doubtful whether you could have remained there if our transportation system had not been shattered. Any landing is possible; the problem is moving reserves and material at the right moment to the right place."

For a whole fortnight after D-Day the weather was most unfavourable for bombing, with continuous low cloud, more often than not completely unbroken. In the circumstances it was far more difficult for the American heavy bombers to operate than it was for my Command; the Americans were compelled to cancel many operations and in those which they were able to carry out many sorties were abortive. On the other hand, Bomber Command was able to attack from below cloud, even when the cloud base was at 2000 feet, in operations in the invasion area. On every one of the seven nights after D-Day Bomber Command was able to operate, mostly against roads and railways of immediate tactical importance, and, with the American heavy bombers largely inactive, this was of critical importance for the success of the invasion. Besides bombing railways, we were able to block essential road junctions by blowing up buildings round them and choking the cross-roads with debris; this is just what the R.A.F. had tried and failed to do in the Battle of France with wholly inadequate forces and no aids to navigation; we were now able to keep the German reserves out of the battlefield during a most critical period by a whole series of heavy and extremely accurate attacks.

But tactical bombing of the German lines of communication was very far from being our sole commitment. Within a few days of the landing in Normandy we were called upon to take part in a long campaign against German synthetic oil plants in Germany and, as soon as the first flying bombs were launched, to give very high priority to the new flying bomb launching sites and supply depots in the Pas de Calais. Besides this there was an even more urgent call to destroy the enemy's large fleet of E-boats and other light naval craft in the Channel which the Navy thought an extremely serious threat to the invading army's sea communications.

There was only one thing to do; I decided at once that my Command should operate on a large scale by day, with fighter cover, as well as by night, and thereby greatly increase the bomb load which could be dropped in any given 24 hours. The first daylight attacks were against coastal targets, where it was unlikely that the enemy fighters would have time to engage our fighter escort in strength. The targets were the enemy's fleet of light naval vessels in Le Havre and Boulogne, which were attacked on June 14th-15th. They were attacked just before sunset, when we could be certain that the vessels would be out of their concrete shelters and collected together in the harbours, getting ready to operate during the night. These attacks were rightly considered of extreme importance by Shaef; the enemy had already shown us how dangerous these light vessels armed with torpedoes could be against shipping in the Channel and if they had been able to operate successfully at this time the results would have been very serious for the invasion.

There could be no more convincing demonstration of the effectiveness of air power than these two operations. Within twenty-four hours, at wholly negligible cost to our forces, the enemy lost all power of seriously disrupting the passage of convoys to Normandy. At Le Havre very nearly every ship in dock, more than 60 all told, were sunk or damaged, and at Boulogne 28 vessels were sunk and many others damaged. In all, some 130 naval and auxiliary craft were put out of action, virtually the whole of the enemy's light naval forces in the Channel area. At the same time the concrete shelters used to house E-boats at Le Havre were damaged by a small number of the new 12,000 lb. medium capacity bombs.

The bombers were also called upon to intervene even more directly in the fighting in Normandy. On the night of June 14th-15th I was called upon to attack a target of immediate and fleeting tactical importance, a road junction at Aunay-sur-Oden, where a great concentration of German troops and vehicles had been reported. The bombers dropped 1168 tons of high explosives, and photographs showed that everything in and around the area had been wiped out. On June 30th it was learned that the 2nd and 9th Panzers division were moving up through Villers Bocage to make an attack that night; there was a network of roads here which it would be almost impossible for the enemy to by-pass and it was therefore the obvious place in which to bomb the Panzer divisions and their equipment—the enemy had also established a supply point there. This time Bomber Command attacked in daylight and dropped 1100 tons of bombs; the Panzer divisions had to call off the planned attack.

A week later aircraft of Bomber Command were used for the first time to prepare the way for offensive action by our army. The 1st Canadian and 2nd British armies were pressing the enemy hard at Caen, the hinge of the German line, but could make little headway against the strong German positions. Bomber Command was called upon to attack these positions and did so in daylight on July 7th; 2350 tons of high explosives were dropped in just under 40 minutes. A full account of the effect of this attack on the German troops was afterwards got from the enemy. It appears that casualties were comparatively light, but the effect on morale was shattering; this was confirmed by the state of the prisoners that were taken then, and by what they said about the bombing. German officers on the staff of Runstedt, Commander-in-Chief in the West, afterwards described the "terrifying immobility on the battlefield" which was produced by what they called our "carpet-bombing." "The troops could not move . . . the communications system broke down; artillery and anti-tank pieces were knocked out; and tanks were immobilized in craters or beneath heaps of dirt and debris." After one such attack it was reported that a whole division was without food or supplies for 24 hours. On this occasion, at Caen, it is clear that the enemy lost, for the time being, all power of offensive action but the army unfortunately did not exploit its opportunities, and our armour did not move forward until the morning of July 8th. The German comment afterwards was that it would have been very different if our troops had shown "sufficient initiative in following up the bombing." As it was, when our armour did go forward, 24 hours later, the first objectives were taken with scarcely a struggle, the enemy in the front line being still in complete confusion. But after the initial success, the armour did not push on.

Shortly afterwards the view was expressed, among staff officers of the Allied Expeditionary Air Force, that as the army did not seem able to take advantage of our tactical bombing, or indeed of our attacks on the enemy's railways, the heavy bombers might be doing more good by returning to the attack on German war industry and at the same time by bombing what bottlenecks could be found in the production or transport of flying bombs. We knew by now that air attack on the railways was having the most serious effect on the fighting power of the German army; fuel and motor transport were being kept from the battlefield, reinforcements were held back for long periods, and the Panzer divisions were frittering away their strength as a result of having to make long journeys by road. However, this advice was not taken, and until the middle of August first priority had to be given to French railways and we had to be ready at any time to smash a way through for the army whenever the Germans offered serious resistance. In point of fact there was hardly an occasion when we did not intervene in the battlefield as soon as the Germans built up a really strong position.

On July 18th the 2nd Army prepared to advance south of Caen, and to prepare the way for this it was decided that Bomber Command, the U.S. Eighth Air Force, and the Allied Expeditionary Air Force should make a very large scale attack on the German army at three points. In all, 6800 tons of bombs were dropped, and of these Bomber Command dropped 5000. Once again the effect was to immobilize a considerable part of the German army. Many troops were found helplessly wandering about, incapable of defending themselves after the shock of the bombing. A Panzer company which had gathered in an orchard with its tanks had all but two of its vehicles seriously damaged; there was a possibility that two tanks could have moved under their own power, but if so, they could have got no distance but would inevitably have been bogged among the craters all round them.

Between D-Day and the middle of August Bomber Command dropped 17,560 tons of bombs on German troop concentrations in the battlefield; eight separate attacks of this kind were made. It was estimated that at any moment Bomber Command's 1000 aircraft could put down a barrage which, for the time being, was equal in weight to the shells of 4000 guns. To bring up such a mass of artillery to the required position in any reasonable time would, of course, have been a physical impossibility, but the bombers could strike without giving the enemy any warning at a few hours' notice.

It is now generally recognised that this "carpet bombing" of enemy concentrations gave the army several opportunities, which for one reason or another were not taken, to break right through the enemy lines. On one occasion armoured formations were delayed by a traffic bottleneck at the bridges across the river at Caen; the enemy had time to set up a screen of guns behind the area which had been bombed. On another occasion the army did get right through the enemy positions, but could not move forward fast enough after this. In the end it was certainly this carpet-bombing which prepared the way for the final break through the German lines, across the Periers-St. Lo highway, which decided the Battle of Normandy. It was concluded after the battle was over that on each occasion the joint air-army operation should have been planned so that the army moved forward the very moment the bombing was over, or even, at some risk from our bombs, that they should begin moving up to the bomb-line before all the bombs had been dropped.

When the use of heavy bombers in the battlefield, very close to our own troops, was first put forward I expressed doubts; it seemed to me that the army had no idea of the risk that the troops would be running. In the event, by extremely careful planning and the extraordinary skill of the crews, we brought down that risk to much less than the soldier ran in the last war when his own guns put down a barrage. The main safeguard was the use of a double check, a carefully timed run by each bomber and a very careful assessment of the position of the target-indicators by a Master Bomber. In one out of the eight such operations there was, in point of fact, a small number of casualties among our own troops. An investigation afterwards discovered that some crews had omitted to make timed runs, in spite of the orders that had been given to them, and aimed their bombs at pyrotechnic signals, which were not markers at all, but were being displayed by the army for some purpose of its own although it had been agreed that such pyrotechnics would not be used when we were bombing. The army commanders were on every occasion completely satisfied by the way in which the bombing had been carried out. I will quote a message of congratulation which Montgomery sent to me after our attack on enemy troop concentrations near Caen on July 7th.

"Again the Allied armies in France would like to thank you personally and Bomber Command for your magnificent co-operation last night. We know well that your main work lies further afield and we applaud your continuous and sustained bombing of German war industries and the effect this has on the German war effort. But we also know well that you are always ready to bring your mighty effort closer in which such action is really needed and to co-operate in our tactical battle. When you do this your action is always decisive. Please tell your brave and gallant pilots how greatly the Allied soldiers admire and applaud their work. Thank you very much."

On an earlier occasion, Montgomery had said that "it was a most inspiring sight to see the might of Bomber Command arriving to join in the battle."

When the enemy began his disastrous retreat from Normandy Bomber Command was able to demonstrate the dominance of air power even more conclusively than before. At this stage of the battle the German plan was to set up a whole series of Tobruks in the Channel ports, and for this he was prepared to sacrifice many divisions of excellent troops to the last man. The enemy hoped, of course, to deny us the use of all the main Channel ports and so present the allies with an insoluble problem of supply and communication as soon as they advanced far beyond Normandy. But the enemy was driven out of these strongholds with astonishing rapidity. Le Havre was held by more than 11,000 enemy troops; after seven attacks had been made by Bomber Command in one week and 9750 tons of bombs had been dropped, the port was captured, and for the loss of some 30 of our own troops, 11,000 enemy prisoners were taken. After one attack by 762 bombers, Boulogne surrendered within a week and 8000 prisoners were taken. Besides these, Brest, Calais, Cap Gris Nez, and the Ile de Cézembre, which was essential for the defence of St. Malo, were all occupied without trouble after attacks by Bomber Command. Brest was also attacked by American heavy bombers and here we also had the task of sinking several large ships before the Germans could tow them into the right position and sink them to serve as blockships. In past wars, without the heavy bombers, these ports could only have been captured after prolonged siege.

The comparatively brief period when the strategic bomber forces both of the R.A.F. and of the U.S.A.A.F. were placed under the control of Eisenhower for all operations related to the invasion of Europe and the defeat of the German air force was absolutely the only time during the whole of my command when I was able to proceed with a campaign without being harassed by confused and conflicting directives. It was in many ways a great relief after two years of working under other directions. When I first took over Bomber Command in 1942 I found that the Air Ministry had lately increased their hold on the Bomber offensive to the point of controlling quite small details. But before long this control, and the responsibility that went with it, was progressively shifting to the Chiefs of Staff Committee and other committees including the War Cabinet itself. In consequence many individuals thought that they enjoyed the privilege of running or trying to run a force without direct responsibility for the results which must, of course, remain with the Commander. Then the Combined Chiefs of Staff in Washington, where as far as the Americans went there were two against the use of air power for one who supported it, also interfered.

When it was very properly decided that all air power necessary for the invasion should be placed at the disposal of Eisenhower, he, being a wise and immensely understanding man, promptly transferred control to an airman—Tedder. The Air Ministry, having by then interposed Leigh-Mallory, found that control of the strategic bomber forces, which had gone pretty well all round the world, was now, being in Tedder's hands, very nearly back whence it had started. This encouraged them to make a further effort to get control again. They went about this by having the control transferred back again, as a preliminary measure, to the Combined Chiefs of Staff in Washington who at once relegated it to General of the Army Arnold and Marshal of the R.A.F. Lord Portal in combination. Portal was on the spot in England and Arnold was not and could not be; they therefore agreed to appoint deputies. Arnold appointed General Spaatz; and Portal appointed his Deputy Chief of the Air Staff, Air Marshal Sir Norman Bottomley. This was unfortunate all round, because Bottomley as a staff officer could not constitutionally exercise control of a force in the field or issue order direct to a Commander in the field. This was got over, after a fashion, by evolving a formula; orders given to me were supposed to come from Portal through the D.C.A.S. who was thus only acting as Portal's staff officer. With this extraordinary lack of continuity and with responsibility so uncertainly poised the natural result was a multiplicity of directives embodying one change of plan after another and so cautiously worded at the end with so many provisos and such wide conditions that the authors were in effect guarded against any and every outcome of the orders issued. They were always in the happy position of being able to challenge any interpretation of any order, if they so desired. The kaleidoscopic changes of plans were in practice less important and less confusing than might be thought, because in actual fact the progress of the bomber offensive was governed nine-tenths by the weather, and one-tenth by my own judgment and decision about which of the alternatives, if any alternative offered, was to be adopted on any given occasion. These decisions I simplified

by installing a senior air staff officer in Eisenhower's and Tedder's
pocket at Shaef and making frequent visits to Shaef headquarters
myself. Having first found out what they wanted—and their
requirements were given priority over any others—I could then
get on with what had to be done elsewhere.

At the time of the invasion a large part of our effort was being
diverted from support of the Allied armies and even more from
the offensive against German industry, as a result of the launching
of flying bombs against Southern England. The date of the first
launching is given as the night of June 15th-16th, but one of these
missiles did in fact reach London in the early hours of June 13th.
Ten flying bombs in all were observed that day, but no more came
over until the night of the 15th-16th, when a considerably larger
number were launched. At once a long prepared plan was put
into operation, and Bomber Command's part in this was to
attack what were known as the "modified launching sites" in the
Pas de Calais. These were small, easily constructed, and extremely
unrewarding targets for air attacks.

The actual battle of the V-weapons had been won by the Allied
bombers several months before. Though the victory was so
obvious and conclusive, the fact remained that long-range
weapons might still be used as a harassing weapon and prove a
sore trial to the people of London and Southern England. The
enemy had originally planned to launch the flying bombs at the
rate of 6000 a day, which would have been perfectly feasible if
he had had the use of the first series of 64 launching sites in
Northern France with an efficient system of communications
behind them. This, of course, would have made the flying bomb
a weapon of vast strategic importance. One thousand heavies of
Bomber Command could just about drop this weight of bombs
on short range targets in 24 hours, but such a rate of attack could
not have been carried our continuously and in absolutely all
weathers; no weather could, of course, prevent the launching of
flying bombs. The enemy intended to use this weapon as a counter-
stroke against invasion, and it is difficult to see how an invasion
could have been mounted with London in ruins, Southern England
laid waste, and every type of communication in disorder. But, as
always, the Germans made an elementary mistake; they planned
what might be described as the weapon of the next war with
extreme efficiency, and showed remarkable powers of invention
and organisation in doing so, but they completely overlooked the
possible effect, though it had already been demonstrated through-

out Germany, of the dominant weapon of the war in which they were actually engaged. This was as bad a mistake as relying on the weapon of the last war, as the Germans did when they put so much of their effort into U-boats and overlooked the fact that aircraft could effectively attack them.

The first launching sites were, as I have already described, so effectively bombed by the American and R.A.F. bombers that the Germans soon abandoned them; they learned too late, in the beginning of 1944, that it was hopeless to rely on anything vulnerable to bombing, especially at so short a distance from bases in England. But the bombing of the French railways also had a profound effect on the V-weapons campaign and made largely ineffective the new dispersed sites which sprang up all over the Pas de Calais. In fact the threat of the flying bomb seemed to have been sufficiently removed that it was judged safe to remove all targets connected with flying bombs from the list of objectives for the allied bombers in the weeks before D-Day; in any case, the bomber forces were wholly preoccupied with the preparations for invasion which in the agreed Allied strategy rightly came before anything else. When the bombs were eventually launched the enemy's supply system was so thoroughly disorganised and the new sites were so ill-adapted to the rapid launching of bombs, that instead of an average of 6000 flying bombs, the enemy was only able to launch an average of 95 a day between the middle of June and the end of August. Of these only two-thirds made landfall and less than one-third reached Greater London after encountering the fighters and anti-aircraft defences of Southern England, but everyone knows how serious a trial these weapons were and can judge for himself what a bombardment more than sixty times as heavy would have been like, especially as the defences would inevitably have been saturated by such a weight of attack and fighters and anti-aircraft guns would have been unable to bring down anything like so large a proportion of all the flying bombs launched.

The flying bombs had only one effect on the progress of the invasion, and this was the diversion of effort from supporting the armies to the defence of England. If the German Air Force had been more combative, the diversion of most of the R.A.F.'s newest and fastest fighters, which alone could catch the flying bombs, would have been a serious matter, and the enormous bomber effort that had to be brought to bear on the launching sites was certainly one of the major contributory causes of the long respite which German industry had from air attack. During the second half of June, Bomber Command dropped more than 16,000 tons on bombs on targets connected with V-weapons, mostly on launching sites, and up to the beginning of September, until the allied armies occupied the Pas de Calais, a further 44,000 tons of bombs. This 60,000 tons of bombs was equivalent to one month's bombing at a time when the bomber offensive was at its height. The launching sites were small and very well concealed, and more than half the operations against them were carried out when they were covered by low cloud; nevertheless, nearly all of them were knocked out. Unfortunately, as one went down another sprang up, for they were very cheap and quick to build. When this happened I was directed to attack the supply depots in which the flying bombs were stored before being distributed to the launching sites. These depots were either caves or reinforced concrete structures, but we succeeded in doing a great deal of damage by dropping both 1000 and 12,000 lb. bombs on them. The roofs of the caves were often smashed in and the stores of bombs buried under rock and earth.

Four enormous concrete structures in the Pas de Calais were suspected of being intended for the storage of firing of V2, the long range rocket. If we had had a large supply of 12,000 lb. bombs no doubt we could have smashed these buildings and as it was we caused severe damage with these bombs. But at the same time, attacks with normal bombs made it impossible for the enemy to complete or repair these buildings. Large numbers of concrete mixing machines round about them were smashed to pieces and the ground was so cratered and torn that it became impossible to bring any repair and building materials up.

On 13th July, 1944, the enemy night fighter force suffered a serious reverse. As I said earlier in this chapter, we had begun to suspect that the enemy had greatly improved his methods of interception and the existence of new equipment was vaguely rumoured. It was, of course, extremely difficult to get information about the work of the German night fighters for the simple reason that they operated over Germany and neither aircraft nor prisoners of war were at all likely to fall into our hands. By an almost incredible stroke of luck the pilot of a Junkers 88 mistook England for Germany in July 13th and landed with his aircraft quite undamaged on an airfield in England. It was a Junkers 88 of the latest type and it contained two wholly new instruments for detecting aircraft in the dark. The first of these instruments, which had the code name of S.N.2, worked on a wavelength such that it could be jammed or confused by a type of Window already in use against the enemy's early warning system. We had in hand a small but sufficient stock of this type of "Window" and decided to use this at once, without waiting for a trial. We used it against the enemy night fighters for the first time on the night of July 23rd-24th in an attack on Kiel and it was at once proved useful. The use of the second new instrument, which had the code name Flensburg, was discovered when a night fighter pilot took up the Junkers 88 and used it in an exercise against our bombers. It was found that by this equipment the enemy could readily home on to the transmissions from a radar set with which most of our bombers had been equipped to give the crews warning of the approach of an enemy fighter. We had this warning equipment modified at once, and sent the Junkers 88 up again to see if it could intercept a considerable number of bombers which had been fitted with the modified warning equipment. It was found that the modification did no good, and the equipment was therefore discarded at once. At the same time the type of Window that was effective against the S.N.2 was tried in the same exercise against the instrument called Flensburg and it was found to be very useful against this as well. Later new types of Window were produced which were even more effective against the new equipment than the type originally intended for use against the early warning coastal radar which had served admirably as a stopgap.

Chapter Ten

THE OFFENSIVE AGAINST OIL

*Panacea targets. A molybdenum mine. Ball-bearing factories.
Tactical objections. The raid on Ploesti. G.H. The Ministry of
Economic Warfare. The oil offensive begins. Miraculously
good weather. The results of the campaign.*

IN THE SPRING of 1944 the Americans began a series of
attacks against German synthetic oil plants, and a week after
D-Day Bomber Command was directed to take part in the same
campaign by attacking the ten synthetic oil plants situated in the
Ruhr. At the time, I was altogether opposed to this further diversion, which, as I saw it, would only prolong the respite which the
German industrial cities had gained from the use of the bombers
in a tactical role; I did not think that we had any right to give
up a method of attack which was indisputably doing the enemy
enormous harm for the sake of prosecuting a new scheme the
success of which was far from assured. In the event, of course,
the offensive against oil was a complete success, and it could not
have been so without the co-operation of Bomber Command, but
I still do not think that it was reasonable, at that time, to expect
that the campaign would succeed; what the Allied strategists
did was to bet on an outsider, and it happened to win the race.

This was very far from being the first time that I had been
pressed to attack the enemy's synthetic oil plants. Ever since the
beginning of the war these had been the favourite targets of the
Ministry of Economic Warfare. They were, indeed, the most
important and most persistently recommended of a whole class
of objectives which at Bomber Command we always called
"panacea" targets. These were targets which were supposed by
the economic experts to be such a vital bottleneck in the German
war industry that when they were destroyed the enemy would
have to pack up. Apart from the single instance of the synthetic
oil plants—and they only constituted a real bottleneck in the last
year of the war—the arguments of the economic experts had
invariably proved fallacious. A good example of this was a
molybdenum mine at Knaben in Norway. We were told that this
produced so large a percentage of all the molybdenum required

by the Germans that its destruction would be a major disaster to the whole of their war effort. We destroyed the molybdenum mine—with a rather small force of Mosquitoes—and no sooner had it been repaired and was producing again, after an interval of a year or so, than the American Eighth Air Force destroyed it once more. But when we asked the economic experts to show us precisely where or when the predicted disaster was overtaking Germany, they confused the issue with a mass of verbiage. The answer, of course, is that molybdenum, though vital—it is used in special alloy steels required in a great many kinds of armament —is needed in such small quantities that no first-class power would be likely to find itself without enough molybdenum, raked up from here and there or smuggled in at a high price, to keep going for many years of war.

Over another panacea target, ball-bearings, the target experts went completely mad. The Germans had at that time the whole vast industrial capacity of the Continent at their disposal and even if we had by a miracle been able to destroy all worthwhile ball-bearing targets in Germany at a time when we were finding it difficult to identify and hit much larger targets, this would only have embarrassed, not stopped, the German war effort. The experts went so far in their special pleading, when they tried to persuade us to attack ball-bearing factories, that they said these could not be put underground because of damp, dust, and so forth. In fact this particular industry was one of the few industries vital to the German war effort that could have been adequately dispersed and hidden underground, and much of it was. And the enthusiasm of the experts was so great that I was actually told that I should be fully justified in accepting such losses to achieve the destruction of Schweinfurt—one of the main centres of the ball-bearing industry—as would put the whole of the bomber force out of action for two months. They paid no attention to the fact that Schweinfurt was too small and distant a town for us to be able to find and hit in 1943.

I hope that some day the history of Sweden's supply of steel, tools, and bearings to Germany will be written. At the time when we were paying Sweden enormous sums of money for not delivering such things to Germany, the Germans were paying enormous sums of money for orders originally given and then paying extra on top of that to have the finished products smuggled out to them. So you could get paid once or twice over for not producing things, and then get paid smuggler's rates for delivering them. It would be interesting to know just how many millions passed into Sweden by both sides during the war.

The enthusiasts who wanted us to concentrate on one particular class of target throughout Germany almost always failed to realise how many factors there were to make such a scheme impracticable. There was first the weather, which up to the last year of the war was always the most important factor to be taken into account when deciding what could or could not be attacked. In Europe the weather is such that even if you were lucky enough to find and destroy two-thirds of any list of panacea targets your chances of finding suitable weather to attack the remaining third would be very small; at the beginning you would be able to choose any one of a long list of targets and there would be a good chance of finding one in some part of Germany where the weather was favourable for attack, but the chances of getting the right weather for the target would decrease as the number of remaining targets decreased. What is more, when you had reduced the number of possible targets to four or five it would become an urgent necessity to knock them out before the targets which you had already attacked had been repaired; otherwise you would have to go round the whole circle again. That being so you could only hope to get an opportunity of attacking the last few remaining targets by keeping the force in a perpetual state of readiness to attack them the instant that the weather appeared suitable. You would thus frequently have to keep a large part of the force, and possibly all of it, standing idle and missing numberless opportunities of doing worthwhile damage elsewhere in Germany.

When the list of possible targets had been reduced to four or five another difficulty would have inevitably faced us. The enemy would know exactly what we were going to do next and with only a very few targets to guard he could have surrounded these with the most formidable defences. Long before this, in fact after the first two or three attacks, the enemy would have known what we were trying to do and would have had ample time to disperse and hide the particular industry concerned, especially as there would have been no general attack on industrial towns as a whole to impede such work by slowing down the whole industrial life and transport of the country.

With the weather went the factor of long and short nights. In June we could only attack within a circle, the circumference of which runs through Emden and Cologne, without getting caught in daylight either coming or going. If your bomber offensive was based on a panacea target system you might well find that after completing a large part of your programme you could not finish it before the nights were too short, and thus the enemy would get several months' respite. This could, of course, have been got over when the Americans had built up their strength and were making heavy daylight attacks, but Bomber Command was being pressed to attack panacea targets long before the Americans came in. Moreover, even when the Americans came to our help, so long as Bomber Command could not operate by day a campaign against panacea targets would have had to be maintained by only half the allied bomber forces during the summer.

An important factor, which the economic experts never grasped, was that it was only in the closing stages of the war that we had navigational aids such as would enable us to identify and hit isolated targets as small as the average large factory.

For these reasons I had consistently refused in the past to use our main striking force for any length of time against panacea targets. I was confirmed in my decision by the fact that whenever we or the Americans did successfully attack such targets, we were always told, just when the enemy ought by rights to have been surrendering unconditionally, that some other manifestation in that particular war industry had just been discovered, or that there was some material or product which the enemy could use and was using as an alternative. Had I paid attention to the panacea-mongers who were always cropping up and hawking their wares, Bomber Command would have flitted continually from one thing to another during the whole period of my Command; the continuity of the offensive as a whole would have been irretrievably lost.

An instance of how costly it could be to listen to the advice of the enthusiasts for panacea targets is the American bombing of the oil refineries at Ploesti in Rumania. Many squadrons of American bombers had to be taken off the main offensive against German industry for long periods, sent to bases in the Mediterranean, and specially trained in order to make a spectacular, low level attack on the oil refineries, which could not be followed up— the refineries were not attacked again until April, 1944—and consequently had so little lasting effect that deliveries of Rumanian oil to Germany persistently increased until the spring of 1944.

The loss of these squadrons for many months materially reduced the American build-up for the main offensive against Germany itself. Even the extraordinarily successful attack against the Möhne and Eder dams did not have so great an effect on the German war economy as was predicted by the economic experts, and I had therefore learnt from bitter experience to regard their predictions with the greatest suspicion and largely to discount their claims in advance.

When Bomber Command was required to begin bombing the synthetic oil plants in conjunction with the Americans in June, 1944, some of these factors were still present, and others were not. But at least we had by then the means to find and hit the targets in reasonable weather. My main objection was that we were swapping horses in mid-stream. Though the bomber offensive had only begun in 1943 and had ended within a year when we were put on to invasion targets, the vast damage that had been done in that short space of time showed that if the available bomber forces—ourselves and the Americans—went on and developed the weight of attack that was by then possible, Germany would then without a shadow of doubt be knocked right out in a few months—this view was completely confirmed when we entered Germany. I therefore strongly objected to stopping the offensive for which we had worked for five years, and which was succeeding hand over fist at the very moment when we at long last disposed of such weight of attack as to put all question of failure out of court. On the one side I saw certainty of success, and on the other side still many chances of failure. We had at that time, in June, 1944, no experience to show whether precision attacks on individual and isolated factories in Germany could be successfully carried out in darkness in any but favourable weather. It is true that we had attacked a great number of small tactical targets and factories in France with remarkable success, but these had only a comparatively few anti-aircraft guns to defend them and it was almost always possible to bomb from a very low level with great deliberation. We had not yet begun attacking in daylight with fighter cover, and when we did begin to do so, shortly after D-Day, it was only against targets on or near the French coast. For us there was no adequate long-range fighter escort force then in sight.

Looking further ahead, I knew that even if we overcame the first difficulties and succeeded in making precision attacks on dark and cloudy nights against targets in Germany, we should have to keep the offensive up through the winter months when bombing efficiency is normally much reduced. If, as seemed almost inevitable, we got the sort of weather we had had during the previous winters, when it proved extremely difficult to make a concentrated attack even on a target as large as Berlin, extending over many square miles, the Germans would almost certainly get a respite long enough to enable them to repair all the damage we had previously done to the oil plants. We learned later that in fact this was exactly what the enemy counted on; it was only by a conjunction of circumstances which amounted to a miracle that we were able to keep up the attack during those winter months and so disappoint the enemy's confident expectations. In war it is not wise to count on miracles.

There was one other factor to be taken into account when weighing up the chances for and against a campaign against the enemy's oil industry, and this was a new navigational aid. This aid was known as GH, and its use had been considered as long ago as 1940, when the re-development of Gee was under discussion. The question then was, which of these two navigational aids should first be introduced. GH was in theory likely to be far more accurate than Gee, but whereas every aircraft in the force could be equipped with Gee and use it simultaneously, only about 100 aircraft at best could use GH in any one operation. When it is remembered that in 1943 we had to be satisfied with a navigational aid, namely Oboe, which could only be used by a dozen or so Mosquitoes in any one operation, it may seem extraordinary that in 1940 GH should have been rejected because no more than 100 aircraft could use it simultaneously. But at that time the principle of using a small Pathfinder Force, which should only be regarded as a measure we were forced to use for want of something better, had not been accepted; the idea then was that every man should be his own Pathfinder and every aircraft have adequate equipment for finding any target. In actual fact things changed so much between 1940 and 1944, and we had to moderate our ambitions to such an extent, that in 1944 the main reason for using GH was the fact that it could be used by as many as 100 aircraft at a time.

GH was put forward not as a navigational aid but as a blind-bombing instrument; its accuracy, we were told, would in theory approach that of Oboe. If so, it would be of the greatest value to Bomber Command, because it could be used against small targets when these were covered by thick, unbroken cloud and ground markers could not be seen. Previously it had been next to impossible to attack small targets such as individual factories in such conditions, except by a handful of Oboe Mosquitoes. H2S was not accurate enough to identify a target of this size; bombing on sky markers dropped by Oboe was too scattered to do effective damage to small targets; ground markers dropped by Oboe could not be seen, and the only possibility was to bomb directly on Oboe, which was not much use when Oboe aircraft could only be guided to the target at the rate of one every five minutes and even then could only drop the bomb-load of a Mosquito. But if we could use a hundred Lancasters to bomb with something like the accuracy of Oboe-equipped Mosquitoes through ten-tenths cloud then it became at least theoretically possible for Bomber Command to maintain an offensive of some sort against the enemy's synthetic oil plants through the winter months. Furthermore, we might with such equipment be able to operate by day over Germany with much greater safety since we should then have the protection of thick cloud against anti-aircraft fire.

On the other hand I had no means of knowing, in June, 1944, whether GH was going to be as accurate as was claimed. Only the most incurable optimist would at this time of day, after all the experience and disappointments we had had with Gee, Oboe, and H2S, base a change of strategy on the theoretical accuracy of a new navigational aid before it had been used on a considerable scale and for a considerable time in the face of the enemy's defences. What was known about GH was certainly enough to make it advisable for me to press for the manufacture and supply of the equipment, since it might well stop an important gap in our armoury. But that was a very different thing from basing all our plans for the future on the hypothesis that it would do all that was claimed for it. And, in any case, GH, like all navigational aids dependent on ground stations, was limited in range, whereas Germany's synthetic oil plants were scattered all over the country and many of them were far to the east.

GH exactly reversed the method of Oboe. Whereas the Oboe ground stations made the first transmissions, which were received by the aircraft and re-radiated back to the ground stations, the first GH transmissions were made by the aircraft. The advantage was that the bomber crew could find their position at any time they chose, and as I said above, that a fair number of aircraft could use GH simultaneously. The main disadvantage by comparison with Oboe, was that the necessary calculations, which, with Oboe, were made at the ground stations, had to be made in the aircraft with GH. Obviously such work would, in general, be more efficiently done in a ground station, where the men could be picked for this particular job and where they would not be distracted by the enemy. As against this, where a number of aircraft bombed on their own GH fixes this would tend to cancel out the cumulative errors that arose from a system that could only be used by one aircraft at a time.

Like everything else, GH was supplied to us some time after it had been promised. But by October of 1943 four Lancaster squadrons, equipped with modified bomb-doors for the dropping of 8000 lb. bombs, could have operated with it. This was too late in the year, at this stage of the war, to make good use of the equipment, since with the winter nights coming on the Command would be required to operate in full strength against distant targets out of range of GH and, in particular, the Battle of Berlin was due to begin.

But one light experimental attack was made with GH on the night of November 3rd-4th against the Mannesmannrohrenwerke on the outskirts of Dusseldorf, and the bombing accuracy, as far as could be estimated in so light an attack, was very good; all the bombs were dropped blind, entirely on GH. As a result of this attack it was decided that such valuable equipment should not be allowed to fall into enemy hands before it could be used by a sufficiently strong force, and I ordered the GH sets to be taken out of the Lancasters for the time being. In the spring one or two very light attacks were again made in order to calibrate the device, and round about D-Day and afterwards some minelaying was done with this equipment.

A particular advantage of GH was that the ground stations could be rapidly moved from place to place and this suggested that as soon as the Allied armies had established themselves on the continent GH would prove an extremely valuable aid for tactical bombing; the ground stations could be rapidly moved forward with every advance of the armies and so increase without delay the range of the device. It was, indeed, for tactical bombing that we now intended to use GH, not primarily for precision attacks on German industrial targets, and it was for this reason that in June I made an urgent request for enough GH sets to equip one bomber Group. I chose No. 3 Group for this. When Bomber Command began to attack the synthetic oil plants of the Ruhr there were nothing like enough aircraft equipped with GH to use for this work, and the first operations, apart from experimental attacks, made with GH were against flying-bomb sites in July and August, when it was essential for the defence of London to continue bombing these without waiting for clear weather. Stirlings were used for these attacks—they were hopelessly out of date for any operation against a well-defended target but could be profitably used at such short range—and they operated in daylight using a new technique which was, in essentials, the same as that used in the much more important daylight attacks with GH which began later in the year. This technique was developed to make up for the severe shortage of GH equipment; two aircraft equipped with GH led a formation of eight aircraft without GH. The eight aircraft followed in pairs in line astern, with a distance of 200 yards between each pair, and each pair was to bomb when the bombs of the preceding pair were seen to leave the bomb doors. As might have been expected, the bombing of most of the aircraft was indifferent; this was because the crews had as yet had very little practice in formation flying, and as time went on, as the formation flying improved, so did the bombing.

In June of 1944 Germany still had the Rumanian oil fields; she lost them to Russia in August of that year and this, of course, contributed a great deal, as did the loss at about the same time of the refineries in Poland, towards the success of the offensive against the enemy's oil. In fact, the loss of the Rumanian fields was, in my view, a pre-requisite for the success of any such offensive. For the time being it was to be hoped that American attacks on the Rumanian refineries, together with the mining of the river Danube, would diminish this important supply. Attacks on these refineries had been resumed in April, a month before the Americans began their major offensive against German oil plants.

When the oil plan was being discussed I described very forcibly my experience with the Ministry of Economic Warfare in the past and expressed my view that if this was anything to go by we should certainly be basing our plans on incomplete information. I had no particular confidence that our economic experts knew how many plants the enemy had, where they all were, and what their building programme was. This criticism was met by the institution of a special committee on oil, and it was lucky indeed that this was done, because the committee very soon began to discover all sorts of alternative sources of oil.

The enemy had, for example, a great number of small benzol and tar distillation plants all over Germany, but especially in the

Ruhr, and our information about these was very inadequate; the committee had at once to get up-to-date and as far as possible complete information about these. Moreover, early in the offensive against oil, Speer put a very competent organiser, Edmund Geilenburg, in charge of the repair, building, and dispersal of oil plants and gave him the highest possible priority for everything that he needed. A corps of 350,000 men worked day and night at this, and it was essential to get the fullest information about the Geilenburg plan, as it was called. The largest oil plants were restored to full production in a few weeks and were often able to produce a fair proportion of their former output in little more than a week after a highly successful attack. The dispersal of small oil plants above and, to some extent, below ground, taxed our intelligence services to the utmost, and it was not surprising to me, that, during the offensive we got news of additional oil sources almost every day. It was a race between the destruction we could do and the building of new small plants and the repair of the large old ones; good intelligence was absolutely vital in such a campaign.

Bomber Command made the first attack on the largest of the ten synthetic oil plants in the Ruhr about a month after the Americans had begun the offensive against oil, and by the end of September had dropped 12,600 tons of bombs on all ten of these plants. Precision bombing on markers dropped by Oboe in average weather proved far more effective than we had any right to expect. It was one thing to bring this off in the face of such ground and air defences as the Germans could spare for tactical targets in France, and quite another to carry out such complicated tactics with success against all the defences of the Ruhr and necessarily at a much greater height. For at this period the air defence of Germany was still intact, though less efficient than in 1943, when such a campaign would have been wholly impracticable. I regard the success of this campaign against the Ruhr oil plants as the highest possible tribute to the efforts, efficiency, and heroism of my crews.

In September, 1944, the air defence of Germany crumbled to pieces; the German army was driven out of France and the enemy's early warning system was lost; at the same time the ground stations for navigational aids could be moved on to the Continent and the range of Gee, GH, and Oboe greatly extended. Every advantage was taken of the desperate position of the enemy defences, and extremely complicated operations were planned which made it next to impossible for the enemy to concentrate his air defences at any given target that we were attacking or on the route of any particular bomber stream. These new, and, in the beginning, largely unpredictable developments which I shall describe in more detail later, had a profound effect on the success of the offensive against Germany's oil supplies.

By October, 1944, a considerable force of Lancasters of No. 3 Group was equipped with GH, the radar aid which was to be of critical importance in the autumn and winter months. These Lancasters began to operate on a large scale in the middle of October, usually between one and two hundred at a time. By no means all the aircraft were actually equipped with GH; in fact only about a quarter to a third of the Lancasters in any one operation usually had it, but by flying in formation in daylight this disadvantage was overcome. Three to five aircraft followed a single aircraft equipped with GH and all the bombs were dropped at the moment when the bombs of the leading aircraft were seen to be released. In case any aircraft should straggle behind or lose formation the GH aircraft normally dropped coloured smoke puffs so that the stragglers would at any rate have something at which to aim. The vast majority of these GH attacks were made in daylight and through ten-tenths cloud, but on a few occasions GH aircraft were used to drop markers by night. An average of three to four attacks a week was kept up by No. 3 Group until the end of the war, and as most of these attacks were made in conditions when no other kind of attack would have been possible, the great access of strength which we gained from the introduction of GH, and its successful application, may easily be appreciated.

The accuracy of the attacks was far beyond all reasonable expectation, but, even so, it proved in practise that GH was really more efficient in area bombing than against single factories. No. 3 Group was able to destroy a whole series of rather small towns, Houffalize, Bonn, Solingen, Witten, and Wesel among them, in single attacks by GH when we were called upon by the army to attack such places for tactical reasons. But it was found that two attacks were often necessary to do really effective damage to a synthetic oil or benzol plant. The concentration of bombing was much greater than in an attack on sky-markers through ten-tenths cloud, but so much less than in an attack where ground markers could be seen that we had to expend a great many bombs to be sure of hitting a small target. In general, a single factory can only be destroyed by a concentration of bombing three or four times as great as that required to devastate a town. As the size of the force was necessarily limited, this meant that No. 3 Group had often to put in a second attack as soon as possible after the first. By the beginning of 1945 No. 3 Group had so far improved in formation flying and in the use of the equipment—it will be remembered that with this device calculations had to be made in the aircraft which with Oboe were done on the ground—that bombing errors were greatly reduced.

But even though these attacks were somewhat extravagant in effort and expenditure of bombs, they were enough to make Bomber Command largely independent of the weather and to destroy the enemy's very reasonable hope of restoring the oil industry in the winter months. In September Speer, in his capacity as Reich Minister for Armaments and War Production, circulated a telegram to the relevant officials in which he predicted that with the bad weather and fogs of autumn and winter "the bombing of synthetic oil plants cannot be carried out with the same precision. . . . In spite of the really considerable damage done, we can in a period of five to six weeks restore production to about two-thirds of the level before the attacks." But the weather was not as bad as the enemy had hoped—in fact, for once it was almost in our favour—and, still more important, GH attacks could be carried out in all conditions so long as the cloud tops were not above 17,000 feet.

With the lengthening nights Bomber Command was able to prosecute the offensive against oil in a whole series of long-range attacks. With the collapse of the German defences, precision attacks could be made by H2S against targets as distant as Politz or Brux in Czechoslovakia; the new Mark III H2S, with more accurate definition of ground detail, proved of great assistance. In Speer's opinion Bomber Command's night attacks were often the decisive factor in putting out of action the largest and most important of the enemy's synthetic oil plants. "Owing to their greater effectiveness," he said, "night attacks caused considerably more damage than day raids," and these night attacks by Bomber Command were, he considered, "more effective in their results than day attacks by reason of the fact that the superheavy bombs caused shattering damage to these plants." Provided that the problem of getting the markers on to the target was solved it was always easier to get a tense concentration of attack on a small target by night than by day, except, perhaps, on the extremely rare occasions when a day attack could be carried out in perfectly clear weather. The American system of bombing in formation, like our own formation bombing by GH, was always dependent on the accuracy with which the pilots kept formation and, of course, on the skill of the bomb-aimer in the leading aircraft. It is also true that Bomber Command used heavier bombs than the Americans, and here I am not referring to the 12,000 lb. and 22,000 lb. bombs for attacking special targets, but the normal bomb-load.

The United States Strategic Bombing Survey says that "in general repeated air attacks, rather than the severity of any single raid, caused the almost complete break-down of German oil production." This is true in general of the American attacks, but not of the most successful of Bomber Command's attacks, where the dense concentration of attack and the heavy bombs used, made the work of repair infinitely more difficult. Leuna, the largest hydrogenation synthetic oil plant in Germany, was attacked twenty times by the Eighth U.S.A.A.F., but when we took over the target in January and February, 1945, Bomber Command had to make only two attacks; it is true, of course, that the cumulative effect of earlier raids made the work of repair increasingly difficult, but there can be no doubt at all that our night attacks, where the bombing was concentrated on well-placed markers, were at once more accurate and far more destructive than any other precision attacks made by either of the Allied air forces in the war.

But I must once again insist that these long-range precision attacks of the winter months could not have been carried out with the required persistence if the German defence system had not crumbled; once this had happened the offensive against oil naturally brought about a vicious circle and for the lack of oil the enemy's fighters were often unable to defend the oil plants. Feint attacks, on nights when there was to be no major attack, with all the apparatus of airborne jamming and aircraft dropping Window to simulate the arrival of a far larger force, were sometimes used to get the night fighters into the air and so waste more aviation petrol, which was in particularly short supply.

There is no need to describe the effect of the offensive against oil in detail; it is a familiar story. From May, 1944, onwards, when the offensive against oil began, the Luftwaffe's consumption of aviation fuel exceeded production and it only kept going at all on its reserves. In June, 1944, Speer was writing to Hitler deploring the "tragic developments" with regard to the supply of aviation fuel, which had been cut to a tenth of its former level by June 22nd; "only through speedy recovery of damaged plants," he wrote, "has it been possible to regain partly some of the terrible losses." It was after this that the Geilenburg plan was adopted, and it undoubtedly made the task of keeping the synthetic oil plants out of action more difficult than before. But in August the Germans had to curtail the period taken to train pilots, to save fuel used in training flights; this had already been cut down once before. The German army, and especially the Panzer divisions, had so much difficulty in getting supplies up, because of the bombing of the French railway system, that this counted for much more than any shortage of fuel at home, but by the end of the year the German army, as well as the air force, was desperately short of fuel. It is known that when the Ardennes counteroffensive was planned the enemy counted on being able to capture allied stores of petrol and so keep the armoured divisions going; when this hope was disappointed many tanks were stranded for lack of fuel. But even more important, in Speer's opinion, was the destruction of German communications by bombing; it was this, he said, which brought the offensive to a standstill. The shortage of fuel was also felt on the Eastern front, where it was a major cause of the Russian victories in Silesia in February and March, 1945.

The enemy's jet-propelled fighters, which were far in advance of anything the allies had and could have disputed our air supremacy—they would, however, have been too fast to operate by night against our bombers—were designed to use an inferior fuel to the aviation petrol used by normal aircraft. Jet-propelled fighters would probably have been able to operate long after the rest of the German air force was grounded, but as a result of stoppages and bottlenecks in the chemical industry, largely the result of our general attack on German industry and communications as a whole, even this fuel was in short supply; the jet-propelled fighters were only able to play a very minor part before the end of the war.

In the weeks just before the end of the war all the German armed forces were immobilised by lack of fuel. The amount of oil produced by the synthetic oil plants and other factories was so little that it would not have paid the enemy to use up fuel in conveying it to the armed forces. The triumph of the offensive against oil was complete and indisputable.

It turned out afterwards that we might have saved a good

deal of trouble, if we had been asked to attack four factories, three in Germany and one in France, which produced ethyl fluid, a small quantity of which has always to be mixed with high-grade aviation petrol. Possibly the Germans would have been able to scrape up enough ethyl to keep going if these four plants had been bombed—they were highly vulnerable to air attack—but in any case here was a panacea target which offered the greatest advantage with no considerable effort. Probably there were many other similar targets which the Germans could have told us about. The difficulty was that we had no means of finding which were the general panacea targets at any given moment, whereas anyone could see for himself that such targets as Essen and Berlin contained a vast number of vital war industries.

Chapter Eleven

THE FINAL PHASE

An overwhelming force. The capture of Walcheren. The attack
on German industrial cities resumed. Shortage of high explosive
bombs. The second battle of the Ruhr. The Dortmund-Ems and
Mittelland canals. The collapse of German industry. Dresden.
A cancelled attack on Berlin. New methods of bombing. More
tactical developments. The defeat of the German defences. The
dispersal of German industry and underground factories. Runstedt's counter-offensive. The sinking of the *Tirpitz*. Views on
battleships. Sea power exerted by Bomber Command.

IN 1944 a single attack by a single Group often did as much
damage as an attack by the whole Command in the previous
year. There were several reasons for this; more efficient
navigational aids, improved tactics, and the disintegration of the
enemy's defences. No. 5 Group, using bombing tactics which they
had worked out for themselves, destroyed quite a number of
industrial cities, and so did No. 3 Group using GH. The devastation caused by such small attacks by a single Group was as widespread as that brought about by a normally successful major
attack by the whole Command the year before. At the same time
the Command as a whole had on the average about 1100 heavy
bombers available, as opposed to about 600 the year before.

But it was not until September, 1944, that I was able to use this
overwhelming force against the enemy's main industrial centres,
which had been given an almost complete respite from bombing
for a period of nearly six months, from April onwards. During
this period I only carried out attacks on German cities when the
weather was unfavourable for operations in France,or when there
was no imperative call for tactical bombing in support of the
army, or attacks on flying bomb sites, railways, U-boat bases,
and oil plants. For the two months around D-Day it was impossible to make any heavy attack on a German city, and all that
could be done was to begin a long offensive against Berlin by
light bombers, Mosquitoes, which subjected the enemy's capital
to a rather heavier bombardment than London was receiving
from the flying bombs; a number of the Mosquitoes were

modified to enable them to carry 4000 lb. high capacity bombs. In all, 85 per cent of the Command's effort was used against targets other than German industrial cities between May and September.

We had seen enough during our offensive against industrial cities in 1943 to know how rapidly the enemy got a considerable proportion of a town's industries working again after a major blitz. I was therefore seriously alarmed by the prospect of what the enemy might have been able to do during this six months' respite; it was, moreover, a period of critical importance when the enemy was getting into production a whole range of new weapons from jet-propelled aircraft to submarines which could re-charge their batteries under water and were largely immune from air attacks when at sea. In point of fact the enemy did make heroic efforts to repair bombed factories and put up temporary dwellings for the many thousands of workers who had been made homeless by bombing. I feared that the enemy might have made so much headway with this that we might have lost all the advantage from the damage we did to his industrial towns in 1943. But in any case the only thing to do was to begin again as soon as circumstances allowed. On 25th September Bomber Command ceased to be under the general direction of the Supreme Allied Commander and operational control passed once again into the hands of the Chief of the Air Staff; and it was round about this date that we resumed the offensive for which Bomber Command's striking force had been called into being. The last flying bomb had been launched from the ground on September 3rd, and a diversion of effort which amounted to 24,000 tons of bombs a month for a period of two and a half months was no longer necessary. And now that France had been cleared of the enemy the army's demands for our services, though by no means few, were rather less frequent; for the moment Bomber Command was only asked to clear the approaches to Antwerp, and when this port could be used the enemy's advantage over the allies in the matter of communications, which had had to be countered by air attack, would no longer be as great as before.

Antwerp had been occupied by the 2nd Army without any serious fighting on September 3rd, but it was useless to the allies while the enemy occupied Walcheren and other fortresses on the mainland at the mouth of the Scheldt. Operations against the enemy positions at the approaches to Antwerp were somewhat delayed by the attempt to force a crossing of the lower Rhine at

Arnhem and Nijmegen by airborne divisions, but Bomber Command began attacking them early in October. Walcheren is almost entirely below sea-level and the water is kept back by a sea-wall more than 200 feet thick at its base, tapering upwards until it is 60 feet thick at the top. On this wall, and inland, the enemy had a number of powerful batteries which would have made any landing a perilous if not impossible operation. Bomber Command was required to attack the batteries themselves, together with others in an old fort on the mainland, and at the same time to breach the sea-wall in a number of places with a view to drowning the batteries inland. During September and October 6000 tons of bombs were dropped on the batteries and on October 3rd the first attack was made on the sea-wall. 243 Lancasters made a breach within an hour, and other Lancasters which I had sent to follow up this first attack with 12,000 lb. bombs were able to report that the object of the attack had already been achieved and to bring back their bombs, which we badly needed, since, as I have said before, these were always in short supply. The sea began to spread over the island and swamped four batteries, but a single breach was not enough to flood the whole island. We accordingly breached the sea-wall on either side of Flushing, threatening seven more batteries, and again on the north-east coast of the island, until the floods had spread over nearly all the low-lying ground. Towards the end of October we attacked those batteries which could not be flooded in preparation for the landings which began on November 1st. By November 6th the enemy no longer commanded the mouth of the Scheldt and the approaches to Antwerp. The flooding of the fertile soil of Walcheren, which it was believed could not be restored to its original condition within many years, was a most unfortunate necessity of war, but access to the port of Antwerp was essential for all future operations by land on the Western front. And, in any case, the wholesale destruction of property is, in my view, always justified if it is calculated to save casualties. After the capture of Walcheren, the Scheldt had to be swept clear of mines, and the first ships were unloaded at Antwerp on November 26th.

We did not wait for the capture of Walcheren to resume the attack against German cities; on the contrary, we dropped 42,246 tons of bombs on industrial cities in October, which was more than twice the weight of bombs dropped on these objectives in any previous month of the war. One reason for this increased weight was that we had to attack the already devastated cities of the Ruhr, both in order to finish off such industries as had begun to produce again during the long respite from bombing at the very time of the year when we should normally have attacked the Ruhr, and for tactical reasons, in order to disorganise the enemy's communications close behind the Western front. In Essen and many other towns almost everything that could be burnt was already reduced to ashes, and we could therefore only attack with high-explosive bombs which in proportion to their bulk weigh far more than incendiaries.

I had some time ago foreseen that this might happen if the bombing offensive went on long enough, and if, as was very likely, the enemy still kept going after enormous areas of his main industrial cities had been destroyed by fire. I had therefore warned the appropriate authorities that the time might come when we should need an enormously larger supply of heavy case high-explosive bombs than before, when our main weapons had been the 4 lb. incendiary and the 4000 lb. blast bomb—this latter was, of course, essentially a weapon for use against intact buildings and was no great use against already ruined cities in which life was mostly going on in cellars and only the essential factory buildings had been partly restored. But in October, 1944, when we had to substitute heavy case high-explosive for incendiary and blast bombs in a large and continually increasing proportion of our attacks, and had already used vast numbers of heavy case bombs in tactical attacks, I found that my warning had been disregarded. For the last six months of the war we were therefore faced with a desperate shortage of high-explosive bombs and had to live all the time from hand to mouth, doing our best with our own supply and with what the Americans could let us have in spite of their own similar shortage.

The use of ordinary high-explosive bombs, which was quite inevitable, was unfortunately less humane than the use of incendiaries and blast bombs, which only caused a large number of casualties when they raised a fire-typhoon, as at Hamburg. A particularly unhappy illustration of this was at Le Havre; when the Germans were still clinging to the port after the Allies had advanced much farther eastwards, on instructions from the army we attacked with heavy case bombs a point of concentration near the docks which we had been assured had been evacuated by the French and was only occupied by German headquarter staffs and troops. Most regrettably the French were still there, and this attack killed and wounded many of them.

Effective additional damage could only be done to the already devastated cities of the Ruhr by an enormous expenditure of bombs, as much as four to five thousand tons in a single attack and sometimes up to 10,000 tons of bombs in two attacks in close succession. It was also difficult to estimate from air photographs either the extent or the value of the damage done, since it was often a question of comparing one ruin with another that had previously stood on the same spot. But we learned in the end that these attacks were astonishingly successful; they not only brought about virtually complete disorganisation close behind the battle-front, but they finally destroyed the war industries of the Ruhr— I am not here referring to the synthetic oil and benzol plants— which had always hitherto been repaired, though with more and more trouble, after each of our attacks. After October, 1944, Krupps ceased production to all intents and purposes until the end of the war and after November the steelworks of Bochum, among the most important in Germany, were equally unproductive.

These are only two examples among hundreds. With the actual, and, as it proved, the final destruction of so many industries in the Ruhr went a grand assault on the communications of the area. The attacks on the Ruhr cities were in themselves disastrous to the enormously intricate railway network of the district; it was not only that railways and railway facilities were themselves seriously damaged, but the whole system became clogged with the extra traffic required by the German army or needed to deal with the disastrous results of Bomber Command's attacks. Perhaps the most effective of all was a succession of attacks on the Dortmund-Ems and Mittelland Canals, which drained them just as fast as the enemy could repair them; the Americans on one occasion took part in this work and successfully breached the Mittelland Canal towards the beginning of the period. These canals were absolutely indispensable to the enemy for the transport of coal, ore, and heavy warlike stores, to and from the Ruhr; the enormous and, as the Germans must soon have realised, quite useless efforts made to repair the canal embankments were in themselves enough to show that we had found an essential bottleneck in the enemy's transport system. As a result of the draining of these two canals —the attacks were made at points where the canals passed between embankments over low-lying ground—and of Allied air attack on the German railways, the stocks of coal in the Ruhr rose from 415,000 tons in August, 1944, to 2,217,000 tons in February, 1945.

But during that period the production of coal in the Ruhr fell from 10,417,000 tons in August to 4,778,000 tons in February; the stocks had risen because it was physically impossible to move the coal to the innumerable factories which then stood idle for lack of it.

There could be no better illustration than the success of our attacks on these canals of the complete change in the whole situation of the bombing offensive that had come about between 1943 and 1944. We always knew that the canals were a first-class panacea target and the Dortmund-Ems Canal had, indeed, been attacked as such in 1940. But it was quite useless to attack the canals unless we could be certain of breaking down the embankments again just as often as the enemy repaired them, in winter as in summer, and within a very few days or even hours of the repairs nearing completion. The enemy could, after all, have rushed fleets of barges, each containing huge loads of coal, past the threatened section of the canal if we had only given him a few days' respite, and Speer himself said in his interrogation that this plan was adopted. He suggests that it was successful and did maintain production in Central Germany, but as he also says that the coal situation became catastrophic in November, 1944, and thereafter caused the most serious dislocation of the whole of the armaments industry, he seems to contradict himself on this point. In any case we kept so close a watch on the canals by photographic reconnaissance and were always so prompt in undoing the work of repair that there can be no question of much coal gaving got through; a little had to be let through since we had to let the Germans get water back into the canals for a few hours on completion of any repair because the water itself was a major factor in force and widening the breaches. If it had been suggested in 1943 that I should divert even the smallest part of the striking force to the task of blocking these canals I should have dismissed the idea as absurd; it was only towards the end of 1944 that we could hope to hit so small a target as the banks of a canal whenever we wanted to, in any weather, and with the enemy knowing, as he must have done, just when and where the attack was due to be made.

It soon became obvious that I had no need to fear a great revival of German war industries during the six months' respite which our preoccupation with the invasion of Europe had given them. In spite of the fact that there were no longer any large cities of the Ruhr to be burnt and that the law of diminishing returns compelled us to use a huge bomb-load to destroy what remained, the industries of the Ruhr collapsed quickly and finally; the second battle of the Ruhr, as it might be called, lasted a much shorter time than the first and was far more decisive in its results. I had to conclude that Bomber Command's main offensive, from March, 1943 to March, 1944, had been more effective than I had judged and that the war industries which the enemy had improvised among the ruins of his towns were far more precarious than I had thought; the Germans could repair Krupps once, twice, or even three times, but the final blow, which was merely part of a shattering attack on the whole Ruhr area left them powerless to restore any of the plant's productive capacity. All the information we have got from Germany since the war goes to show that it was in the autumn of 1944 that air attack on German war industry as a whole began to have a decisive effect. Here, for example, is a significant passage from Speer's interrogation:

"Until the autumn of 1944, the diversion of man-power to A.R.P. construction work and the clearance of air raid damage had a disturbing effect on production, for up to that time there was a shortage of man-power in industry. From the autumn of 1944 onwards the effects of air attack were so considerable that a rapidly increasing surplus of man-power became available. The total man-power engaged on work arising from air-raid damage can be estimated at between 1,000,000 and 1,500,000 persons."

What Speer means, of course, is that in the autumn of 1944 so many workers were idle because the factories they worked in had been destroyed that they constituted a large reserve of men for the clearance and repair of air-raid damage; since this reserve was continually increasing this implies a situation which was manifestly a vicious circle.

From October 1st until the end of the war, Bomber Command dropped 153,000 tons of high explosive or incendiary bombs on the industrial cities of Germany, many of them new targets, and many others targets that had often been attacked before. In 1944, the heaviest attacks were made in October, since in November we had to concentrate largely on synthetic oil and benzol plants, while in December and January we had to make heavy attacks on the communications which Runstedt was using for his counter-offensive in the Ardennes and on his troop concentrations. But

B.O.   Q by December of 1944 we had devastated or very seriously damaged 80 per cent of all the cities in Germany with a population—before the war—of more than 100,000; yet more cities, especially in the east of Germany, were devastated in 1945.

With the German army on the frontiers of Germany we quickly set up GH and Oboe ground stations close behind the front line and this ensured the success of attacks on many distant objectives when the weather would otherwise have prevented us from finding the target. At the same time the bombers could fly with comparative safety even to targets as distant as Dresden or Chemnitz, which I had not ventured to attack before, because the enemy had lost his early warning system and the whole fighter defence of Germany could therefore generally be out-manœuvred. In February of 1945, with the Russian army threatening the heart of Saxony, I was called upon to attack Dresden; this was considered a target of the first importance for the offensive on the Eastern front. Dresden had by this time become the main centre of communications for the defence of Germany on the southern half of the Eastern front and it was considered that a heavy air attack would disorganise these communications and also make Dresden useless as a controlling centre for the defence. It was also by far the largest city in Germany—the pre-war population was 630,000—which had been left intact; it had never before been bombed. As a large centre of war industry it was also of the highest importance. An attack on the night of February 13th-14th by just over 800 aircraft, bombing in two sections in order to get the night fighters dispersed and grounded before the second attack, was almost as overwhelming in its effect as the Battle of Hamburg, though the area of devastation—1600 acres—was considerably less; there was, it appears, a fire-typhoon, and the effect on German morale, not only in Dresden but in far distant parts of the country, was extremely serious. The Americans carried out two light attacks in daylight on the next two days. I know that the destruction of so large and splendid a city at this late stage of the war was considered unnecessary even by a good many people who admit that our earlier attacks were as fully justified as any other operation of war. Here I will only say that the attack on Dresden was at the time considered a military necessity by much more important people than myself, and that if their judgment was right the same arguments must apply that I have set out in an earlier chapter in which I said what I think about the ethics of bombing as a whole.·

In this winter of 1944-1945 we did not, as in all previous winters, use the long nights mainly for deep penetration of Germany; we attacked in the East and West with equal weight. Other important industrial centres in the East, such as Dessau and Chemnitz, were successfully attacked for the first time, and in the West we found new targets in many of the smaller industrial towns, such as Solingen and Pforzheim. Such targets were often attacked as much for tactical as for strategic reasons, because they were not only of industrial importance but had become centres of communication for the Western front or were occupied by troop concentrations or headquarters staffs and organisations.

The application of methods developed for precision bombing to area bombing greatly increased the average area of devastation in the average successful attack. I have already referred to the use of GH, originally intended for attacks on single factories, for the bombing of towns, and quite different methods were also worked out by No. 5 Group; these were developments of "offset marking," whereby the bombs were aimed at a marker some distance from the aiming point and therefore clear of smoke from the target, the bomb-sights being set in such a way as to ensure that the bombs did not actually hit the marker or fall near it but overshot and offset it by the right amount to hit the real aiming point. When this technique was first used against tactical targets the Master Bomber made calculations which he broadcast to the main force to ensure that the bomb-sights were corrected, but this, together with the placing of the marker and the Master Bomber's check of its position, took some time; even against tactical targets in France the inevitable delay caused rather heavy casualties and it was obvious that no force could afford to orbit the target for ten or more minutes in Germany, with fighters coming up all the time and many anti-aircraft guns in the target area continually firing. A modification of this technique was therefore adopted for use against well defended targets in Germany, and at the same time the technique was adapted in a quite simple fashion to ensure that the bombs were distributed over a much larger area than that of a single factory. The actual target was first illuminated and marked, without being visually identified, by means of H2S. In the light of the flares so dropped the crews of a small force of aircraft, between five and nine in number, identified a previously chosen marking point which might be anything between a 1000 and 2000 yards away from the centre of the area which was to be attacked. This marking point was marked with 1000 lb. target indicators, and the Master Bomber checked their position, dropping target indicators of a different colour to cancel any that might be wide of the mark. The main force were then instructed to approach the marking point on a definite track and release their bombs just so many seconds after the markers on the marking point were in the bomb-sights as to ensure that the bombs would overshoot into the area to be attacked. This saved a great deal of time but it also had the enormous advantage, for area bombing, that the main force could distribute their bombs far more evenly over the area to be attacked than by any previous method. By the method used throughout 1943 the bombs were distributed roughly over a circular area, but most densely in the centre of it; in a successful attack the centre of this circle corresponded with the aiming point. This meant that if we wished to do as much damage towards the circumference of the circle as towards the centre, we had to use an excessive number of bombs, since far more bombs normally fell near the centre than towards the edge of the area to be attacked. Further-more, if that area should be long and narrow, as some objectives were, a great many bombs would have to be wasted to ensure hitting both ends of the area. To overcome this difficulty 5 Group divided the attacking force into a number of sections and instructed each of them to approach the marking point by different lines of approach and to bomb a different number of seconds after the marking point, with the markers burning on it, had appeared in the bomb sights. In an attack on Bremerhaven, for example, a very straggling and difficult target, on the night of 18th-19th September, 1944, the force was divided into five sections, each with separate instructions, which in fact meant that the force bombed five separate aiming points to which they were guided by only one marking point; it would, of course, have taken a long time and have been excessively dangerous for low-flying aircraft to place actual target indicators accurately on all five aiming points. The reason for using this procedure against Bremerhaven in particular was that it is a long and narrow town and if the bombs had been aimed at a single aiming point in the centre of this elongated area a great number would have had to be wasted to ensure the destruction of the place.

This attack was a comparatively primitive example of 5 Group's methods of area bombing. A further development, on use against targets which were not elongated in shape, was to distribute the bombs, by exactly the same methods but by a further sub-division of the force, not merely between several aiming points lying on a single line, but between several aiming points lying on several lines; these lines fanned outwards, as it were from the marking point and crossed the target in various directions. In an attack on Munich on the night of November 26th-27th, 1944, the aircraft dropped their bombs along five such lines, and in a later attack on the same town on December 17th-18th along five such lines; both attacks were highly successful.

Finally each aircraft in the force could be given a separate heading on which to approach the target area from the marking point and a different interval of time at which to bomb after the marking point was in the bomb-sight. This meant, in effect, that the bombs from each single aircraft in the whole force were aimed at a separate aiming point, which ensured that the bombs were yet more evenly distributed over the whole area. In this way Brunswick was most successfully attacked on the night of October 4th-5th, 1944, and Heilbronn on the night of December 4th-5th, 1944.

All this sounds complicated enough and it did require considerable mathematical ability and the issue of very detailed instructions when planning the attack. But for the individual airman it was no more complicated to follow the separate instructions issued to each crew than when all the crews followed the same instructions, while however elaborate might be the planned distribution of the bombs the Master Bomber and the marking crews had only to make sure of one marking point outside the target area.

Apart from Mosquito attacks, which became increasingly heavy, Bomber Command carried out no further operations against Berlin, though in the late summer of 1944, when the German army was in headlong retreat from France and it seemed conceivable that the war might end at any moment, there was a plan to carry out a vast Anglo-American air attack on Berlin in daylight; the idea was that this might cause the German Government to panic at a critical moment. General Doolittle came up to Bomber Command on the afternoon before the projected attack and he and I and our staffs examined the final plan together in the Operations Room. The routes were decided and the whole operation pretty well cut and dried when I discovered that the Americans, whose long-range fighters were required to protect Bomber Command's striking force as well as their own Fortresses, were unable to raise enough fighters to give what I considered adequate cover for our aircraft during such a deep penetration of Germany. The greater part of our striking force was unable to fly in formation and in an operation involving the whole or most of the force the bomber stream was inevitably very long, stretching to sixty miles or more, so that a large fighter force had always to be assembled when we attacked a German target in daylight. There had been some misunderstanding about this in the earlier stages of planning the operation, since it was only on the day before the operation was to take place that I discovered that an American long-range fighter force sufficient to cover both our own and the American bombers all the way to Berlin was not available. Although Jimmy Doolittle did his utmost, as always, to meet our requirements I had to refuse to subject my force to a risk far greater than usual—I had particularly in mind our obsolete .303 calibre defensive armament—The whole operation was therefore cancelled.

If I were asked what were the relations between Bomber Command and the American bomber force I should say that we had no relations. The word is inapplicable to what actually happened; we and they were one force. The Americans gave us the best they had, and they gave us everything we needed as and when the need arose. I hope, indeed, I know, that we did everything possible for them in turn. We could have had no better brothers in arms than Ira Eaker, Fred Anderson and Jimmy Doolittle, and the Americans could have had no better commanders than these three. I was, and am, privileged to count all three of them as the closest of friends. As for the American bomber crews, they were the bravest of the brave, and I know that I am speaking for my own bomber crews when I pay this tribute.

When once the Allied armies were near the frontier of Germany and we had reorganised our tactics to take advantage of this fact, the enemy was almost always unable to put up any serious resistance against our night attacks but this, of course, was only because of our increased power of manœuvre, and not because of any reduction of the still formidable night fighter force. The most serious blow to the enemy was the loss of his early warning stations on the Channel coast; the only stations he now had were on the German frontier, or on the coast of Holland, and these latter could always be avoided by sending the bombers over France on a route which was out of range of radar stations in

Holland. The bombers could therefore approach to within 40 miles of the German frontier before the enemy knew of their approach, and usually the enemy had less than an hour's warning. The enemy's night fighters were now based on new airfields and had lost all the elaborate communication and control centres in France and Belgium. It was estimated that they needed at least forty minutes warning of the approach of our bombers if their opposition was to be effective. The fighters therefore had scarcely enough time as it was, and we decided to deny them even this by jamming the early warning stations with airborne apparatus carried in Stirlings which flew at a distance of about 60 miles from the German frontier. This jamming was very effective, and it only remained for us to take every possible advantage of it when planning our attacks so that the enemy not only had too little·time in which to get his night fighter force together, but would also find it impossible to decide, in the few moments he was given, which was the real attack and which were feints. We increased the number of feints, and also the number of real attacks, and the most complicated operations were repeatedly undertaken. An actual example will give the best idea of the sort of thing that happened.

On the night of February 14th-15th, 1945, the main targets were Rositz and Chemnitz, both in Saxony, and therefore at a distance from the frontier which would normally have put our force in great peril; Rositz was to be attacked by 224 heavy bombers, and Chemnitz first by 329 heavy bombers and then, after an interval of three hours, by another force of 388 bombers. Fifty-four heavy bombers were also to lay mines that night in the Baltic. Berlin was to receive yet another attack by Mosquitoes, a force of 46 of them being dispatched.

The enemy's early warning system was on that occasion jammed, and reduced in range, from Arnhem to Luxembourg. The minelaying force flew across Denmark to the Baltic while at the same time the Mosquitoes flew across North Germany to Berlin. In addition, 95 heavy bombers made a diversionary sweep over the North Sea. Then two separate forces, each of 12 Mosquitoes, broke from the cover of the jamming screen, and, as soon as they were within range of the early warning stations dropped bundles of Window which, on the enemy's radar, simulated the approach of large bomber forces; these two small Mosquito forces made for Duisburg and Mainz with the object of attracting the fighters based in the Ruhr and North-East

Germany. At this stage, the enemy controllers were therefore aware of two main threats, the one somewhere up in the North and towards the East, the other in the general direction of the Ruhr. And at this moment in the enemy's confused affairs the two main heavy bomber forces broke cover from behind the screen of jammers and flew on the same course in the direction of Coblenz. Just north of Coblenz, the two main forces diverged, one flying to the North-West and the other to the South-East, but after an interval they converged again and both made for Saxony.

The enemy's first reaction was to decide that we were threatening the Ruhr and to send fighters there; the controllers had been deceived by the 24 Mosquitoes which were the first to break out from the jamming screen. The deception did not last for long, and fighters which had been sent to the Ruhr were hurriedly sent further South to orbit a beacon near Cologne. By this time, when the two main forces had reached Coblenz, the enemy had accurately plotted this very large number of heavy bombers, and when the two forces diverged near Coblenz, both of them continued to be plotted and the fighters followed both forces until they came together again, which was at a point about 40 miles west of Chemnitz. After this, the fighters only followed the force which was to attack Chemnitz. But all this was too late. A large number of fighters had eventually collected at the beacon near Cologne, but when they were sent after the main bomber streams not one of them was able to catch up with them. Meanwhile the mine-laying aircraft flying over Denmark had engaged the attention of some fighters based there and the enemy, after plotting the diversionary sweep across the North Sea and deciding that some 350 aircraft were approaching—the real number was 95—sent some fighters to a beacon near Hamburg to be ready for this threat; these fighters were not used again. From stations near Berlin the enemy did send a number of fighters to Chemnitz, but these were scarcely more effective than the fighters sent from the Cologne beacon; they arrived so late that only a very few combats took place. When the bombers were on their way back from Saxony, other fighters came up from the south, but these also failed to catch up with the two bomber streams.

We had naturally stopped jamming the enemy's early warning stations as soon as this was no longer necessary, but three hours later we began to jam them again, this time concentrating on stations rather farther to the south. It will be remembered that the plan was for a second large force of heavy bombers to make a second heavy attack on Chemnitz, which was now the only real objective. This force flew on a route which passed to the south of Mannheim but in advance of it there flew a small force of Mosquitoes dropping Window, and as soon as these broke from the screen put up by our airborne jamming these diverged from the route assigned to the heavy bombers and flew in the direction of Mainz and Frankfurt. There were then three feint attacks in this second phase of the night's operations; eight Mosquitoes attacked Frankfurt, 11 attacked Nuremburg, and 14 Dessau, which is about 75 miles north-west of Chemnitz.

As many night fighters as the enemy had previously sent to the beacon near Cologne were sent up in this second phase of operations, and nearly half of them had been airborne three hours before. But the Window-dropping Mosquitoes effectively prevented the fighters from intercepting the bombers near the German frontier, and when the fighters were eventually directed towards the main bomber stream very few of them reached it, partly because we were using effective measures to jam the apparatus they carried for detecting aircraft in the dark and partly because there was cloud over part of the route.

In all, the total losses that night were only 1.3 per cent of all sorties, including the aircraft used to carry apparatus for jamming the early warning stations, Mosquito fighters sent against the enemy's night fighters, and the diversionary sweep.

It was, of course, essential for the success of such tactics that the enemy should have no warning of the approach of bombers except from his own radar stations, and such warning might have been given him by any transmission, including the transmission from our own H2S equipment, from the bombers themselves. But crews now had the use of Gee right up to the front line, since the Germans could no longer jam it over France, and they had little need of H2S on the earlier stages of any flight. I therefore ordered a complete "signals silence," with no use of H2S or any other equipment making a transmission which the enemy could pick up, until the aircraft were within 50 miles of enemy-held territory and therefore had broken through the jamming screen. When the weather allowed, the main force was often instructed to fly at a low level on the way to the German frontier in order to make it still more difficult for the early warning stations to detect its approach.

During this period, from September, 1944 till the end of the war, the enemy discovered no new defensive measure, in spite of the fact that absolutely every form of radar or system of signals which was of any real value to the defence was being jammed or interfered with in some other way by us. Consequently there was no need for us to bring in anything new; we needed only to keep the enemy controllers guessing by similar means as those used in the attack on Chemnitz and Rositz on the night of February 14th-15th, and to see to it that we never became systematic or regularly repetitive in our planning of operations. It is probable that if the war had continued the enemy would have devised something new, possibly in the use of short-wave radar, or possibly in the use of infra-red rays, but as it was there was nothing to worry us and in the last few months of the war the night fighter force, in addition to all its other troubles, began to be starved of petrol. I have already described how we used feint attacks, on nights when there were no major operations in order to get the enemy to use up still more petrol by dispatching fighters to meet an imaginary threat and to wear down the morale of his night-fighter forces.

The only defence the enemy could offer was purely passive; it was an attempt to disperse or bury underground the most important of his war industries. One of the most elaborately organised of such industries was the manufacture of pre-fabricated U-boats, which we first detected when air photographs showed that a U-boat had left the stocks in a U-boat building yard in an unprecedently short time, about a quarter of the usual time, which meant that the parts of the submarine must have been manufactured elsewhere and quickly assembled in the building yard. U-boat building yards had always in the past proved a rather hopeless target for air attack, as I continually but ineffectively pointed out to the Admiralty when continually pressed to attack them, while in the present there were too many other urgent calls upon us; with the new method of manufacturing all the parts of U-boats in a great number of workshops scattered all over Germany it looked as though the enemy had made things still more difficult for us. As the new U-boats did not come to the surface, where they could be detected by radar, o re-charge their batteries, but breathed in air through a tube running up to the surface of the sea, there was some reason for fearing that a new and very serious threat to our shipping might develop. The threat never came to anything for two reasons. The change of plan and design in the middle of a war caused endless delays, and

by the time that the industry was ready for a considerable production of the new U-boats, German communications were in such
a state of disorganisation as a result of air attack that dispersal,
instead of protecting the industry, made it all the more inefficient. Many U-boat hull parts manufactured inland were too
big for anything except transport by barge, and the blocking of
the Dortmund-Ems and Mittelland Canals took care of that. In
varying degree these two factors constantly worked against the
dispersal of industries, and by 1945 there was absolutely no
industry which we could not be confident of attacking with
success by one means or another, provided only that we could
afford to give that industry first priority as a target for an
adequate period; I should say that a fortnight would have been
about enough for all but the very largest, most essential, and most
widespread industries such as the oil industry, coal mining, or
steel production. Here the opinion of Speer is of great importance;
referring to dispersal and underground factories, "I was not of
the opinion," he said, "that the effects of planned air operations
against industrial targets could be avoided by measures of this
nature. The choice of when to deliver attacks on industrial
objectives and of sustaining these raids as consistently as might
be required lay exclusively with the enemy bombers." In
particular, Speer thought little of the German attempts to put
essential industries underground. "One cannot meet air attack
with the slogan ' Concrete versus Bombs.' The opponent in the
air is able to choose his objectives and in so doing he can plan to
concentrate on any vital target such a weight of attack as hitherto
has never been possible in the whole history of war. There was
consequently no means of defence."

The situation was even more clearly described by General
Engineer Spies. "Ultimately," he said, "delay in getting semi-
finished products to the assembly factories progressively slowed
down production until it came almost to a standstill early in
1945. The fact that semi-finished products had to be carried over
long distances was due, in the first place to the bombing of
factories which forced dispersal, and secondly to the attacks on
transport."

Underground factories are, of course, as dependent on communications as any other and in the last year of the war it would
have been perfectly easy to attack by concentrating on the railways running to them. But at the same time we were prepared,
in the closing stages of the war, for more direct measures if these

should be needed. We already had Wallis's 12,000 lb. medium
capacity bomb, which was capable of breaking through the roof
of a railway tunnel or a very thick concrete roof, and when the
success of this bomb was proved Wallis designed a yet more
powerful weapon, the 22,000 lb. bomb, the most destructive
missile in the history of warfare until the invention of the atom
bomb. This 22,000 lb. bomb did not reach us before the spring of
1945, when we used it with great effect against viaducts or railways leading to the Ruhr and also against several U-boat shelters.
If it had been necessary, it would have been used against underground factories, and preparations for attacking some of these
were already well advanced when the war ended. Even where a
factory was too deeply buried for the bomb to go right through
the earth or rock overhead, these large bombs would certainly
have brought down the rock ceilings, as happened when we
attacked with ordinary 1000 lb. bombs the caves in which the
Germans hid their flying bombs in France, on the machinery
below. But in general a great deal of nonsense was talked about
underground factories in the last year of the war; the fact was
that not one per cent of one per cent of German industry had
either got underground or could ever have been put underground,
and even if more had been buried this would not have made it
much more difficult to keep them out of action. For example,
the vast concrete structures, for launching "secret" weapons,
which were built by the enemy at Mimoyeques, Watten, and
elsewhere in Northern France, were almost impregnable to
bombs but were put out of action by the simple process of deny-
ing access to them. This we did by ploughing up all the ground
all round them with moderate-sized bombs. Because of all the
craters even a goat would have found it difficult to get to the
site, and trucks and railroads never had a hope.

From October, 1944, until the surrender of Germany our main
commitment was the destruction of German industrial cities,
attacks on individual factories, and the bombing of the enemy's
communications, but we had to be always ready to support the
armies in the field. As soon as the port of Antwerp was freed, the
Allied armies began a limited advance to the Rhine, in preparation
for the crossing of the river and deep penetration into Germany.
Bomber Command was required to prepare for the advance in the
Aachen Sector—Aachen surrendered on October 21st and gave the
Allied armies their first sight of a German town destroyed by
fire bombs—and we were called upon to destroy three fortified

towns on the River Roer, Düren, Jülich, and Heinsburg, which covered the approach to the Cologne plain. On the 16th November, in daylight, we dropped 5689 tons of bombs on these towns, and though we had expected to make a second attack, for the army wanted complete destruction, we were told that nothing more was needed. When the Ninth Army reached the River Roer a new obstacle appeared. The enemy still held two dams, at Urft and Schwammenauel, which controlled the flooding of the Roer valley, and if the Americans had crossed the Roer waters the enemy could have trapped them by releasing the flood waters behind them. We were therefore asked, at short notice, to break the dams down. The structure of the dams was very similar to that of the Sorpe dam which had been accurately attacked in 1943 when we breached the Möhne and Eder dams but had not been broken down because the retaining wall of earth proved invulnerable to any weapon then in our possession. As with the Sorpe dam, there was just a chance that an explosion or series of explosions on the Urft and Schwammenauel dams would cause seepage and eventually lead to the complete disintegration of the structure, but I did not think much of this chance and, moreover, the enemy was in a position to adjust the water level so as to avoid erosion of the dam. I therefore told General Eisenhower that there was no hope that the operation would be successful, but that we should make the attempt; the dams were bombed five times between December 3rd and December 11th and were repeatedly hit, but nothing happened. The only alternative was for the army to capture the dams and this they were about to do when Runstedt's counter-offensive began on December 16th.

It was the essential condition of this counter-offensive that it should be carried out in such bad weather that the German army would be largely immune to air attack and for a considerable time there was fog and low cloud over very large areas. But even in the first week after December 16th, when the weather was appalling, Bomber Command, and Bomber Command alone, was able to operate against communications used for the counter-offensive on four nights and two days; all were large-scale operations. Attacks on communications were maintained until the enemy was withdrawing as rapidly as possible, and the extremely heavy damage that was done in railway centres behind the German lines, as, for example, in the Nippes marshalling yard at Cologne, undoubtedly had a profound effect on the whole situation. The enemy's roads were blocked by an overwhelming attack on St.

Vith on December 26th. Many roads met in this town, which was right in the centre of the bulge made by the enemy advance, and every one of them was blocked by our attack; it was not even possible to clear a way through the side-streets of the town. Two whole divisions on their way up to critical areas in the battlefield had to make a wide detour and were so much delayed that many units were unable to dig in before the allies counter-attacked. Troop concentrations at Houffalize were afterwards bombed, on the night of December 30th-31st and once again on the night of January 5th-6th; the town was almost entirely destroyed and bomb craters over a large area hampered the movements of troops and supplies at another focal point.

The Runstedt counter-offensive was of particular interest to us at Bomber Command because it was quite clear from the reports of prisoners of war taken during the battle that the German army was getting very short of fuel and of its best tanks; the Panzer divisions invariably went into battle with many fewer tanks, and less fuel in these, than they were intended to have; they were often forced to tow each other into the battle areas. After the war the Ardennes counter-offensive was cited by Speer in answer to the question whether the German High Command were ever forced to modify, postpone, or abandon any operations because of the effects of strategic bombing. His answer to this question was a curious one; he said that the High Command never altered any plan for a projected operation on account of the effects of our air attacks. But this was not because these attacks had no effect; it was because the High Command simply refused to admit their existence or their effect. So the Ardennes counter-offensive was punctually carried out on the appointed date although Model and Dietrich had already pointed out that many essential supplies were wanting. We all now know, as we then knew, what a forlorn hope that offensive was.

In February and March the Allied armies reached the Rhine, and Bomber Command was called upon to make yet more attacks on the ruined cities of the Ruhr and Rhineland with a view to creating further chaos in the rear of the German armies who were holding the east bank of the Rhine. The rubble of Cologne, Duisburg, Dortmund and Essen was stirred up once again. Troops packed into the ruined town of Wesel were bombed on 6th March and on the following night. In the week which ended on March 25th Bomber Command made seventeen attacks on railway centres, bridges, troop concentrations, and strong points to prepare for the crossing of the Rhine by the 21st Army Group. After we had bombed Wesel once again the Rhine was crossed and the town was occupied by a Commando force which sustained only 36 casualties; it had been expected that this would prove a very costly operation. In a message to me after the attack on Wesel on the night of March 23rd-24th, Field Marshal Montgomery said: "My grateful appreciation for the quite magnificent co-operation you have given us in the Battle of the Rhine. The bombing of Wesel last night was a masterpiece and was a decisive factor in making possible our entry into that town before midnight." When the allies had crossed the Rhine and struck deep into Germany we were ordered to stop all strategic bombing, since the end was obviously at hand, but we continued to attack by day and night such centres of organised resistance, together with road and railway communications, as still confronted the advancing armies.

During all this period the Admiralty continued to worry about the German navy and in particular, in the autumn of 1944, about the *Tirpitz*; our own battleships with their usual large complement of ancillary craft, were kept hanging about at home in case the Germans should decide to send the poor old lone *Tirpitz* to sea, and it was felt that some use might be found for these large units of the Royal Navy in the Pacific. I was accordingly asked to intervene in this fantastic "war" between these dinosaurs which both sides had just managed, at great expense and after vast argument, to preserve from their long overdue extinction. I was quite willing to do so, but only if this did not seriously interfere with more important operations; I gave an undertaking that we should sink the *Tirpitz* in our spare time. In September the *Tirpitz* was lying in Alten Fjord, in the North of Norway, and out of range of Lancasters carrying a normal bomb load. I dispatched No. 617 and No. 9 Squadrons to a base in Russia with orders to attack the *Tirpitz* on the way back to England with 12,000 lb. medium capacity bombs; by attacking from the East there was a good chance of taking the enemy by surprise and of aiming a good proportion of the bombs before the smoke-screen which had been set up for the protection of the battleship could provide effective cover. The plan worked fairly well in so far as one bomber crew got a sight on her and the *Tirpitz* was hit by one 12,000 lb. bomb in the bows, the only place in which she could stand such a wallop. The damage was not very obvious in air photographs, though there could be no doubt that the ship had sustained a direct hit. We had very good reason to believe that the ship could never be made fit for operations before the probable end of the war and was therefore quite useless to the enemy; this was confirmed by German reports that came into our hands after the war. As this solitary dinosaur had been equally useless as a warlike weapon for a long time before this new development did not seem to cut much ice with the Admiralty; I was therefore pressed to attack the *Tirpitz* again. The *Tirpitz* was then moved at slow speed in her damaged condition, she was only capable of doing 8-10 knots—to Tromso, which was just within range of Lancasters based in England but which was still so far North that during winter the darkness would be almost continuous and a daylight attack would therefore be impossible; unless we were to wait for the spring we should have to act quickly. A second attack was made, also by No. 617 and No. 9 Squadrons, but this time there was unexpected bad weather and complete cloud cover over the ship. In a third attack the ship capsized after at least two direct hits by 12,000 pound bombs and a number of near misses. One hit amidships tore over 100 feet out of her side.

During the remaining months of the war Bomber Command disposed of nearly all the rest of the enemy's collection of large warships, often with ordinary 1000 lb. bombs, which was certainly preferable to drawing on our small stock of 12,000 lb. bombs. In a single raid on Kiel in April 1944, the *Admiral Scheer* was capsized at the quayside and the *Admiral Hipper* was hit while in dry dock by three bombs, which made her entirely unseaworthy. The battleship *Schlesien* had to be beached and the *Elbe* was burnt out and beached. In the same month we attacked the pocket battleship *Lutzow* in the canal at Swinemunde and sank her. In December, 1944, the cruiser *Koln* was attacked and damaged when in Oslo Fjord; she returned for repairs to Wilhelmshaven where the Eighth U.S.A.A.F. finally bumped her off.

This exertion of sea power by aircraft, in the last year of the war, cannot be said to have been of vital strategic importance, though it certainly served to demonstrate the hopeless fragility of battleships and may therefore influence the course of future wars if not the naval mind. One recalls pre-war years in which the Admiralty scoffed at the very idea of an aircraft ever succeeding in approaching a warship. The destruction of 88 of the enemy's light surface craft in attacks on Le Havre and Boulogne on June 14th and 15th, 1944, was of much greater import, since it ensured our lines of communication across the Channel, than the death of these futile capital ships. Even more important an exercise of sea-air power was Bomber Command's prolonged minelaying campaign which, on a very conservative estimate, sank or damaged over 1000 enemy and enemy-employed ships between February, 1942 and May, 1945. This has a great effect on the course of the war as a whole, and was of vital consequence at such critical stages of the war as the invasion of North Africa and the invasion of Normandy. Mines laid off the West coast of France in November, 1942, largely prevented the large force of U-boats held in the bases on that coast from operating against our convoys on the way to Gibraltar, and immediately after the invasion of Normandy Bomber Command was once again called upon to blockade the same bases on the Atlantic coast of France; the result of this and the magnificent work of Coastal Command was that the enemy was unable to use his U-boats with any effect against our cross-Channel convoys and, when these bases were threatened from land, found great difficulty in evacuating to Norway what serviceable U-boats remained in the French ports. Just before the invasion we laid mines in certain areas in the English Channel and off the Belgian and Dutch coast to prevent light surface craft from getting out to attack our convoys, and just after D-Day we anticipated that the enemy would withdraw troops from his army of occupation in Norway for use in Normandy and laid mines in the Kattegat and elsewhere south of Norway; it is known that these measures were particularly successful.

But the greater part of our minelaying was directed against the German merchant navy and supply shipping. The mines were laid over a very wide area, and the campaign was designed to obstruct all Germany's sea communications, but there were also two particular objectives. When the Ruhr was being most heavily bombed we made every effort to obstruct the supply of iron ore to that area from Sweden, by way of Rotterdam, and from Spain, by way of Bilbao and Bayonne. The route from Sweden eventually became so dangerous that the Swedes decided to withdraw their ships, at a moment when the enemy could ill afford the loss. A second objective was the sea communications in the Baltic by which supplies and reinforcements reached the German army in Russia.

As might have been expected, it was just about the time when the bomber offensive began to have a really decisive effect, in the last year of the war, that the minelaying campaign also proved the most serious drain on the German resources, and this in spite of the fact that throughout this period our operations had to be curtailed because of a shortage of mines. During this last year some 40 per cent of all the men in the German navy were employed in minesweeping and escort duties, but even this large force was quite unable to clear a passage for essential convoys. Danzig bay was once closed for 15 days, and a single operation by Lancasters of No. 5 Group, which dropped mines in the Konigsberg ship canal, closed the ports of Konigsberg and Pillau for 13 days. The Kiel canal was twice blocked during that year when Mosquitoes of the Pathfinder Force dropped mines in it, a daring and extremely skilful operation. In September of 1944 the Naval Liaison Officer at the German Air Force Operations Division summed up the catastrophic position which the minelaying in the Baltic had brought about: "Without training in the Baltic, and safe escort through coastal waters and the routes to and from operations in mid-ocean, there can be no U-boat war. Without sea-borne supplies, it is impossible to hold Norway. Without freedom of movement in the Baltic we cannot use transport in German coastal waters. . . . But already we no longer command the sea routes within our sphere of influence, as, is shown by the day and week long blocking of shipping routes in the Baltic approaches."

Chapter Twelve

SUMMING UP AND THE WAR
OF THE FUTURE

A Bombing Survey. The effects of bombing. The Japanese war.
Bomber Command's casualties. Obsolete weapons in future wars.
Atomic explosives. Battleships and the atom bomb. A single
service.

AS THE Allied armies entered Germany they were closely
followed, and often accompanied, by the 300 civilian experts,
350 officers, and 500 enlisted men who formed the United
States Strategic Bombing Survey; this body had been established
in the previous November by the United States Secretary of War
who had rightly insisted that the value of their work would be
in direct ratio with the speed with which it was executed. With
far less promptitude, a dozen or so observers—all that we at
Bomber Command could then gather up or were permitted to
send—did their best to get some information with which to assess
the result of the R.A.F.'s bombing offensive; three months after
the surrender of Germany I was still pointing out that for lack
of any scientific and properly organised inquiry it was daily
growing more difficult to judge the effect of our campaign as a
whole and that it would soon become impossible to do so.

The American survey was naturally concerned before anything
else with the results of American attacks and some bias in favour
of their own methods of bombing single factories and railway
targets, even though the method was abandoned when the
Americans began to bomb Japan in strength, was only to be
expected. For example, the American conclusion about area
attacks is that the losses inflicted by them "fell mostly on industries relatively inessential to the war effort," which is demonstrably inaccurate. Naturally the most important factories, and
only these, were chosen as targets for individual attack, and some
of the most recently constructed of these were well away from
the centres of the towns. But the main bulk of German war
industry was exactly where one would expect to find it, and where
it is in every country in the world, in the great industrial cities;
one has only to look at the list of factories destroyed after any one

of our successful attacks on a single large town to see that this is so. After all, Krupps was in Essen—was Essen, Rheinmetall-Borsig in Dusseldorf, the Bochumer Verein steel works in Bochum, and so on. At the same time it did not always happen that a successful attack on the main factory for the production of a particular weapon had as much effect on reducing production as an area attack on a district in which there were a number of apparently less important factories. After an attack by the U.S.A.A.F. on the large factory at Fallersleben which was then producing the flying bombs, most of the work was transferred to other factories, and a much greater loss of production resulted from our subsequent attacks on the Ruhr. The production of flying bombs was cut by between 20 and 30 per cent of what was intended because of shortage of sheet metal manufactured in the Ruhr and the disorganisation of the railway system.

The main work of the American survey was to consider the effect of bombing on each industry one by one, and though an attempt was made to estimate the effects of attacks on cities as a whole, this was admittedly very incomplete and great difficulties were experienced in getting at the truth. For the general survey of the separate war industries many German records were consulted and many German war-leaders, generals, and industrialists were examined. In considering such evidence a difficulty at once arises; the Germans were not always in a position to judge whether at attack was really aimed at a single factory or at a town. On the one side American attacks on single factories quite often destroyed a large number of buildings in the neighbourhood of the actual target, or elsewhere, and on the other hand our attacks on industrial towns often destroyed factories of such size and importance that it might well have appeared to the German authorities that our attacks were in fact aimed particularly at these factories. On the night of 15th-16th March, for example, the accumulator factory at Hagen was destroyed together with most of the town, and this is how Speer referred to the matter—he was discussing the result of our attacks on targets connected with the production of U-boats: "The factories at Hagen and Vienna manufacturing accumulator batteries were destroyed and Posen was lost to us, but the largest accumulator factory (Acfa) at Hanover remained intact. If the last-named factory had been destroyed, the construction of U-boats would have had to be abandoned four weeks later." Speer was, in fact, assessing the results of attacks which were partly directed against industrial cities and partly against specific factories as though this had been a campaign against a single class of industrial objectives; it was, in fact, nothing of the kind, and our economic experts had not even put the last remaining factory at Hanover, on which the whole U-boat industry then depended, on the list of factories which the Anglo-American bomber forces were required to attack.

There is often a marked discrepancy between the observations of the United States Strategic Bombing Survey and the assessment made by members of the Operational Research Section of Bomber Command when they examined our targets on the spot, and this discrepancy even extends to the simple question of what percentage of houses in a town were destroyed; possibly the word "destruction" was defined in two different ways, or possibly outlying districts were considered part of the town in one survey and not in the other. Thus the United States survey says that we destroyed 31 per cent of the houses in Hamburg, and 22 per cent of the houses in Dusseldorf, but our Operational Research Section worked it out as 61 per cent in Hamburg and 50 per cent in Dusseldorf.

The representatives of our Operational Research Section in Germany were able to revise the measurements of the extent of devastation in German cities which we had obtained during the war from air photographs; these were taken under operational conditions and did not always give complete cover of the areas concerned. Seventy German cities were attacked by Bomber Command. Twenty-three of these had more than sixty per cent of their built-up areas destroyed and 46 about half of their built-up areas destroyed. Thirty-one cities had more than five hundred acres destroyed, and many of them vastly more than 500; thus Hamburg had 6200 acres, Berlin 6427—this includes about 1000 acres of destruction by American attacks—Dusseldorf, 2003, and Cologne 1994. Between one and two thousand acres were devastated in Dresden, Bremen, Duisburg, Essen, Frankfurt-am-Main, Hanover, Munich, Nuremburg, Mannheim-Ludwigshafen, and Stuttgart. As an indication of what this means it may be mentioned that London had about 600, Plymouth about 400, and Coventry just over 100 acres destroyed by enemy aircraft during the war.

It was, of course, much more difficult to get sufficient information to measure the loss of production in the devastated areas, but some assessment of this was attempted for a few sample towns.

The information obtained confirmed what we already knew from the statements of German generals and politicians, that it was only on the last year of the war, in spite of such catastrophes as the burning of Hamburg and the ruin of great areas in Berlin, that our bombing really began to affect the whole German war machine. In Dortmund, for example, production was reduced by bombing by about 30 per cent over the whole period from March, 1943 till the end of the war, but the loss of production was most unevenly distributed over this period; in the last seven months of the war production was reduced by 60 per cent, and in March, 1945, was set down as nil. It was the same at Bochum, where the loss of production was even more severe; over the whole period from May, 1943 till the end of the war production was cut by 45 per cent, but in the last five months of the war it was cut by 86 per cent.

Some attempt was also made by the Americans to assess the loss of production in Germany as a whole which resulted from our attacks on cities, but this assessment admittedly left so many factors out of account that it can only give a very vague indication of the situation. The figures arrived at do not, for example, show "to what extent Germany's capacity to continue producing, working, and fighting may have been undermined in the process of meeting these attacks and making good, or trying to make good, the losses incurred." Since between a million and fifteen hundred thousand people were engaged solely in work arising from air-raid damage, and since the attempt to restore the great industrial towns to some semblance of life must have cost Germany a vast expenditure of other labour and material, this is a considerable omission from the assessment. Nor does the American survey take into account the cumulative effect on German production as more and more cities were ruined. But in spite of all these omissions the American figures once again bear out the general conclusion that in the last months of the war the loss of production resulting from the destruction of cities became really disastrous.

The R.A.F. was not in a position, as it most emphatically ought to have been, to judge the result of its main offensive in the light of a sufficient body of indisputable evidence, gathered by people who knew what to look for and before such evidence had disappeared. But no one who surveys the evidence that has been collected, contradictory and confusing though it often is, can fail to be struck by two main points. In the first place, the towns which were devastated in 1943 proved surprisingly resilient. In the second place, even though the Germans had had five months respite in which to rebuild factories and rehouse the workers, the resumed offensive in the autumn of 1944 had an immediate effect on production several times as great as the effect of the offensive of 1943. The reason for this is obvious enough; it was not until 1944 that our strength and equipment was anything like equal to our task, though even then we only had a force of between a third and a quarter of what had been originally estimated as necessary for the bombing offensive against Germany.

In the last three months of 1944 a greater weight of bombs was dropped than in the whole of 1943. Moreover it was only in the last few months of 1944, just when production in Germany began to fall most rapidly, that we were allowed to use any considerable part of our force against German industrial cities. Over the entire period of the war only 45 per cent of the Command's whole effort was against German cities, so that in fact we were using for the main offensive a force which was not only less than one-quarter of the strength originally planned, but nearer one-eighth.

It is an obvious and most certain conclusion that if we had had the force we used in 1944 a year earlier, and if we had then been allowed to use it together with the whole American bomber force, and without interruption, Germany would have been defeated outright by bombing as Japan was; the two atom bombs only added three per cent to the already existing devastation, and their use against two cities merely gave the Japanese, as all American authorities agree, a pretext for immediate surrender when they had already been defeated by area bombing of the same kind as that used against Germany. To have had the force we built up in 1944 a year earlier would have been perfectly feasible, and this is not an absurd speculation like wondering what aircraft could have done in the Battle of Waterloo. We were only prevented from having that force by the fact that the Allied war leaders did not have enough faith in strategic bombing. As a result, the two older services were able to employ a large part of the nation's war effort and industrial capacity in the production and use of their older weapons, and were also able, when the older weapons failed, to get what amounted to more than half our existing bomber force used for their own purposes.

All this was sufficiently obvious, in the closing stages of the war against Germany, to bring about a revolutionary change of plan in the conduct of the Japanese war. The Americans were so much impressed by the achievements of strategic bombing in Europe that they decided to put a far larger share of the national resources into air power than had been previously intended. And although they had rigidly adhered to the theory, if not always to the practice, of precision bombing of factories in Europe, they used against Japan exactly the same method of devastating large industrial cities by incendiary bombs as was used in Europe by Bomber Command. Admittedly one reason for the rejection of precision bombing was that it was even more difficult to get information about Japanese than about German industry, but in my opinion, as I have emphasised in an earlier chapter, we never had sufficient information about German industry to offer any certainty of success in a campaign against key factories. In any event it was not until the last year of the war that we had the technical equipment for such attacks.

But, as Major A. P. de Seversky has pointed out in his published report to the United States Secretary of War, the Americans were far from exploiting air power to the full even in the Pacific War. A great many lives were lost in capturing air bases by combined operations, and this "island-hopping" could have been done by air if the right islands had been chosen, or, as Major de Seversky says, aircraft with the range of the B-36 could have been produced earlier and Japan could if necessary have been bombed from India, Australia, or Alaska. There was just as intense a struggle in America as in England between those in the air force who were anxious to develop a stragetic bombing force, and the army and navy who made every effort to restrict the development and use of the new weapon.

The best of our own four-engined bombers, the Lancaster, had all the range that was wanted for the strategic bombing of Germany, which was the purpose for which it had been built, but until the nearest bases to Japan had been captured the ordinary Lancaster could have played no part in the bombing of Japan, and when those bases were captured they were so restricted in size that it is doubtful whether it would have been profitable to operate more aircraft from them than the Americans themselves proposed to use. But we had our plans, long before the end of the Japanese war, for increasing the range of the Lancaster.

Japan did not have the industrial strength of Germany and its war production was more easily reduced by bombing. Dispersal of industry was even more disastrous an expedient there than in

Germany; in Germany dispersal greatly added to the enemy's difficulties as soon as his communication system began to break down, but in Japan much work was farmed out, as a protection against air attack, and carried on in the flimsy and highly inflammable houses of the Japanese people instead of in concrete factories which would have been far more difficult to destroy. Nor had the Japanese the great organising ability of the Germans. For these and many other reasons it is probable that it would have taken longer to reduce Germany than Japan by bombing alone; it is also possible that some sort of landing on the Continent would have been necessary before the enemy's final surrender. But I am certain that if we had had an adequate bomber force to attack Germany a year earlier, that is, in 1943, or if we had not had the pre-invasion bombing and the bombing of the V-weapon sites to divert us in 1944, we should never have had to mount an invasion on anything like the scale that proved necessary. Once again let me point out that in the last three months of 1944 Bomber Command had dropped as great a weight of bombs as in the whole of 1943; there was no reason at all why we should not have been as ready for the offensive in 1943 as in 1944 except that we did not get the men, aircraft, and equipment when we asked for them, and we were always being diverted from the main offensive by the demands of other services. As the Americans also suffered continuously from similar diversions without these diversions the result would have been the inevitable and total collapse of Germany and there would have been no need for the invasion.

The greater part of this book has been occupied with our actual achievements, not with what we might have done if we had had the means. But it may be as well to summarise those achievements here. In 1940 Bomber Command's attacks on the invasion ports on the coast of France convinced the Germans that no attempt to invade England could be made without complete air superiority over the Channel, and this, because of Fighter Command, was demonstrably unattainable. Later the Command, by successful attacks on French factories working for the enemy, did much to prevent the Germans from converting all Western Europe into an arsenal, and while doing so supplied Coastal Command and our Air Force in the Middle and Far East with many squadrons and additional air-crew. The main attack of 1943, before its interruption by the invasion, compelled the enemy to use more and more of his air force for the defence of Germany, thereby depriving the Luftwaffe of all power of taking offensive action and fatally weakening it on the Eastern, Mediterranean, and eventually the Western front. Scarcely less important was the diversion of more and more guns, all of them dual-purpose weapons, for the defence of German cities, and Speer himself was of opinion that the German armed forces were "considerably weakened" by this. At the same time our main offensive, by the unprecedented devastation which it caused in the largest German industrial cities, reduced every form of war production and prevented the development of many new war weapons and industries. It caused the enemy to divert a major part of his effort to defence. It made heavy demands on science and manpower.

Bomber Command's attacks in the three months before D-Day were so effective, and the new means and tactics of precision bombing were so rapidly mastered (I myself did not anticipate that we should be able to bomb the French railways with anything like the precision that was achieved) that the invasion proved an infinitely easier task than had been expected; not even the most hopeful of the Allied war leaders had thought that the casualties would be so light or the setbacks so few. When the beachhead was established, the bombing of railways continued and a method of using heavy bombers in the battlefield was rapidly and successfully improvised; by this means the most strongly defended positions were taken by the army with incredibly slight losses. In this way the Channel ports, which it had been an essential part of the enemy's defensive strategy to retain, were captured with extraordinary speed and scarcely any casualties after preliminary bombing; the island of Walcheren fell in a few hours after the enemy's defences had been attacked by our bombers, and the port of Antwerp was opened to the Allies. The crossing of the Rhine at Wesel, which had been expected to prove a difficult and expensive operation, cost us only 36 casualties after the reduction of Wesel by air attack. When the bombers returned to the assault on German cities the Ruhr was rapidly made completely unproductive and, in a campaign in which Bomber Command joined with the U.S.A.A.F., had nearly all its communications cut. In the Allied victory over Runstedt's counter-offensive our heavy bombers not only played a most important tactical role, but the results of our strategic bombing were immediately apparent in the enemy's shortage of weapons and fuel. In the last phase of the war Bomber Command, in conjunction with the U.S.A.A.F., carried out a campaign against the enemy's oil supplies which in the spring of 1945 left all the German armed forces without fuel. In the war at sea our minelaying campaign sank or damaged over 1000 ships, and bombing virtually destroyed the enemy's light surface forces in the Channel and about half the number of heavy warships—including the *Tirpitz*, the *Lutzow*, and the *Scheer*—sunk by all methods during the war.

These far-reaching successes were not gained without grievous casualties. During the whole period of the war approximately 125,000 members of air-crew entered Bomber Command units. During the period of my Command alone it is estimated that nearly 44,000 men were killed, about half that number injured, and in addition more than 11,000 men held prisoner by the enemy. Seven thousand one hundred and twenty-two aircraft were lost on all operations during this period. Yet these casualties were far lighter than were anticipated and the rate progressively fell as against the steady increase which was expected.

There are no words with which I can do justice to the air-crew who fought under my command. There is no parallel in warfare to such courage and determination in the face of danger over so prolonged a period, of danger which at times was so great that scarcely one man in three could expect to survive his tour of thirty operations; this is what a casualty rate of five per cent on each of these thirty operations would have meant, and during the whole of 1942 the casualty rate was 4.1 per cent. Of those who survived their first tour of operations, between six and seven thousand undertook a second, and many a third, tour. It was, moreover, a clear and highly conscious courage, by which the risk was taken with calm forethought, for their air-crew were all highly skilled men, much above the average in education, who had to understand every aspect and detail of their task. It was, furthermore, the courage of the small hours, of men virtually alone, for at his battle station the airman is virtually alone. It was the courage of men with long-drawn apprehensions of daily "going over the top." They were without exception volunteers, for no man was trained for air-crew with the R.A.F. who did not volunteer for this. Such devotion must never be forgotten. It is unforgettable by anyone whose contacts gave them knowledge and understanding of what these young men experienced and faced.

No award could be commensurate with the achievements of the men who flew our aircraft, but I did ask, at the close of the war, that everyone in Bomber Command, both those who flew and those who worked on the ground, should be granted a Bomber Command campaign medal just as the Eighth Army were awarded a special distinction; as it was, the only decoration that most of our ground crews could wear was the "defence" medal. Few people realise that whereas some 50,000 air-crew, before and during the period of my Command, were killed in action against the enemy, some 8000 men and women were killed at home in training, in handling vast quantities of bombs under the most dangerous conditions, in driving and dispatch riding in the black-out on urgent duty and by deaths from what were called natural causes. These deaths from natural causes included the death of many fit young people who to all intents and purposes died from the effects of extraordinary exposure, since many contracted illnesses by working all hours of the day and night in a state of exhaustion in the bitter wet, cold, and miseries of six war winters. It may be imagined what it is like to work in the open, rain, blow, or snow, in daylight and through darkness, hour after hour, twenty feet up in the air on the aircraft engines and airframes, at all the intricate and multifarious tasks which have to be undertaken to keep a bomber serviceable. And this was on wartime aerodromes, where such accommodation as could be provided offered every kind of discomfort and where, at any rate during the first years of the war, it was often impossible even to get dry clothes to change into between shifts. We never had more than 250,000 men and women at any one time in Bomber Command, so that the total of some 60,000 casualties among air-crew and ground staff should give some idea of what the Command had to face in maintaining an offensive for which the great majority were awarded the "Defence" Medal. I know that among the people concerned the award was, and is, the subject of much bitter comment, with which I was and am in entire agreement. Every clerk, butcher or baker in the rear of the armies overseas had a "campaign" medal.

Every commander must be prepared to ask himself, after every campaign, whether the results were worth the casualties. The only answer that can usually be given is to point to the contribution which that campaign made to final victory, and it is often possible to argue, as with most battles of the war of 1914-1919, that victory might have been more cheaply gained by some other means. But without exception our bomber operations were designed to reduce the casualties of all the services or of the civilian population (as in attacks on V-weapon industries and sites) and in almost every instance our operations demonstrably had that effect. Without the intervention of Bomber Command the invasion of Europe would certainly have gone down as the bloodiest campaign in history unless, indeed, it had failed outright—as it would undoubtedly have done. Without the preliminary bombing, the assault on the German prepared positions at Caen would have cost the army as many lives as an offensive in the 1914-1918 war, and the capture of the Channel ports, the landing at Walcheren, and the crossing of the Rhine were all operations that could only have been undertaken at a vast sacrifice if it had not been for the intervention of air power; as it was, these enormously strong positions were taken with astonishing ease, and at Le Havre, for example, which was captured after a week's bombing, 11,000 prisoners were taken for a loss of some 50 Allied soldiers. Sea battles between modern battleships, which are apt not to sink until after they have become red hot furnaces, are often indescribably horrible; a few bombs on the German navy in its bases largely put an end to such warfare. As to our main bomber offensive, the extent to which it saved the lives of the armed forces on every front by depriving the enemy of weapons is less easily calculable. But no one can doubt that it was enormous; the incidental effect that the German air force was kept out of the battlefields as well as prevented from bombing England in the later stages of the war, must by itself have saved innumerable lives. It cannot therefore be doubted that everyone of the 60,000 of Bomber Command who died saved many of his fellows by his death; over and above this is to be added the contribution of all our multifarious operations to the final victory of the Allies.

In the war of 1939-1945 England could just, though only just, afford to neglect to the extent that she did the weapon which at the time should have dominated all her strategy. The fact that both her enemies neglected this weapon to a markedly greater extent, and also that their folly gave England two great allies, made it possible for us to win the war even though the greater part of our national resources went into the production of less powerful and sometimes wholly obsolete weapons.

In both Germany and Japan the older services maintained a rigid control of the design, production, and use of aircraft and took every possible step to prevent independent strategic action by either force, with the result that when such independent action had to be attempted as in the Battle of Britain or in the Japanese air attacks on Okinawa, there were no aircraft suitable for the purpose. The Germans had, of course, allowed their soldiers to dictate the whole policy of the Luftwaffe, which was designed expressly to assist the army in its rapid offensives; the appropriate outcome of the decision was that before long the German army had to be deprived of all air cover and air support on every front in order to provide some defences for Germany against independent strategic action in the air. Much too late in the day the Germans saw the advantage of a strategic bombing force, but their attempts to produce four-engined bombers, which continued even in 1945, only served to impede the production of fighter aircraft urgently needed for defence. The attempt to bring about the results of strategic bombing by other weapons, the V1 and V2, was sound strategy, but clearly the enemy did not have time or the opportunity to work out the supply or the tactical employment of such weapons in the face of a bomber force which at that time dominated the situation; it is as if someone had attempted the experimental development and production of the rifle in the very middle of the Battle of Agincourt.

In Japan things were even worse; there both the admirals and the generals had control of the air force, so that it was split into two and misused by two contending parties. As with the German air force, its only successes were against totally unprepared opponents. The faults of design extended from the aircraft themselves to the bombs. The Japanese navy's biggest bomb was a characteristic product of the naval mind; it was quite heavy and weighed about 1800 pounds, but the navy did everything it could to make it resemble a naval shell, and filled it with the small quantity of high explosive that naval shells contain. The Japanese army's biggest bomb only weighed 1100 pounds. Both services designed and used their aircraft wholly for tactical support of their own operations. As with the Germans, the Japanese decided late in the day to produce aircraft capable of independent stragetic bombing, with the range and bomb load required; they were even more behind the times than the Germans and built only three four-engined bombers which were still making test flights when the war ended.

Such obliquity of vision was not the prerogative of our enemies. In Great Britain, as I have tried to show, it was a desperate struggle to maintain any kind of strategic bombing force and still more, when we had such a force, to use it for the purpose for which it was built. In the years of peace between the wars of 1914 and 1939 the Royal Air Force repeatedly escaped destruction at the hands of the other two services only by the skin of its teeth. In America, which has no air force dependent of the other two services, the struggle to operate independently was still more intense and the right to do so was achieved still later in the day. Before the war the American navy had exacted the concession that no aircraft of the U.S.A.A.F. should fly beyond a limit of 300 miles from the nearest coast, and they tried to forbid any aircraft whatever from operating over any water unless under naval control. The American Air Force leaders had to risk their careers when the agitated for big bombers. There was more than one Billy Mitchell. In France there was no attempt whatever to develop aircraft for anything except army support, but as no aircraft fit for anything in modern war were in any case developed, the only effect of this way of thinking was, as I have said in an earlier chapter, that Bomber Command, in order to fulfil a promise exacted by the French, sustained heavy casualties in a futile attempt to hold up the German invasion of France.

In no future war can we count on such folly as the Germans and the Japanese showed or such neglect by our enemies of whatever may be the most powerful weapon to hand. In 1939, as no one needs reminding at the present time, we risked losing the war outright because we had no adequate supply of weapons of any sort, rather than because we had not developed the right weapon, and it is possible, though unlikely, that our hairbreadth escape from total destruction may have taught us a lasting lesson; that particular danger, the danger of confronting a fully armed enemy with no adequate weight of arms, may perhaps not recur. But in the future it will be as fatal to rely on an antiquated weapon as to have no weapons at all, and, as I see it, there is a very great danger of this happening. For in the next war whoever has charge of the most powerful weapon then developed will have a worse time than the Air Force had in the 1939 war. He will have not only the admirals and the generals against him, but the air marshals as well. Already there has been a far too easy acceptance of the idea that the atomic explosive is necessarily an atomic bomb, a weapon to be carried in aircraft, from which it is argued that the bomber is what is now required for modern warfare. I myself regard the bomber as having had its day in the last war, when it was undoubtedly the predominant weapon, just as the U-boat was the predominant weapon of the 1914 war and was only prevented from winning it by the stupidity of the old German admirals and generals who would not give it a chance. They missed victory only by weeks—that is history not opinion. But I have not the slightest doubt that the Air Force will go the way of the other services and tend to cling to the antiquated weapons with which it will conceive its interests to be bound up; an obvious line of defence for the bomber will be to insist on its use for the dropping of atomic bombs.

It is true that the atomic explosive has to be carried by some-thing, and perhaps a few very fast, very long-range aircraft would provide a convenient means of carrying it. But it is much more efficient if put into a missile which has no crew and is directed by radar and mechanical means. It does not necessarily have to be carried by anything resembling a missile within the meaning of the act. There is no doubt that it is becoming, and will continue to become, easier and simpler to produce, and to disguise the production of, atomic explosives; my own opinion is that an ordinary embassy official, or, for that matter a commercial traveller or tourist, will eventually prove just as good, and potentially more secretive, a conveyer of atomic explosives as any aircraft, rocket, or other machine.

There is no reason why the parts of an atomic bomb, or rather let us not call it an atomic bomb but an atomic exploder, should not be brought in bit by bit by seemingly innocent people and assembled anywhere where cover can be found, in an Embassy, attic, lodging, or in a ship in harbour. The threat of its presence could then be used to back an ultimatum, or it could be used to destroy outright the area in which it was placed. So let us not imagine that wars—once an affair of small professional armies and just lately the concern of entire nations—are necessarily to remain within the province of what are called the "armed forces." Most probably wars will be mainly taken over by the scientists, the diplomats, and the "cloak and dagger men." With weapons potentially so lethal as atomic explosives there is no need to em-broil millions in production and in battle for many years when decisions can be brought about in a few seconds by the exercise of a little chicanery on the part of a very few persons.

There has already been a significant attempt to scout the idea of the employment of agents for carrying atomic explosives. Major de Seversky makes a far-fetched comparison between the agent with the atomic explosive and the Japanese piloting a suicide aircraft; the Japanese suicide pilots failed, and Major de

Seversky concludes that the agent, who stands a good chance of blowing himself up, will also fail. He rests the argument on the point that it is more difficult to produce good pilots than aircraft, so that the Japanese made a mistake when they threw away their pilots, but this does not apply if the explosive is so enormously powerful that by throwing away one pilot one can produce as much effect as an attack by a thousand bombers. If the Japanese suicide aircraft had contained atomic explosives their use would have obviously been worthwhile and decisive—after all, the loss of one man in an attack which did as much damage as a full scale attack by a force of four-engined bombers would not be considered excessive. The argument is, in fact, so weak that it sounds suspiciously like special pleading for the retention of aircraft with which to drop atomic bombs.

There is only one answer to this otherwise inevitable tendency in each of the services to get tied to a particular and invariably obsolete weapon, and all weapons are obsolete as soon as they are in use. There must be only one service; the survival of three of them at this stage in the development of armaments is wholly idiotic, and there never was any reason or need for them at any time. There was at one time only one service, in those long past days when generals commanded sea battles and the scum of the seaports, described as "sailors," were forced by the roughest and readiest discipline to work the ships under the real fighting men, the soldiers, who fought and directed the battle. But during and after the Napoleonic wars the sailors, who have never been backward in propaganda, built up their reputation to such a degree that they even had the effrontery to nominate themselves the "senior" service, though what that means, and why they should have awarded themselves that title, no one knows. The armies of the world fought and conquered or lost long before human beings learned to launch a ship or even to float on an inflated bladder, and the armies of England were levied long before there was any navy. But once it had acquired this prestige, or rather, had taken it to itself, the Navy—and not only our Navy, for the same thing happened in America and in other countries—set itself apart as a service which should be independent of the other offensive and defensive requirements of the country; the result is that the other services have either been inclined or have been forced to do the same thing, more or less in self-defence.

None of this mattered in the days when the evolution of

B.O. S

weapons was slow and it took centuries before any major change occurred which could affect the routine strategy and tactics; Nelson's guns had just about the same range, the same mechanism, and fired a projectile of just about the same weight, as the guns of Francis Drake. But nowadays strategy and tactics are again and again revolutionised within a year or two as the result of the invention of a new weapon, so that the consequence of insisting on the survival of a weapon in order to ensure the survival of the service which uses it are as immediate as they are disastrous. There is no better example of the tendency to cling to old weapons than the history of the battleship in the last quarter of a century. Even now, when the absolute mastery of the aircraft over surface ships has been completely demonstrated, the American admirals have staged an exhibition of atom bombing against capital ships, as though there could be any need to study the effect of atom bombs on warships when a 12,000 pound bomb filled with ordinary explosive had already taken 100 feet out of the side of the *Tirpitz* and capsized and sunk her in a matter of minutes. And, as if this was not enough, there is the example of the *Bismarck*, which was reduced to perambulating slowly in a circle, with no power to protect herself, by a torpedo from a single aircraft which hit her in the rudder, and the example of what remained of the German navy after the *Tirpitz* had gone, when most of the rest of the enemy's major units were sunk, set on fire, or capsized by ordinary 1000 lb. bombs. And in the Pacific, too, there were many examples of aircraft defeating capital ships. The army's reaction to the atom bomb is not less optimistic; it is argued that such bombs cannot be used in the battelfield without wiping out all the troops on both sides, a theory which overlooks the fact that modern armies are useless without an industrial civilisation behind them and that such a civilisation would obviously be the first objective for the atom bomb. After this had done its work, an enemy army could be arrested by the police.

The consequence of being tied to one weapon were often very tragic. I shall never forget how Admiral Tom Philipps and his men went down with the *Prince of Wales*. He and I had worked for years together on the Joint Planning Committee and shared the same lodgings in Ebury Street. He was a delightful man, and very able and hard working. But he would never bring himself to admit that air power could have any serious effect on naval operations; Joint Planning Committee papers signed by him and myself always set out his ideas of what the navy should do without any serious regard to the air, with a subsequent qualification by me of his opinion.

I said good-bye to him after a meeting of the Deputy Chiefs of Staff in King Charles Street in 1941, just before he left for the Far East and I for the United States. After the loss of the *Prince of Wales*, Colonel "Joe" Hollis, then our secretary, reminded me of my parting words to Tom Philipps; what I had said was: "Tom, you've never believed in air. Never get out from under the air umbrella; if you do, you'll be for it. And as you flutter up to heaven all you'll say is—' My gosh, some sailor laid a hell of a mine for me! '" Poor Tom Philipps—he was the bravest of the brave. He and John Leach, captain of the *Prince of Wales*, and another old and valued friend of mine from Staff College days, walked down the side of the ship together and into the sea as she rolled over and sank.

He could have had some fighter cover, though there would not have been much of it and it would probably have been ineffective, from Buffalo fighters based at Singapore. But he would not break wireless silence to ask for fighter protection when he saw a Japanese aircraft shadowing the *Prince of Wales* the evening before. Well he knew that he was looking for trouble with only two ships against the Japanese fleet, but he did not regard the air as dangerous. When a second shadowing aircraft appeared the next morning he still would not break wireless silence, but the captain of the *Repulse*, astonished by the omission, signalled on his own responsibility. The fighters arrived only in time to see the ships sinking. So died a dear friend, a brave man, a most able man, with no thought but of his duty and of his country.

Now that the Japanese war is over, the sailors of both the English and American navies are declaring that Japan has been defeated by sea power. I am quite prepared to admit that Japan could not have been defeated in the precise way that she was defeated without sea power being used to provide transport facilities. But there were other ways of going about it. It would have been perfectly possible, by choosing the right islands, to hop from one to the other under cover of air power, and this would have been much quicker than using ships; in fact, aircraft did most of the Fleet's work. Full advantage could also have been taken of the increasing ranges of aircraft so that island hopping would have largely become unnecessary. It has for some time been quite possible to design an aircraft which would fly right round the world without stopping, but there is no need for it; if it can go halfway round the world it can get at anything on the earth's surface by going either one way or the other, and in point of fact a radius of three to four thousand miles is all that is generally necessary.

The real answer to all these disputes is that sea power is of course vital, but that it is not necessarily exercised by ships. It can be, and indeed nowadays it mostly is, exercised to a far greater extent by aircraft—here I need only point to the record of Bomber Command against the German navy and the German merchant fleet, or to the record of Coastal Command in their battle against the U-boats. It will in future be exercised by directed atomic missiles.

The navy with its battleships—the most expensive and the most utterly useless weapons employed in the whole of the last war—provide the outstanding example of that parochial spirit which springs from the existence of separate services. I do not for one moment suggest that the army has not shown the same proclivities, and, as I have said, the same thing will certainly happen with the Air Force now that bombers, as we know them, have, as far as one can see, become obsolete. As to the army, heaven knows that we have suffered enough from what is known in the services and outside them as the "cavalry mind." For the past century and more, even up to the outbreak of war in 1939, nobody had much chance of promotion to high command in the army unless he was a cavalry soldier, and it is perfectly well known that, in order to get cavalry soldiers as far as high command, it was often necessary to excuse them from the more difficult qualifications in the intervening stages of their career. Unfortunately they were too apt to develop the mentality of the animals they were so enthusiastic about. If some such provision had not been made, the working infantry, sappers, and gunners would generally have reached the higher posts first, but, as it is, how many of the high commanders of the last 150 years, up till 1939, were not cavalry officers? Because of the cavalry influence, and consequently, of this system of making appointments, the idea of using cavalry inevitably persisted for a quarter of a century after the presence of a horse on a battlefield could only be considered a symptom of certifiable lunacy. It was the cavalry mind which abolished the Tank Corps and the Machine Gun Corps after the last war, and it was the cavalry mind which, when I was at the Army Staff College, attached as much, if not more importance to the student's prowess as a horseman than to anything else he might achieve on the course. This was in 1927, and in the army of the nation which had invented tanks; it is no wonder that twelve years later you would have thought that it was the Germans who had invented them.

Separate services not only fight for the preservation of their own favourite weapons; they do all they can to hold in check anyone who may want to use a new and more powerful weapon which might threaten them. Shortly after the 1914-1918 war it was the Air Force that had such a weapon, or rather was in a position to develop it. In 1919 the Air Force was allowed £15,000,000 a year, the cost of one day's war, but even this had shrunk to £11,000,000 in 1922, and in that year the R.A.F., which in 1918 had a front line strength of 3300 aeroplanes, could only raise 371 front line aircraft. This was the moment when the army and the navy struck. By intrigue resulting in the formation of the Fleet Air Arm, which afterwards became an integral part of the Navy, the Air Force was split in two. The army's plans were, however, far more destructive, for the War Office proposed that the Air Ministry should have control of nothing but civil aviation, research, experiment, and supply, which meant that in fact the Air Force should cease to exist. But in this the soldiers, who are vastly inferior to the sailors in the arts of propaganda and politics, badly over-reached themselves, and the proposal was successfully resisted.

Thereafter, for nearly twenty years, I watched the army and navy, both singly and in concert, engineer one deliberate attempt after another to destroy the Royal Air Force. Time after time they were within a hairbreadth of success; time after time Trenchard, and Trenchard alone, saved us. If they had succeeded they would have abolished our air power as they succeeded in abolishing our tank power, while retaining the Camberley drag hunt, and, as the pinnacle of our sea power, those scarcely more useful battleships whose bones now lie where air power so easily consigned them, littering the floors of the ocean or obstructing the harbours of the world. And had they succeeded in suppressing the Air Force, we should have entered the war with one fighter as we entered it with one tank, we should have lost the Battle of Britain, and the Nazis would have ruled Europe—if not the world—for centuries.

After the last war, with the results of the Battle of Britain and the bomber offensive still fresh in everyone's mind, the army and navy realise that there is not the smallest hope of abolishing the

Air Force, so they now speak incessantly of "co-operation" between the services; they realise too well that the only alternative is their own abolition as services. The orthodox opinion, in every inquest on the campaigns of the last war, is that none of them could have been won without the co-ordinated use of all weapons, a theory which makes for the preservation of all sorts of useless articles. Personally, I quite agree with the principle of co-operation, but only on the lines of abolishing all three services and having only one defence force; it would probably have to be called the Defence Force, though I do not like the term "defence." "Defence" is a gesture not of war but of inferiority.

Such a service must obviously become more and more dependent on science, and must make it its main business, as the only condition of winning the next war, to exploit the best contemporary weapons that science has to offer, with no more regret when it relinquishes an older weapon than a scientist shows when a hypothesis is exploded, or when he finds a quick and easy method to replace one that was inefficient and laborious. This does not mean that the scientists should have complete control of the single service. Obviously its commanders, under the government, must make the final decisions, but they must be intelligent enough and sufficiently free from that prejudice which has always been a disease of the professional fighting man to make the best use of every invention. And as science flits from one overwhelming weapon to another the slightest prejudice in favour of an obsolete weapon will be fatal to the country whose commanders allow themselves to act on it.

With modern science what it is, it is clear that there must be fundamental revolutions in tactics at frequent intervals, but I have no reason to believe that the strategy, as opposed to the weapon on which Bomber Command's main offensive was based, should be abandoned; on the contrary, any new weapon which science is likely to put into our hands should make this strategy yet easier of application and yet more certain and swift in its effect, as the atom bomb itself has most certainly done. This strategy entirely reverses the old principle that wars are to be won only by seeking out and overcoming the enemy's armed forces where these are strongest; at sea, the commonest illustration of this principle is that commerce raiding is unprofitable if the enemy's main fleet is not engaged. But what we had proposed to do with our projected, but never attained, 4000 heavy bombers first line was to ignore alike the German army and the German navy, except in so far as it was necessary to defend England and secure our bases and sea communications, while striking continuously at the enemy's industrial potential; the old principle only applied in that it was necessary either to overcome, or better still to evade, the enemy's air defence. Aircraft were the first weapons to make such a strategy possible, though sea power was often less directly applied in the past to much the same ends by means of blockade and the cutting of sea communications. The weapons of the future threaten the destruction of a country's industries in a matter of hours rather than years, and if we attempt any other application of them we shall probably find that our enemies have been before us and destroyed all those resources on which the mere existence of armed force depends.

For the moment we have to maintain such forces as we have, or a reasonable proportion of them, with such weapons as they possess. But there is no doubt that to-day the atom bomb momentarily holds the field, though there is a possibility that what has hitherto been a by-product of the atom bomb, the radioactive particles which send out lethal rays, might be produced independently of the explosion of such a bomb and used as a deadly weapon against the people of large cities or large concentrations of troops. But as things stand now, we may regard with equanimity the threats, or even the warlike gestures and advances, of any powers anywhere in the world, provided we have a few atom bombs and the means of using them. This situation will quickly pass as the scientists provide all and sundry with the new weapons and the counter-measures against them. The whole key to our defence is encouragement of science and the scientists. Whoever gets far enough ahead in science will prevail —for the time being.

Quarrels do, of course, occur within a single service and often amount to quite serious feuds between the advocates of one weapon or another. These we must expect to continue, but I do not think we need fear that if we organise a single service the quarrels between the ex-soldiers, ex-sailors and ex-airmen who have been forced to wear the same uniform will be just as destructive as before. For one thing, new men will enter the single service who will have no reason to practise the old totem worship of the horse, the battleship, the tank, or the heavy bomber. And for another there is the example of the Air Force, which in the beginning was mainly composed of ex-soldiers and ex-sailors who settled down very well together to work for the advancement of the new weapon. I myself began my service career as a soldier; I have never been accused of any undue partiality for the army, much as I like soldiers.

My part in the next war will be to be destroyed by it; I cannot doubt that if there is a war within the next quarter of a century it will certainly destroy a very great part of the civilised world and disrupt it entirely. Perhaps, after all, that may be the best solution. Any part of the human race that imagines that its survival is either necessary or outstandingly desirable must indeed, in the light of history, be thought to have an extraordinary conceit of itself. The only alternative to such otherwise inevitable destruction is world federation, a government of the world powerful enough to determine the policy of every country. Such world federation might well develop from a first and partial federation of a few of the most powerful states. That seems as yet too good to be true, but it is the only alternative. Meanwhile, and at last, I am back in Africa, which I left unwillingly, though as a volunteer, in 1914, and to which I have always longed to return. Like most of us, I was dragged into war by accident —an accident made in Germany—and by accident I stayed longer than most in the business of war.

THE END

INDEX

Aachen, 147; capture of, 252

Abbotsbury, 26

Acoustic mines, 139

Adams, Ronald, 25

Addison, Lord, 115, 118

Admiral Hipper, 256

Admiral Sheer, 256, 267

Advanced Air Striking Force, 33, 41

Afghanistan, Amir of, 19

Air Defence of Great Britain, 142

Air Ministry, Planning Department, 14, 25; responsibility in Palestine and Transjordan, 29-31; secret files, 37; staff of, 49-51; relations with other services, 57-8; and bomber offensive, 214-5

Aircraft factories attacked, 46, 165, 185, 193-4, 199

All Hallows School, 15, 16.

Alten Fjord, 255

Aluminium plants attacked, 45-6

America, missions to, 27-9, 59 *et seq.*; and strategic bombing, 53-4, 264; entry into war, 66; aircraft production in, 117; bombing survey by, 259 *et seq.*; *see also* United States Army Air Force.

Anderson, General Frederick, 246

Antwerp, 236, 237, 266

Ardennes counter-offensive, 233, 241, 253 *et seq.*, 266

Area bombing, switch to, 77

Army, de-mechanisation of, 11-12, 24, 276

Army Co-operation Command, 110

Army Staff College, Camberley, 11, 23-5

Arnhem, 237

Arnold, General Henry, 28, 56, 215

Atlantic Wall, 195 *et seq.*, 205, 207

Atom bombs, 75, 271 *et seq.*, 279

Augsburg, 141, 194

Aunay-sur-Oden, 210

Baghdad, 22

Ball-bearing factories, 221-2

Barrett, Air Marshal Sir Arthur, 41

Bath, 122

Battles, 33, 34

Battleships, 274 *et seq.*

Beaverbrook, Lord, 27

Bedneall, Colin, 157

Bennett, Air Vice-Marshal D. C. T., 25, 203; and H2S, 127; in command of Pathfinder Force, 128; appreciation of, 129-30

Berlin, 179, 183; attacks on, 67, 135, 136, 180-1, 185, 186 *et seq.*, 225, 235-6, 248; first daylight attack on, 142; first H2S attack on, 180-1; projected mass attack abandoned, 245-6; area destroyed, 261

Bismarck, 60-1, 274

Blenheims, 33, 69, 104, 110, 114

Blind Marker Illuminators, 170

Bochum, 147, 239, 260, 262

Bomb-aimers, introduction of, 96, 97

Bomber Command, strength of, 53, 73, 76, 92-3, 99 *et seq.*, 101, 104, 108, 134, 191, 255; headquarters, 70; casualties, 84, 85, 96, 105-6, 112, 115, 117, 122, 123,